1977

ot

N DAYS

THE FACES OF EVE

THE FACES OF EVE
Women in the Nineteenth Century
American Novel

Judith Fryer

NEW YORK
Oxford University Press
1976

For Lynn and Deborah, the new Atalantas

Contents

Acknowledgments   vii

Preface   ix

I. The Myth of America as New World Garden
   of Eden   3
The Garden   3
The American Adam   5
The American Eve   8

II. The Temptress   27
Elsie Venner: The Literary Convention with
   Psychological Trappings   29
Beatrice Rappaccini: The Literary
   Convention as Allegory   40
In Which the Ambiguities of the Dark Lady
   are Compounded by the Appearance of the
   Pale Maiden: Melville's Isabel   47
Celia Madden: The Temptress as "Greek"   54
Hawthorne's Miriam: The Temptress as Jew   62
Hester Prynne: The Dark Lady as "Deviant"   72

Contents

III. The American Princess   **85**
  The Pale Maiden   87
  Daisy Miller   97
  Milly Theale   101
  Maggie Verver   112
  Isabel Archer   126

IV. The Great Mother   **143**
  The Archetype: Olive Chancellor   143
  The Mother-Surrogates   153
  The Neglecters   173
  The Real Witch-Bitches   182

V. The New Woman   **204**
  The New Myth of Atalanta   204
  Zenobia: The New Woman as Tragedy-
    Queen   208
  The Unnatural Lady Reformers of Boston   220
  Through the Eye of the Needle   234
  Edna Pontellier: The New Woman as Woman   243

Notes   **259**

Bibliography   **276**

Index   **289**

Acknowledgments

The idea with which this book begins is not new; it is the myth of America as New World Garden of Eden, which I believe to be the dominant myth of American culture. This subject has occupied my thoughts, conscious and unconscious, for a very long time, and during that time my ideas have been influenced by others who have dealt with this myth. I am especially indebted, however, to the community of scholars at the University of Minnesota, several of whom have helped to shape this study in a major way.

David Noble was the first to introduce me to the idea of America as New World Garden: fortunately, only Adam resided there, and so in Professor Noble's intellectual garden, the germ of this study was born. Mulford Sibley sparked my interest in utopia and helped me to see the attempt to establish sacred communities in this profane world as living myth. Bernard Bowron imparted to me the skill of reading a novel, and that he is pleased with this piece of work shows that I learned well the lesson he had to teach—despite the fact that we shall never agree about Olive Chancellor. That I have not been able to convince Chadwick Hansen of the duplicity of Mrs. Bread, Mrs. Grose and Mrs. Wix does not mean that his criticism has not been invaluable. In fact, without his patient guidance and generous support this study might never have come to fruition. It is impossible to express

Acknowledgments

my debt to Mary Turpie, mentor of countless American Studies scholars. From the inception of this book, when she
helped me to prune the weeds from the garden of my own
thought, to its culmination, when her wide-ranging knowledge of American art guided my choice of illustrations, her
influence has been prevalent.

Several people helped with the preparation of the manuscript in its final stages, and while it is impossible to name
everyone who participated in one way or another, I would
like to mention here Alice Crozier, whose careful reading and
helpful suggestions strengthened the book; Spiro K. Peterson
and Charles Skipper from Miami University who provided
funds for typing the manuscript; typists A. Delphine Swanson
and Cheryl Beavers; Ravina E. Gelfand and Mary Farrell
Bednarowski who helped to read the galley proofs; James
Raimes and Ellen Royer of Oxford University Press, all of whom
made valuable contributions. Lynn and Deborah Fryer deserve
a special thank you for their countless proofreadings of the
notes and bibliography.

Preface

What is not-I, not masculine, is most probably
feminine, and because the not-I is felt as not
belonging to me and therefore as outside me,
the anima-image is usually projected upon women.
—Carl Jung, *The Archetypes and the*
Collective Unconscious

During the years from 1840 to 1900 the ideas and images
which shaped the American mind were those having to do
with the urge toward perfection. From the men and women
who experimented with alternative life styles in utopian
communities at the beginning of this period to those who
designed fictional utopias at its close, to the writers of imaginative literature, who in novel after novel re-created the Garden, either in its newborn pristine and somewhat sterile innocence or in its Old World state of decadent experience, the
myth of America as New World Garden was so central to the
American imagination that it permeated all levels of culture,
consciously and unconsciously.

The "American Adam" has become a stock figure of cultural interpretations of America by intellectual historians and
literary critics. These scholars, products of their patriarchal
culture, have depicted "the authentic American as a figure of

heroic innocence and vast potentialities, poised at the start of a new history." [1] But they ignore Eve, and strangely so, for she was a figure of primary importance to nineteenth-century thinkers, and especially to novelists. This, then, is a study of the American Eve.

Unlike the American Adam, a single image cannot contain the American Eve. Sometimes simple, sometimes complex, she was perceived in a variety of ways by her creators. Rarely is she a whole woman; usually, as we shall see, male writers tended to cast her as a type. Writers like Hawthorne and James, of course, drew on literary conventions established well before the nineteenth century, yet their works are uniquely products of American culture as well. This is an analysis, therefore, not only of the nineteenth-century American heroine, but of the culture which shaped the perceptions of the authors whose creation she was, and of the authors themselves, who projected their own images upon their heroines.

THE FACES OF EVE

～ I ～
The Myth of America as New World Garden of Eden

Sigh no more, ladies.
                    Time is male
and in his cups drinks to the fair.
Bemused by gallantry, we hear
our mediocrities over-praised,
indolence read as abnegation,
slattern thought styled intuition,
every lapse forgiven, our crime
only to cast too bold a shadow
or smash the mould straight off.

—Adrienne Rich,
"Snapshots of a
Daughter-in-Law"

THE GARDEN

The myth of America is the myth of the New World Garden.
It has its roots, as Leo Marx has shown, in the Elizabethan
vision of the New World, in Crèvecœur's *Letters from an
American Farmer* and Jefferson's republic. "In its simplest,
archetypal form," he writes, "the myth affirms that Europeans experience a regeneration in the New World. They
become new, better, happier men—they are reborn. In most

3

versions the regenerative power is located in the natural terrain: access to undefiled, bountiful, sublime Nature is what accounts for the virtue and special good fortune of Americans. It enables them to design a community in the image of a garden, an ideal fusion of nature with art. The landscape thus becomes the symbolic repository of value of all kinds—economic, political, aesthetic, religious." The American myth of a new beginning, then, may be a variant of the primal myth: "a separation from the world, a penetration to some source of power, and a life-enhancing return." [1]

Marx's Edenic symbol is Hawthorne's 1844 description of "Sleepy Hollow," which concludes with "the shattered ruins of a dreamer's Utopia." In nineteenth-century America the force which shatter the dream-life of a pastoral people was the Civil War and its concomitant urbanization and industrialization. But the sense of the failure of that dream in real life only intensified the longing for perfection in the American imagination. On a literal level pre- and post-Civil War utopians attempted to re-establish the actual Eden state in the many experimental communities which flourished across the country, especially between 1840 and 1880, or wrote utopian "novels," beginning with Edward Bellamy's *Looking Backward* in 1888, which are actually schemes for the socialist reformation of America. Looking back on these decades of utopian experimentation, John Humphrey Noyes reflected, "As a man who has passed through a series of passional excitements is never the same afterward, so . . . these socialistic paroxysms have changed the heart of the nation; and . . . a yearning toward social reconstruction has become a part of the continuous, permanent, inner experience of the American people." [2] These communitarians were engaged in nothing less than living myth; theirs was the attempt to take the raw material of literature and of dreams and turn it into the basis for real life. On an imaginative level this myth attains its first ripeness in the works of Hawthorne, who gave such titles to his stories as "The New Adam and Eve" and "The Tree of Knowledge" and whose *The Marble Faun* is a literal

4

retelling of the Fall of Man; it culminates in the works of Henry James, who traced repeatedly the progression from innocence to painful experience and whose cultivated or decaying gardens are often the scenes of spiritual stress and temptation.[3]

The notion of America as New World Garden is a Romantic notion. It is Hawthorne's "moonlight in a familiar room." It is Henry James defining *The American* as "romance" in the Preface to that novel: "The real represents to my perception the things we cannot possibly *not* know, sooner or later, in one way or another; it being but one of the accidents of our hampered state. . . . The romantic stands, on the other hand, for the things that, with all the facilities in the world, all the wealth and all the courage and all the wit and all the adventure, we never *can* directly know; the things that reach us only through the beautiful circuit and subterfuge of our thought and our desire." [4] By the turn of the century this Romantic myth of America as New World Garden would give way to the new realism, first in Howells's detailing of "the smiling aspects of American life" and then in the more sordid reality of the new myth, the Waste Land.

THE AMERICAN ADAM

The American myth, R. W. B. Lewis writes in *The American Adam*, "described the world as starting up again under fresh initiative, in a divinely granted second chance for the human race, after the first chance had been so disastrously fumbled in the darkening Old World." Its hero is "an individual emancipated from history, happily bereft of ancestry, untouched and undefiled by the usual inheritance of family and race; an individual standing alone, self-reliant and self-propelling. . . . Adam was the first, the archetypal, man. His moral position was prior to experience, and in his very newness he was fundamentally innocent. The world and history lay all before him." [5]

5

One is reminded of an old riddle about two Indians—a big Indian and a little Indian, sitting on a fence. The little Indian is the big Indian's son, but the big Indian is not the little Indian's father. How can this be? David Potter, who recounts this riddle, points out that social conditioning prevents us from seeing immediately that the big Indian is, of course, the little Indian's mother, and illustrates his thesis that generalizations most often made to explain American culture are conceived from masculine perspectives which do not take women into account at all.[6] The attempt of Americans to live out in their lives as well as re-create in their imaginative and historical literature the myth of America as New World Garden is just such a masculine conception, which Potter does not, but well might have analyzed. This myth, as envisioned by our poets and philosophers, by our seers and reformers, and especially by our novelists, is the myth of the New World Adam. If Eve was the cause of the original Adam's downfall, the role of the New World Eve must be minimized. This time she must be kept in her place so that in the American version of the myth there will be no Fall. America is to be the realization of the myth of the eternal return. In the language of Mircea Eliade, one might say that in the sacred space of the New World the American Adam will exist in a state of timeless perfection; it will be possible for him to recover in the present a primordial, mythical time.[7]

The American Adam, then, is Emerson's self-reliant man who lives in harmony with nature; he is Thoreau, first self-consciously living out his role at Walden and then deliberately re-creating it as literature; he is John Humphrey Noyes, seceding from the Union to found a society of Perfectionists, as he writes to William Lloyd Garrison: "I am writing that all men should know that I have subscribed my name to an instrument similar to the Declaration of '76, renouncing allegiance to the United States, and asserting the title of Jesus Christ to the throne of the world." He is Huckleberry Finn and Billy Budd; and he is Christopher Newman and Adam Verver. In *The American*, for example, James's Christopher

Newman, with his suggestive name, awakens suddenly "from a sleep or from a kind of reverie" a changed man. "I spent the morning looking at the first green leaves on Long Island," he says. "I seemed to feel a new man inside my own skin, and I longed for a new world." His "sole aim" in life had been "to make money," but now he comes to the Old World "as simple as a little child" and sees the treasures of Europe with "an eye in which innocence and experience were singularly blended." But such a man can have nothing to do with a *real* woman; Newman has come to Europe to buy a wife, and she must conform to his notions of what a woman ought to be. "I have succeeded," he says, "and now what am I to do with my success? To make it perfect, as I see it, there must be a beautiful woman perched on the pile, like a statue on a monument. She must be as good as she is beautiful, and as clever as she is good. . . . I want to possess, in a word, the best article in the market." [8]

Newman is, according to his compatriot Mrs. Tristram, "the great Western barbarian." He is the ancestor of the male heroes—fictional and actual—whom Theodore Roszak calls the "bully boys"; their "hairy-chested bravado . . . is the full and hideous flowering of the politics of masculine dominance" which leads finally to the Fall of the Western World: World War I. [9] To such men, women have been "the objects of crushing masculine contempt," but at the same time deified, like Christopher Newman's pedestaled ideal woman. "Earth Mother, Muse, love goddess, siren, nymph, angelic maiden," Roszak writes, "in one form or another, all the feminine qualities have been elevated to the highest cultural status. . . . Mythologizing woman has been a standard method of gilding her cage." [10]

Roszak argues that the rise of "masculine dominance" in the nineteenth century was paralleled by, and in fact a result of, the increased pressure for woman's emancipation building from the 1830s and 1840s and extending far beyond the issue of the ballot. He cites, for example, this passage from the much translated *Sex and Character* by the highly regarded scientific authority Otto Weininger, as evidence of the passion with which men tried to dismiss women:

> Women have no existence and no essence; they are not; they are nothing. Mankind occurs as male or female, as something or nothing. Woman has no share in ontological reality, no relation to the thing-in-itself, which, in the deepest interpretation, is God. . . . Woman has no relation to the idea, she neither affirms nor denies it; she is neither moral nor anti-moral; mathematically speaking, she has no sign; she is purposeless, neither good nor bad. . . . she is as non-moral as she is non-logical. But all existence is moral and logical existence. So woman has no existence.[11]

The "woman question," however, was the burning issue of the day—to both feminists and antifeminists. It represented to Henry James's Basil Ransom, for example, what was wrong with his America: "The whole generation is womanized; the masculine tone is passing out of the world; it's a feminine, a nervous, hysterical, chattering, canting age, an age of hollow phrases and false delicacy and exaggerated solicitudes and coddled sensibilities, which, if we don't soon look out, will usher in the reign of mediocrity." [12] It was the focus for writers of serious and popular novels, newspapers and magazines, lectures and pamphlets, and for the reformers who agitated for equal rights and who formulated alternative life styles for themselves in experimental communities.

THE AMERICAN EVE

Woman's Place and the Emergence of the New Woman

It is interesting to take Roszak's point, that the masculine dominance at the turn of the century—a direct response to the threatened disturbance of the traditional relations between the sexes—led to the suicidal bloodbath of World War I, and apply it to the earlier decades of the nineteenth century. The real impetus of the women's movement began half a century earlier. In 1843 Margaret Fuller had set forth her program for women in "The Great Lawsuit: Man versus Men; Woman versus Women," subsequently published as *Woman in the Nineteenth Century*. Appropriating Emerson's vision of true manhood, Fuller argued that woman's proper education began with a return to her original freedom. Seeing "renunciation" not as a "piercing virtue" but as a dreary waste, she described the bourgeois home as bleak and dreary and was convinced that the central evil of her society, which condemned such women of genius as Mary Wollstonecraft and George Sand as outlaws, was its sexual code.[13] Five years later the first Convention on Women's Rights, held in Seneca Falls, New York, resolved that "The history of mankind is a history of repeated injuries and usurpations on the part of man toward women." [14] If the later agitation over the ballot, which was merely a symbol of the upheaval of traditional sexual roles, made "bully boys" of the men of the turn of the century, their bravado leading them ultimately into World War I, what of America's own war, the Civil War? And what of the rapid industrialization and urbanization of the postbellum decade?

The tone of those decades is apparent in the pessimism underlying the buoyant optimism of Whitman's *Democratic Vistas* and Mark Twain's *The Gilded Age*, in E. L. Godkin's label, "the chromo civilization." Traditional historians, in assessing the aftereffects of the war, stress the "hurried, aggressive growth" which gave birth to "an alarming public and private corruption," [15] the clash of Paganism and Puritanism,[16] and of Yankee and immigrant culture.[17] Stephan Thernstrom, in his "dissenting essay in American history," shows that the most important phenomenon of the post–Civil War era was the move from country to city, a "great social transformation" which *upset traditional patterns*. Even Thernstrom, however, focuses on the male population. In asking "who moved to the city?" he attacks his predecessors who have focused on the "more exotic" immigrants from foreign

9

cultures and stresses the importance of the farm *lad* who moved from a rural to an urban setting within the culture.[18] Thernstrom is right about the great social transformation which took place as old values were uprooted. But the most significant change of all goes unnoticed, like the fact that the big Indian is the little Indian's mother: the breakup of the traditional home with the emergence of the "new woman."

Wendell Phillips had said, "After the slave, then the woman."[19] Potter argues that woman's chance came with the move from country to city. With the potential of economic independence open to her, not only was the basis for her subordination diminished, but the stability of the family was challenged as well. The last part of his point is more valid than the first. Whether the city presented more opportunity for independence than the frontier is open to speculation. Recent historians such as Gerda Lerner make clear that pioneer women had to be not only independent, but often heroic, that frontier men and women were interdependent. Helen Papashvily points out that the letters, diaries and newspapers of the eighteenth century show that women kept taverns and shops, managed farms, manufactured, processed, traded; they were printers, editors, teachers, doctors, nurses, druggists and writers. The city, on the other hand, meant that the shop, the office, the factory moved out of the home, that women lost their chance for vocational and professional training and business experience—that men's and women's spheres became separate and distinct.[20] This upsetting of traditional patterns was disturbing to both men and women, then. It represented, as Henry James perceived, a real separation of the sexes. This sense of confusion and upheaval following the Civil War was a challenge to the whole structure of American society. If the move to the city meant that the family, once the most important unit of production, would now surrender its functions to institutions outside the home—manufacturing to the factory, control over property to the state, the education of children to public schools—it also meant that new roles must be learned by both men and women. For American writers of the nineteenth century, who wrote primarily for and about the middle and upper classes, this "new woman" was a subject of grave concern.

One can judge the extent of the preoccupation with the "new woman" and the threat she posed by the proliferation of conservative propaganda meant to counteract new trends by glorifying home life as a "profession." Harriet Beecher Stowe, for example, as the most famous woman of her day, might have been expected to take up Wendell Phillips's cry. But in her portrayals of the "new woman" in such novels as *My Wife and I*; as editor of *Hearth and Home*, the dominant interest of which was manifested by the woodcut under its title of a rustic cottage with children playing around the door; as contributor to her brother Henry Ward Beecher's *The Christian Union*; as co-editor with her sister Catharine Beecher of the best-selling book, *The American Woman's Home*, she showed herself to be a great conserver and preserver of woman's traditional sphere. In *The American Woman's Home*, the "family state" was called "the aptest earthly illustration of the heavenly kingdom, and in it woman is its chief minister. Her greatest mission is self-denial." [21] But it was more: "Woman's *distinctive profession*," Catharine Beecher wrote in 1865, "includes three departments—the training of the mind in childhood, the nursing of infants and of the sick, and all the handicrafts and management of the family state." [22] In a time of transition, when the West, the new urban growth, and the influx of immigrants threatened the stability of the family, this American housewife could nurse, cook, educate, protect, save.

These sentiments were echoed in gift books, ladies' magazines, newspapers and periodicals, sentimental novels and best sellers like *The Mother at Home*, in popular manuals on home building like Andrew Jackson Downing's *Architecture of Country Houses*, and in the arguments of ministers like Horace Bushnell and Henry Ward Beecher. [23] Willard Parker, M.D., wrote in 1869, for example: "Woman has an internal organization which fixes the great purpose of her life," [24] while H. S. Pomeroy, M.D., declared in 1888: "The key to the question, 'What is woman's work?' is the fact that Nature has imposed on her the most of the burden of reproduction. The rest of woman's work follows naturally. . . . the woman is the home-maker and house-keeper, and this is just what God meant her to be—just this and nothing more." [25] And Horace Greeley wrote in *Hearth and Home:*

> I hold that the appointed sphere of man is broader, not higher than that of woman—that the household is her kingdom, within which her influence should be paramount. . . . Of course, a true wife should consult her husband on all matters of importance, and will evince great deference to his wishes, tastes, feelings, aversions. . . . I hold that there is an immensity of work to be done that specially pertains to the sphere of women. . . . If the "Girl of the Period" could only be induced to leave the piano unafflicted and devote the next year or two to . . . the kitchen range, I feel very sure that her happiness as well as that of mankind, would thereby be signally promoted. [26]

At about the same time, however, a dramatic conversation appeared in the *Atlantic Monthly,* in which a character named *Sang-Froid* prophesied: "Puritanism has so long held us in rigid subjection, depriving us of even innocent amusements, that human nature is sure to be revenged. The pendulum will swing as far to one extreme as it has swung to the other." [27]

A sexual revolution was taking place through these decades, despite wishful thinking. Compare the observations of Alexis de Tocqueville in his classic treatise, *Democracy in America* (1835), with those of James Bryce in *The American Commonwealth* (1888). Tocqueville wrote, "In America, more than anywhere else in the world, care has been taken constantly to trace clearly distinct spheres of action for the two sexes, and both are required to keep in step, but along paths that are never the same." Women took no part in business or politics, according to Tocqueville; they never managed "the external relations of the family," but were confined to "the quiet sphere of domestic duties." The duties of man were carefully divided from those of women "so that the great work of society may be better performed." [28] Fifty-three years later Bryce could report (perhaps idealistically) that American women had gained access to virtually all of the professions. "It is easier for women to find a career, to obtain remunerative work of an intellectual as of a commercial or mechanical kind, than in any part of Europe," he wrote, perceiving the result as "a new kind of womanhood," the effect of which on American society at large was profound. [29]

Between the time of Tocqueville and the time of Bryce the "new woman" had begun to permeate all levels of American culture. New magazines appeared, devoted exclusively to her: *Godey's Lady's Book, Harper's Bazar, Woman's Journal*, the *Ladies' Home Journal*. The function of *Godey's Lady's Book*, edited by Mrs. Sarah Josepha Hale, was to act as a kind of arbiter of taste and fashion, but it did prepare the way for a greater feminine interest in the outside world. One of the first issues of *Harper's Bazar*, in 1868, devoted a double-page spread to drawings of "women at work"—not in the home, but making artificial flowers, paper boxes, hoop-skirts, envelopes, umbrellas, paper collars, preparing candies, setting type, burnishing silver, mounting photographs. [30] The *Women's Journal* was Elizabeth Cady Stanton and Susan B. Anthony's magazine, which later came to be called the *Revolution*. E. D. Draper, one of its founders, in 1870 offered free silk to all who would wear bloomers. [31] The *Ladies' Home Journal* by 1885 was the most heavily subscribed of all of the ladies' magazines, having a circulation of 170,000. [32] Except for the *Woman's Journal*, however, these magazines were usually dominated by strongly antifeminist editors, such as Edward Bok of the *Ladies' Home Journal*. They attempted to make housekeeping into a science, and even *Harper's Bazar*, which favored woman's suffrage and other progressive reforms, exalted the ancient and honorable profession of the homemaker.

In 1868 Julia Ward Howe founded the first formally organized club for American women in Boston, the New England Woman's Club, while Mrs. J. C. Croly founded the Sorosis of

New York City that same year when she was excluded from a press dinner for Dickens because of her sex.[33]

In the field of education, Vassar was established in 1865, Smith and Wellesley in 1875, to give young women advantages equal to those of men,[34] and in 1882 M. Carey Thomas, later president of Bryn Mawr College, became the first American woman to earn the degree of Ph.D.[35] The educated woman did not take her place in American society with ease. Although the land-grant colleges encouraged co-education, sentiment against higher education for women was such that Thomas Wentworth Higginson felt obliged to publish in the *Atlantic Monthly* the satirical essay, "Should Women Learn the Alphabet?" [36] And when Vassar College opened, the *Round Table* commented:

> To compel the female brain to do the work of the male brain is just as much to unsex the fair sex as to make her arms or her back perform masculine labor. . . . Banish the barbarous curriculum proposed by your committee—dead languages, higher mathematics, metaphysics, and similar studies. . . . Substitute belles lettres . . . This is the appropriate field for women.[37]

By 1883 Henry James had decided that this "new woman" comprised the distinctively American topic and recorded his fascination with "the agitation on their behalf" and the failure of "the sentiment of sex." [38] The popular counterpart of the James "new woman" was the dime-novel heroine, who first departed from gentility in the late 1860s with Eulalie Moreau clad in male attire in Frederick Whittaker's *The Mustang-Hunters; or The Beautiful Amazon of the Hidden Valley.* Whittaker capitalized on the Amazon-heroine in *The Jaguar Queen: or, The Outlaws of the Sierra Madre,* 1872; while Edward Willett's Dove-eye, alias Kate Robinette, in *Silver-spur; or, The Mountain Heroine,* became the first heroine to commit violence. These female counterparts of the Western cowboy were a real departure from the refined and genteel females of the traditional novel. Even in the tales of Cooper, from whom these adventures probably derive, no lady had been capable of "the remotest approach to indelicacy of thought, speech or action." [39] The full-fledged dime-novel heroines are Hurricane Nell, who appeared in 1878 almost simultaneously with the first appearance of Deadwood Dick, and her successor, Calamity Jane. This Amazon-heroine has all the skills of the Western hero: she is just as capable of revenge and violence and just as aware of sex. [40]

To medical experts and educators writing in the *North American Review, Popular Science Monthly* and the *Educational Review*, to intellectuals like Henry Adams and C. Stanley Hall, the new woman threatened not only the American home but the very survival of the race. "Turning an energy properly altruistic and collective into individualistic self-consciousness," wrote Hall, "deflecting blood to the brain from the 'generative organs,' with atrophied mammary glands and irregular periodicity," she had lost touch with the sacred primitive rhythms that bound her to "the deepest law of the cosmos." His acme of femininity, as was Adams's, was the "madonna conception," and he dreaded the race suicide that the sexless, neurotic modern woman portended. [41] As late as 1902, the nation was still worried about race suicide, for its president, Theodore Roosevelt (one of the "bully boys") wrote:

> . . . fundamentally infinitely more important than any other question in this country—that is, the question of race suicide.
> . . . desires to be "independent"—that is, to live one's life purely according to one's own desires—are in no sense substitutes for the fundamental virtues, for the practice of the strong, racial qualities. . . . the woman who deliberately avoids marriage, and has a heart so cold as to know no passion and a brain so shallow and selfish as to dislike having children, is in effect a criminal against the race, and should be an object of contemptuous abhorrence by all healthy people. [42]

American Eves in American Edens

The period between the times of Tocqueville and Bryce, during which the traditional relationships between the sexes were being questioned and disrupted, coincided almost exactly with the utopian impulse in America: most communal experiments with alternative modes of living began in the 1840s and Bellamy's influential fictional utopia was published in 1888. In these Edenic schemes, actual or literary, there was a new role for Eve; she was released from her confining roles of doll, wife and mother by the condemnation of sexual pleasure as "impure," by the abolition of monogamous marriage, or by the abolition of private property. In the case of the Shakers, the most notable example of celibate living, the concept of a bisexual God made logical the equality of the sexes and the belief that the attempt of one sex to dominate the other could only prove disastrous. As for the revivalist movement, which flourished chiefly in the "burned-over district" of western New York and often spawned free-love communities, Whitney Cross asserts that reformers like Elizabeth Cady Stanton, Amelia Bloomer, Susan B. Anthony, Antoinette Brown Blackwell, the Grimke sisters and others soon to lead the woman's rights movement served their apprenticeships in the reforms that flourished there: temperance, abolition, moral reform, all of which were led largely by women because women played such an important part in religion.[43] On the other hand, R. Palme Dutt argues that the struggle for the emancipation of women is "inextricably bound up with the struggle for socialism." The conditions of a private property society, he asserts, "of the individual household, of economic dependence, of the exploitation of the weakest, of the conflict between the social needs of motherhood and the care of children and the individualist laws of property and the anti-social conditions of the wage system" all underlie the oppression and servitude of women, and can only be overcome through social organization, through, in other words, a communist form of society.[44] The religious utopian communities, then, concentrated on the regeneration of the soul, while the secular communities tried to reform society by adapting the ideas of European socialists to the New World.

Most of the communitarians were concerned with sex and

sexual roles in one way or another. Those religious groups which enforced celibacy were often preoccupied with sexuality by default. In theory a woman fared better in celibate communities than she did in the profane world because she could no longer be considered a sexual object; instead of being confined to the sphere of home and children, she could hold positions of leadership and responsibility equal to those of men. Yet there was something childlike about her dependence upon a charismatic leader like Mother Ann, and something self-defeating about the denial of her own sexuality. Mormonism, on the other hand, which gave free reign to the polygamous sexual desires of men, could hardly be said to improve the status of women. John Humphrey Noyes, also a charismatic leader, combined Mother Ann's rhetoric about sexual purity with the polygamous practices of the Mormons. On a spiritual level at least, he was deeply concerned with the treatment of women as human beings, devising, for example, the system of "male continence" to free women from the pain and subsequent burdens of childbirth. For Noyes, the variety and multiplicity of sexual expression possible for the Perfectionists in complex marriage outweighed the advantages of personal intimacy. The Oneida Community was both the most radical nineteenth-century experiment in women's liberation and the most blatant example of hero worship at the expense not only of women, but of that individualism which Americans hold dear. In his insistence on mutual communism in economics and sex, Noyes had much in common with such twentieth-century writers as Alice Rossi and Carolyn Heilbrun who propose androgynous paradigms. But in his attempts to achieve spiritual perfection through sexual "purity," based on a personality cult that centered on himself as romantic hero, he was very much a man of his time.

Many, though not all of the socialistic communes believed with Noyes that a community of love demanded sexual equality and sexual freedom for both men and women. Like the Mormons and the Perfectionists, these communitarians were vigorously excoriated by the upholders of puritanical mores as advocates of "free love." Either way—in a celibate or a "free-love" community—woman was released from her confinement to the home, on the one hand because sex was sinful, on the other because private property, and thus private, monogamous relationships were not compatible with the general good. Both were abhorrent to Victorian America, which "exalting home and family, found the 'unnatural' restraints of the Shakers as objectionable as the 'licentious' sex mores of the Perfectionists." [45]

Most American secular communities were living implementations of the philosophies of Robert Owen or Charles Fourier. With no tyrannical God to appease for the Fall of Man, they dared to seek a new happiness by abolishing the Christian code of the dual nature of man: he was not by nature sinful, they believed, but perfectible. In this and in proclaiming the emancipation of women they were revolutionary; but when they experimented with free love they were considered outrageous, often bringing down the wrath of both church and state. Both Owen and Fourier were subversive in their views of marriage and family; both proposed the economic independence and equality of every member of the community. Although Owen based his communism on the home, and Fourier his joint-stock system on business principles, the main idea of both was the enlargement of the home, the extension of the family from the little man-wife circle to the larger corporation. Secular communities like those of New Harmony and Brook Farm understood intellectually the logic of complete equality among men and women as they understood the logic of industrial reform and abolition. Robert Dale Owen of New Harmony, in fact, went beyond the community to the Indiana legislature with divorce and property reform bills for the benefit of women which became law in that state. Brook Farm was the community of the intellectuals: Emerson (although he did not join), Hawthorne, the Channings, Charles Dana, Orestes Brownson, Theodore Parker, Bronson Alcott, John Sullivan Dwight,

Isaac Hecker, Margaret Fuller, Elizabeth Peabody were a few of those who were drawn to George Ripley's plan for a cooperative community in which "Equality before God of all of us was the central principle." [46] Margaret Fuller, whom a Brook Farm resident described as "the most wonderful woman of her age," [47] found it not surprising "that it should be the anti-slavery party that pleads for woman," considering that her economic dependence on man makes her "a child, or ward only, not an equal partner." [48]

The leaders of all of the utopian communities, interestingly, were men, with the exception of Mother Ann Lee and Jemima Wilkinson. In every case these communities were self-conscious attempts on the part of the leaders to create new sexual roles for their followers in much the same way as novelists create roles for their characters. In nearly every case the communities disbanded when their leaders died or left the community. But Emerson had predicted their demise as early as 1842. "The Reforms have their high origin in an ideal justice," he wrote, "but they do not retain the purity of an idea. They are quickly organized in some low, inadequate form, and present no more poetic image to the mind, than the evil tradition which they reprobated. This then is our criticism on the reforming movement; that it is in its origin divine; in its management and details timid and profane." [49]

The year 1880, when the members of the Oneida Community voted to become a joint-stock company and divide the shares of the corporation among its members, marks the end of the major phase of the American utopian communities. But John Humphrey Noyes's concern with sexual equality and his belief that in "vital society" men and women will "mingle at their labors" [50] was not dead. Eight years after the demise of the Oneida Community, Edward Bellamy began with Noyes's concern with the alienation of men and women from one another in American life. Although he did not go so far in his utopian novel as Noyes had gone in reshaping the actual lives of men and women at Oneida, his *Looking Backward* became one of the most popular books ever published in America: many millions of copies were printed in the United States and it was translated into twenty languages; forty-six more utopian novels were published in this country and many in Europe as well; one hundred and sixty-five "Bellamy Clubs" sprang up throughout the United States, devoted to the discussion and propagation of the aims expressed in the book; and the Populist party, which reached its peak during this period, was greatly influenced by Bellamy's ideas and got many of its votes from his adherents.[51]

The renown of *Looking Backward* cannot be ascribed to its literary qualities. Strictly speaking, like all the other utopian "novels" for which it served as a model, it is not a novel at all; it is a barely fictionalized socialist tract with cardboard characters whose "literary" function is to make the espoused philosophy palatable to the reader. But neither was it popular because its ideas were radical or new. *Looking Backward* was not the first American utopian romance. Hawthorne's *Blithedale Romance*, for example, had recorded the author's experience at Brook Farm, but his perspective was that of a member of a failed community, while for Bellamy the new Eden state was possible. The promise of American life which the book held out is only part of the reason for its success, however; another factor was its essentially middle-class, and therefore acceptable point of view. Although Bellamy saw with Noyes (and with Marx and Marcuse) [52] the alienation between work and life created by Western industrial society and the resulting gap between the respective social roles of the two sexes, and although he would correct this situation by having men and women work side by side, dress similarly to one another and participate equally in the political process, his utopian vision in this book is not really radical. His utopia would utilize the tools of the new technology to create a conventional sort of heaven-on-earth. Thus, although women are allowed to express their sexuality—"The girls of the twentieth century tell their love," even occasionally proposing to men—and despite Bellamy's belief that the whole mating process had been transformed by the new social, political and economic equality, in the world of *Looking Backward* there is no real experimentation with new sexual roles and with alternative life styles.

Aware of the relationship between economic and sexual dependency, the twentieth-century spokesman, Dr. Leete, finds it "shocking to the moral sense" that any person should be dependent for the means of support on another person. Thus, every man, woman and child receives the same living wage in credit hours for work done, but women have their own feminine regime in the industrial army, headed by their own general-in-chief. They do only work that is "perfectly adapted, both as to kind and degree of labor," to their sex, their hours of work are shorter than those of men, and they are permitted to work at all "only because it is fully understood that a certain regular requirement of labor . . . is well for body and mind." Not only do the difference and separation of men's and women's work mark Bellamy's views as conventional insofar as the role and status of women are concerned, but more importantly, both *Looking Backward* and *Equality,* its sequel, espouse traditional views of marriage: men and women apparently marry only once, for life; they live together, like traditional nuclear families, in private dwellings; women cannot pursue full careers because they must take several years out for maternal duties. Nowhere are the possibilities of divorce, nonmarriage or state child-care explored. Radical though such ideas may seem, all of them had been tried in real life by utopian communitarians half a century before.

Much more courageous is the book of Edward Bellamy's brother, Charles Bellamy. His *An Experiment in Marriage* is the story of a journey to another place, rather than to another time like Edward Bellamy's books. In Grape Valley there is a totally new relationship between the sexes. Women are truly as independent as men. Economically self-sufficient, they marry only for love, never for reasons of dependency. Divorce, moreover, is easy; there are no questions of maintenance to be settled and children are the wards of the state, cared for and educated at the general nurseries and schools. For these utopians, "Anything less than love uniting husband and wife is bondage. Any other relation except that founded on absorbing and controlling passion is mutual slavery." [53]

Edward Bellamy did in fact share his brother's ideas, but he was reluctant to make them a part of *Looking Backward* or *Equality* because he felt that they would diminish the attractiveness of his ideal state. He told his wife Emma, for example, that he had written one chapter which he would have to omit because the world was not yet ready for its contents.[54] Bellamy was so cautious about what the reading public would accept that he even substituted the word "nationalism" for "socialism" in *Looking Backward* because, as he wrote to William Dean Howells in 1888, " 'socialism' suggested to Americans 'the red flag,' an abusive tone about God and religion, and all manner of sexual novelties." [55] He likewise decided to omit a chapter that drew conclusions similar to this one from an unpublished story: "If God had depended for volunteers, there would have been no women. But he conscripted souls for that duty." [56] Other published and unpublished material suggests, however, that in his view that woman gives the race continuity and acts "as the centripetal force in bringing man, the individualist, back to the race," teaching him to "love his fellows . . . develop his nobler qualities, and achieve . . . social solidarity," [57] Bellamy was very much a man of his time. The idea of woman as culture-carrier can be traced throughout the nineteenth century, from Hawthorne, who worshipped in his Sophia those very qualities Bellamy cites, to Henry James.

If the utopian novel, for which Bellamy's *Looking Backward* stands as a model, merits the same kind of judgment which Emerson had leveled at the communities—that in its origin it is divine, but in its management and details timid and profane—how much greater is the extent to which this can be said of the imaginative literature of the nineteenth century. The great novels of the period of American utopianism were an imaginative rendering of the shared myth of the New World Garden. That the heights to which their authors aspired, and which they often achieved in a literary sense, were so much greater makes their timidity or insensitivity to women the more obvious. It is the novel—the imaginative reflection of the collective unconscious—which takes the raw material of myth and transforms it into a work which the people of a culture can understand and identify with on a conscious level. Significantly, the women in the novels of Hawthorne, Melville, Oliver Wendell Holmes, Harold Frederic, Henry James and William Dean Howells are not women at all, but images of women. They are reflections of the prevailing images of women in the nineteenth century, and like the predominantly male creators of utopian schemes, their male creators perceive with cultural blinders the women in the New World Gardens of their imaginations.

The Faces of Eve

Eve in the New World Garden, despite Adam's wish to ignore her, restrict her role or enshrine her on a pedestal, is the most important phenomenon in nineteenth-century America. In the novel she is no single figure, easy to trace like Adam. A woman of mystery, connected to Time as Adam is not, she is like a prism: turn her this way and you see one facet; turn her that way and you see another. Sometimes she is threatening, alluring, yet dangerously suggestive of Adam's fall from purity, like Eve the original temptress. Thus Hawthorne, for reasons similar to those of celibate communitarians who deny Eve's sexuality in the attempt to restore woman to her original status as female godhead, condemns her as a deviant from society. Sometimes she is Eve before the Fall, the pure and asexual preserver of American society. Sometimes she is the mother of us all, a manipulating and possessive figure to such novelists as Henry James, looming large as Ann Lee, mother of all the Shakers. Sometimes she is the "new woman," saying "No!" as the first rebel Eve did to the sphere prescribed for her by the original Patriarch. These, then, are the faces of Eve projected by the predominantly male novelists of the nineteenth century between the time of Tocqueville's observation about "the quiet sphere of domestic duties" and that of Bryce about the "new kind of womanhood" and concurrent with the utopian impulse which led American reformers and writers to attempt actual and imaginative returns to the sacred space and primordial time of the Garden. The images of Eve which appear in the major novels of this period are rooted deeply in contemporary attitudes toward women. In some cases the novelists borrow from real life in their portraits—Hawthorne and Henry James, for example. In some cases the utopians borrow from novels in creating new roles for their characters; Ann Lee and Fanny Wright, the milieux of the Mormons, Perfectionists, Brook Farmers and communitarians at Fruitlands seem more like characters and scenes out of novels than like real life. And in many instances these settings and characters did become the materials of novels and plays. Somewhere, then, in that place between fiction and reality—the place of "moonlight in a familiar room"—the faces of Eve emerge as the images of woman in the nineteenth century: the Temptress, the American Princess, the Great Mother, the New Woman.

The Temptress is the most obvious face of the Eve paradigm. She is Hawthorne's "dark lady"—Beatrice Rappaccini, Hester Prynne, Miriam; Oliver Wendell Holmes's Elsie Venner, poisoned prenatally by a snake-bite; Melville's Isabel and Harold Frederic's Celia Madden. An American counterpart of the *femme fatale* in nineteenth-century Romantic literature, she is deadly because of her alluring yet frightening sexuality, which threatens to destroy the self-reliant hero. Her tragedy is inherent in her posture of defiance to societal mores.

The American Princess is Eve before the Fall. Delicately beautiful and innocent, she is the psychosexual opposite of the Temptress. She is the "pale maiden" of Hawthorne and Melville—Priscilla, Hilda, Lucy—and Henry James's Daisy

Miller, Isabel Archer, Milly Theale, Maggie Verver. When she stands alone, she is self-reliant as well as innocent, but her self-reliance is more theoretical than actual. Unlike her dark antipode, she is never threatening to men. A descendant of the sentimental heroine, her project is to get her man.

The Great Mother is a woman even more threatening than the Temptress because she is more powerful. I borrow the term "great mother" from the title of Erich Neumann's brilliant book which traces the myths of the feminine through artifacts and expression from prehistoric times. In the novels of Henry James, the mother figure is manipulative and destructive; she would commit the ultimate Jamesian sin of possessing the very soul of the hero or heroine. Olive Chancellor is the archetype of the Great Mother in this chapter, serving as an introduction to the surrogate mothers—the Governess, Mrs. Grose, Mrs. Bread, Mrs. Wix; the mother-neglecters—Mrs. Farange, Mrs. Moreen, Mrs. Touchett; and "the real witch-bitches"—Rose Armiger, Madame de Bellegarde, Madame Merle.

The New Woman is the "free" and "equal" woman of the utopian communities and novels. Ironically, she is not a person at all, but a caricature. Whether she is deprived of her sexuality as a Shaker or a Bostonian, or of possibilities for intimacy at Oneida, or whether she is still basically the sentimental heroine of *Looking Backward,* one cannot believe in her. Hawthorne's Zenobia, the "most complete creation of a person" according to James, commits suicide. The others—James's Bostonians: Olive Chancellor, Miss Birdseye, Mrs. Farrinder, Dr. Prance; and Howells's Dr. Breen and Eveleth Strange—range from vicious to sentimental portrayals. Only Kate Chopin's Edna Pontellier is a woman, not an image; but she too commits suicide—a comment on the possibilities of a full life for a woman in nineteenth-century America.

In this study of nineteenth-century novels, the omission of Cooper, Poe, Mark Twain and especially of Howells, the "dean of American letters" whose study of the American girl was thought to be definitive in his day, may puzzle some readers. While Cooper's and Poe's dark ladies are certainly predecessors of Hester Prynne, most of Cooper's novels were written before the temporal boundaries of this study, and Poe's dark ladies appear in his short stories and poetry; his one novel has no women. Mark Twain created no really significant women; his Roxanna in *Pudd'nhead Wilson* is the most interesting, but even she is little more than a literary stereotype. As for Howells, although women are important in most of his novels, his primary aim was to present "the smiling aspects of American life," his own definition of "realism," and the Edenic myth is essentially a *Romantic* notion. Howells figures in this study only in a limited way, therefore: his Dr. Breen is an example of the professional "new woman" and his Eveleth Strange of the utopian "new woman."

With the exception of Kate Chopin, it will be noticed, the novelists to delineate these faces of Eve are all male. This is not so surprising as it may seem, for literature is a reflection of culture, and culture in nineteenth-century America was still predominantly male. The awakening of female writers to a sense of their own identity (with the notable exception of Emily Dickinson, whose poetry is beyond the scope of this study of novels) begins at the turn of the century, and is properly the subject of a study of women in twentieth-century literature.

"Maria Catherine Smith," by Captain John Smith, c. 1680. Courtesy, the American Antiquarian Society, Worcester, Massachusetts.

The Temptress

Adam: ". . . nothing lovelier can be found
In Woman than to study household good,
And good works in her Husband to promote."

Eve: "But to Adam in what sort
Shall I appear? Shall I to him make known
As yet my change, and give him to partake
Full happiness with mee, or rather not.
But keep the odds of Knowledge in my power
In Female Sex, the more to draw his love,
And render me more equal, and perhaps,
A thing not undesirable, some time
Superior: for inferior who is free?"

—John Milton, *Paradise Lost* [1]

Critics of American literature who equate Eve the temptress with "the Dark Lady of Salem" [2] limit the complexity of her image. Her province, for one thing, is wider than Salem; Cooper and Poe make use of her in their tales, probably borrowing her from Milton, Coleridge, Keats and Trollope, and she appears as far away as Norway in the plays of Ibsen. In fact her literary prototype can be traced to medieval tales of courtly love, and beyond to Latin literature and Roman comedy. A recent poster advertising the French film *Eve* carried this caption: "Mysterious—tantalizing—alluring—wanton—but deep within her burning the violent fires that destroy a man." [3] But the dark lady is, for another thing, more than temptress: she has within her the seeds of liberation—her own and, as we shall see, vicariously her author's.

Milton's Eve, like later literary temptresses (especially those of Hawthorne, who admits in the preface of *The Marble Faun* to having "laid felonious hands upon a certain bust of Milton"), is a person who acts out her feelings in ways that depart from the plan of the patriarchal community. She is, in other words, what Kai Erikson would call a "deviant"—one whose conduct "the people of a group consider so dangerous or embarrassing or irritating that they bring special sanctions to bear against the persons who exhibit it . . . a person whose activities have moved outside the margins of the group, and when the community calls him to account for that vagrancy it is making a statement about the nature and placement of its boundaries." [4] In literature, the dark lady exists outside the boundaries of the community, while the pale maiden typifies the traditional values of the community: they are creatures of the same culture, inventions of the same imagination.

This chapter traces the image of the temptress in the nineteenth-century American novel from simplicity to complexity: Oliver Wendell Holmes's Elsie Venner, Hawthorne's Beatrice Rappaccini, Melville's Isabel, Harold Frederic's Celia Madden, Hawthorne's Miriam and Hester Prynne. Zenobia is an obvious omission from this list, but despite her voluptuous beauty and her deviance from the norms of the community, which link her to the other heroines of this chapter, hers is really the face of the "new woman." Hawthorne's own equivocal position on the boundary of the community—his own participation in a utopian experiment—puts him in a special position as a commentator on his society. His Zenobia, also a participant in a utopian experiment, is more than a deviant from societal norms; she is a shaper of mores in a new community.

ELSIE VENNER: THE LITERARY CONVENTION WITH PSYCHOLOGICAL TRAPPINGS

Elsie Venner is so lavishly and so unsubtly endowed with Eve-like qualities that she is little more than stereotype. But precisely because all of the components of the myth are so clearly delineated, this novel provides the clearest definition of "temptress."

Holmes states in all three of his prefaces—1861, 1883, 1891—that he is dealing with the doctrine of Original Sin, and furthermore that he is writing not psychological realism [5] but "romance," claiming thereby all of the privileges which Hawthorne assumes in "The Custom House" preface to *The Scarlet Letter*. "The real aim of the story," Holmes says in the second preface, "was to test the doctrine of 'original sin' and human responsibility for the disordered volition coming under that technical denomination. Was Elsie Venner," he asks, "poisoned by the venom of a crotalus [rattlesnake] before she was born, morally responsible for the 'volitional' aberrations, which translated into acts become what is known as sin, and, it may be, what is punished as crime? If, on presentation of the evidence, she becomes by the verdict of the human conscience a proper object of divine pity and not of divine wrath, as a subject of moral poisoning, wherein lies the difference between her position at the bar of judgment, human or divine, and that of the unfortunate victim who received a moral poison from a remote ancestor before he drew his first breath?" [6] His heroine clearly is Eve—"a physiological conception fertilized by a theological dogma." Holmes links her in this preface to Keats's Lamia, a woman changed into a serpent (and in the novel to Coleridge's Christabel, a vampire, as well), and to Hawthorne's Miriam, although he disclaims Hawthorne as a model, stating that his own work was well advanced before the publication of *The Marble Faun* (but not, I might add, before the publication of "Rappaccini's Daughter" and *The Scarlet Letter*).

By 1891, in his preface to the third edition, Holmes was

openly calling his heroine Eve and using her to challenge orthodox theology:

> Believing, as I do, that our prevailing theologies are founded upon an utterly false view of the relation of man to his Creator, I attempted to illustrate the doctrine of inherited moral responsibility for other people's misbehavior. I tried to make out a case for my poor Elsie, whom the most hardened theologian would find it hard to blame for her inherited ophidian tastes and tendencies. How, then, is he to blame mankind for inheriting "sinfulness" from their first parents? May not the serpent have bitten Eve before the birth of Cain, her first born? That would have made an excuse for Cain's children, as Elsie's antenatal misfortune made an excuse for her. But what difference does it make in the child's responsibility whether his inherited tendencies come from a snake-bite or some other source which he knew nothing about and could not have prevented from acting?

In the novel, the two theological responses to "original sin" are personified by the Reverend Dr. Honeywood and Brother Fairweather. Elsie recognizes Dr. Honeywood's compassion (she sends for him on her deathbed despite her membership in Brother Fairweather's church), as do her two friends, old black Sophy, who represents the opposite of Puritan repression and is the only one who understands Elsie emotionally, and Dr. Kittredge, the only one who understands Elsie intellectually. (He understands, for example, that "Elsie would have been burned for a witch in the old times.")

Elsie Venner is the unwitting temptress in this nineteenth-century puritanical New England Village: Holmes takes great pains to describe that "community" and to place Elsie outside its boundaries. The town of Rockland is a rocky version of the Garden. Several paragraphs of description are given to its pastures, its various bushes of bayberry, blackberry, huckleberry, barberry, its trees, ponds and tumbling brook. The town is set against The Mountain, home of Rattlesnake Ledge and the terror of all the village. At the foot of the mountain stands Dudley Mansion, the home of Elsie Venner

and her father Dudley Venner, descendant of Governor
Thomas Dudley of the Massachusetts Bay Colony. Before the
story begins the Venner garden had been a wilderness of
roses and the scene of the "young and fresh and beautiful"
love of Dudley and his bride. At the time of the story the garden is "somewhat neglected, but not in disgrace." "The
flower-beds were edged with box, which diffused around it
that dreamy balsamic odor, full of ante-natal reminiscences of
a lost Paradise, dimly fragrant as might be the bdellium of
ancient Havilah, the land compassed by the river Pison that
went out of Eden." The way out of Eden, then, is either the
wildness of The Mountain with its threatening avalanches
and its rattlesnakes or the town—a place "with residences
which had pretensions to elegance, with people of some
breeding, with a newspaper, and 'stores' to advertise in it,
and with two or three churches."

Towns, for Holmes, are not bad. Their core amounts to a
"Brahmin caste of New England," a caste "not in any odious
sense—but by the repetition of the same influences, generation after generation, it has acquired a distinct organization
and physiognomy." This "harmless, inoffensive, untitled ar-
istocracy," is known especially by the prevalence of scholars
among its male members. Such a man is Bernard Langdon,
the hero of the story and the master of the school which Elsie
attends. The female member of the Brahmin caste would
seem to be a "light-haired girl with dark eyes, hazel, brown,
or of the color of that mountain-brook . . . where it ran
through shadowy woodlands," an "opening bud" waiting
"on the rock of expectation" for her man with her "monosyl-
lable ready for him."

In Elsie's school, the "Apollinean Female Institute," there
are three distinct types (Holmes calls them "classes") of females, all within the boundaries of the community:

Hannah Martin. Fourteen years and three months old. Short-
necked, thick-waisted, round-cheeked, smooth, vacant forehead, large, dull eyes. Looks good-natured, with little other

expression. Three buns in her bag, and a large apple. Has a habit of attacking her provisions in school-hours.—

Rosa Milburn. Sixteen. Brunette, with a rareripe flush in her cheeks. Color comes and goes easily. Eyes wandering, apt to be downcast. Moody at times. Said to be passionate, if irritated. Finished in high relief. Carries shoulders well back and walks well, as if proud of her woman's life, with a slight rocking movement, being one of the wide-flanged pattern, but seems restless—a hard girl to look after. Has a romance in her pocket, which she means to read in school-time.—

Charlotte Ann Wood. Fifteen. The poetess before mentioned. Long, light ringlets, pallid complexion, blue eyes. Delicate child, half unfolded. Gentle, but languid and despondent. Does not go much with the other girls, but reads a good deal, especially poetry, underscoring favorite passages. Writes a great many verses, very fast, not very correctly; full of the usual human sentiments, expressed in the accustomed phrases. Undervitalized. Sensibilities not covered with their normal integuments.

These three descriptions, almost medical case histories in their terseness, are meant to stand as a contrast to Elsie Venner, who enters the schoolroom next. And they do. Elsie is as different from her classmates as the language used to describe her.

A girl of about seventeen entered. She was tall and slender but rounded, with a peculiar undulation of movement, such as one sometimes sees in perfectly untutored country-girls, whom Nature, the queen of graces, has taken in hand, but more commonly in connection with the very highest breeding of the most thoroughly trained society. She was a splendid scowling beauty, black-browed, with a flash of white teeth which was always like a surprise when her lips parted. She wore a checkered dress of a curious pattern, and a camel's hair scarf twisted a little fantastically about her. She went to her seat, *which she had moved a short distance apart from the rest,* and, sitting down, began playing listlessly with her gold chain, as was a common habit with her, coiling it and uncoiling it about her slender wrist, and braiding it in with her long delicate fingers. Pres-

ently she looked up. Black, piercing eyes, not large,—a low
forehead, . . . —black hair, twisted in heavy braids,—a face
that one could not help looking at for its beauty, yet that one
wanted to look away from for something in its expression, and
could not for those diamond eyes [emphasis added].

Elsie, then, dresses differently from the other girls; she is un-
commonly beautiful; she sits apart from the rest; she is associated with a rare alpine flower (which is found only in one
spot among the rocks of The Mountain—on Rattlesnake
Ledge); and there is something altogether repellent about
her—her teacher must instantly fling away the flower Elsie
has given her and wash the tips of her fingers which Elsie
has touched. For all her difference from her peers in this
story, however, Elsie has sisters in other Romantic literature
of the period—the heroines of Keats and Coleridge mentioned earlier, and with her black hair, her black eyes, her
wild beauty, her exotic, almost foreign qualities as expressed
in her personal adornments, the dark ladies of Poe, Hawthorne and Melville. Holmes comes as close as possible to
naming her Eve—through her initials, the hisslike sound of
"Elsie" and the venomous quality of "Venner." Elsie's own
speech is nearly a hiss: "She did not lisp, yet her articulation
of one or two consonants was not absolutely perfect." She
undulates when she moves; she coils and uncoils a gold
chain about her wrist; the diamond-patterned skirt which
she usually wears beneath another skirt of some diaphanous
material is like the diamond pattern of a snake's multiple
skins; her piercing diamond eyes hypnotize her victims. The
association with snakes is not metaphorical, but literal. Elsie's mother, we learn, was bitten by a snake when she was
pregnant with Elsie. "Poor Catalina" died after Elsie's birth,
but Elsie imbibed the poison of the serpent and bears the
marks of its fangs (always covered with a necklace) upon her
neck.

The snakelike qualities of Elsie are what make her deviant.
The incomparable brilliance of her compositions is tied to her
intimate knowledge of the savage scenery of The Mountain

(she literally knows Rattlesnake Ledge) and she so terrifies her teacher that it makes Miss Darley ill. "Tell me," Miss Darley asks Mr. Langdon, "are there not natures born so out of parallel with the lines of natural law that nothing short of a miracle can bring them right?" Elsie's snakelike qualities noticed in the schoolroom are even more apparent when she appears at a party dressed with such special splendor that groups naturally part to make way for her. Her long black hair is a braided coil; round her neck she wears a golden torque; her dress is a "grayish watered silk"; her collar is pinned with a flashing diamond brooch with "the silver setting of a past generation." On her wrists she wears bracelets: "one was a circlet of enameled scales; the other looked as if it might have been Cleopatra's asp, with its body turned to gold and its eyes to emeralds." It is partly her dressing and behaving to please her own fancy, "with small regard to the modes declared correct by the Rockland milliners and mantua makers," that makes her draw "a circle of isolation around herself," just as she had sat apart in the schoolroom by her own choice. But more than that, it is the "strange, cold glitter in her eyes" with which she looks at the crowd babbling and moving before her that isolates her.

Her peculiar habits, her strong will, her piercing eyes make her independent of the customary patterns of behavior and subject to no influence but her own. Since childhood she has been a hard creature to manage, often manifesting the most extraordinary singularities of taste or instinct. Her father has been able to influence, but not govern her. Old Sophy, "said to be the daughter of a cannibal chief," succeeds best with her; except for one Spanish dancing teacher, all the other servants are afraid of her. Her friend Dr. Kittredge recommends that her father get her a foreign governess—someone, in other words, not bound by New England traditions of repression. The doctor, like Sophy, has watched her closely. Once, for example, while in the Venner garden, he has been startled by the sound of a sharp prolonged rattle, and moving toward the sound, discovers Elsie, alone, dancing a wild Moorish fandango. She emanates a "passionate fierce-ness," rattling her castanets, "her lithe body undulating with flexuous grace, her diamond eyes glittering, her round arms wreathing and unwinding," flinging herself finally in a "careless coil."

> At last, when the veins of the summer were hot and swollen, and the juices of all the poison-plants and the blood of all the creatures that feed upon them had grown thick and strong, . . . about this time of over-ripe mid-summer, the life of Elsie seemed fullest of its malign and restless instincts. . . . At this season, too, all her peculiar tastes in dress and ornament came out in a more striking way than at other times. She was never so superb as then, and never so threatening in her scowling beauty. The barred skirts she always fancied showed sharply beneath her diaphanous muslins; the diamonds often glittered on her breast as if for her own pleasure rather than to dazzle others; the asp-like bracelet hardly left her arm. She was never seen without some necklace,—either the golden cord . . . or a chain of mosaics, or simply a ring of golden scales.

Elsie's scowling beauty, then, is emblematic of her threat; her sexuality equals deadly poison for men who succumb to her.

The first man whom Elsie "tempts" is her cousin Dick Ven-ner, orphan son of a South American trader and a lady of Spanish descent. The two cousins have been raised together and are "as strange a pair as one roof could well cover. Both handsome, wild, impetuous, unmanageable, they played and fought together like two young leopards, beautiful, but dangerous, their lawless instincts showing through all their graceful movements." Elsie, however, is the wilder of the two, and Old Sophy, watching them in their play, always seemed to fear more for the boy than for the girl, warning him often not to overexcite her. One day Dick does vex Elsie into "a paroxysm of wrath." She springs at him and bites him. That incident ends Dick's stay at the Dudley mansion for some years, but he returns as a young man who would like to become master of the estate. He doesn't love Elsie; his motives are pecuniary, but as a youth tired of easy conquests he is fascinated by her, especially by that irresistible quality in her eyes which makes him feel "drawn to her by a power which seemed to take away his will." It is not only Elsie's snakelike eyes which draw Dick, however; it is her sexuality. Both of them feel "a renewal of that early experience which followed the taste of the forbidden fruit—a natural blush of consciousness, not without its charm." In using the word "forbidden," Holmes is implying the incestuous quality of the sexual attraction between Dick and Elsie. They had been raised like brother and sister until Elsie's father became aware "that it would never do to let these children grow up together. They would either love each other as they got older, and pair like wild creatures, or take some fierce antipathy, which might end nobody could tell where. It was not safe to try." Dick cannot come too close to Elsie, in fact, without provoking the dangerous aspects of her sexuality. At one point, for example, when he attempts to remove the golden coil from her neck, she throws her head back, narrows her eyes, "her forehead drawing down so that Dick thought her head actually flattened itself," and reminds him so vividly of the little girl who had struck him with those sharp flashing teeth that the two white scars begin to sting just as they had the first time. Dick is in no real danger from Elsie, however; he is already fallen. Symbolically, his half-foreign background prevents him from being one of the elect; but more than that, he courts Elsie in cold blood without loving her, he attempts murder (but is foiled by Abel the gardener), and he is likened to the devil himself—"that strange horseman . . . looking so like Mephistopheles galloping hard to be in season at the witches' Sabbath-gathering."

The attraction which Elsie exerts on Bernard Langdon is more enticing, but the schoolmaster is safe because he is one of the elect who knows what he wants—the perfect helpmeet Miss Letitia Forrester, granddaughter of Reverend Honeywood, a "wholesome and hearty" girl, "so full of life, so graceful, so generous, so vivacious, so ready always to do all she could . . . for everybody, so perfectly frank in her avowed delight in the pleasures which this miserable world offered her in the shape of natural beauty, of poetry, of music, of companionship, of books, of cheerful cooperation in the tasks of those about her." Those New England Brahmins always choose the pure maiden over the dark lady whose dangerous sexuality both entices and frightens them. The typical Adam, Bernard is at first drawn to Elsie, both aroused and disturbed. The glitter of her diamond eyes affects him strangely. He dreams of her, wondering, ". . . —by what demon is she haunted, by what taint is she blighted, by what curse is she followed, by what destiny is she marked, that her strange beauty has such a terror in it, and that hardly one shall dare to love her, and her eye glitters always, but warms for none?" Because Bernard does not want to risk involvement with Elsie himself, he chooses to see only the luster of ice in the light of her eyes, and nothing of the passion which burns for him. He sees her as a creature who might hate, but can never love, and is relieved when she ceases to focus her glittering eyes upon him. The climax of his struggle with his own feelings about Elsie occurs when she saves his life on Rattlesnake Ledge. He has gone for a tramp on The Mountain, seeking the place where Elsie's rare flower grows. Seating himself on a rock, he looks about for a straw to bite on, "a country-instinct,—relic, no doubt, of the old vegetable-feeding habits of Eden," and finds instead a hairpin of Elsie's. He feels a thrill of excitement shoot through him, and begins to look about for some cave fitted up as her retreat. The real threat of Elsie's sexuality is suddenly made abundantly clear to him: what he sees at the mouth of the cave is "the glitter of two diamond eyes, small, sharp, cold, shining out of the darkness, but gliding with a smooth, steady motion towards the light, and himself. . . . Then for the first time thrilled in Mr. Bernard's ears the dreadful sound that nothing which breathes, be it man or brute, can hear unmoved,—the long, loud, stinging whirr, as the huge, thick-bodied reptile shook his many-jointed rattle and adjusted his loops for the fatal stroke." He is saved by Elsie: her power is greater even than the snake's. When Bernard feels the charm of the snake dissolving and is able to turn away, he sees Elsie, "looking motionless into the reptile's eyes, which had shrunk and faded under the stronger enchantment of her own."

Elsie has saved Bernard's life, but she has revealed to him her poisonous essence, and from this point on he will study her rather than love her. Grateful to her for saving his life, he shudders when he recollects the scene and dreams of being "pursued by the glare of cold glittering eyes,—whether they were in the head of a woman or of a reptile he could not always tell, the images had so run together." It is after this incident that Bernard tells Dr. Kittredge that he does not love Elsie, but pities her; that he writes to his professor, the narrator of the tale, for information about Christabel and Lamia; and that he procures some caged rattlesnakes to study, which like Elsie in her final illness, live on nothing but air. Bernard's rejection of Elsie's love—love which might have saved her but might also have destroyed him—brings about her death, but also her release from the curse which has poisoned her existence. After she declares her love for him and he replies that he is her true friend, but nothing more (in language reminiscent of Isabel Archer's "sisterly" devotion to Ralph on his deathbed), she takes to her bed and does not get up again. It is the antidote sent by Bernard, the leaves from the white ash, that makes her violently ill and finally extinguishes both her poison and her life, the two being inextricably entangled.

I have so far focused on Holmes's description of Elsie Venner as "a physiological conception fertilized by a theological dogma," but the author's psychological insights into the "dark lady" should be mentioned at this point, for they identify another dimension of Eve the temptress present in more complex characterizations. I refer specifically to Elsie's relationship with her father. It is interesting that none of the dark ladies have mothers. Perhaps this is one reason why they are deviants: they have no models. But more important, this makes the relationship with their fathers special. Holmes says of Dudley Venner that "the woman a man loves is always his own daughter." Living in isolation with his daughter—having sent Dick Venner away, perhaps because of sexual jealousy—he avoids her. "Are there not fruits," he wonders, "which while unripe, are not to be tasted or endured?" Whether because of his incestuous fears, or because Elsie reminds him painfully of her mother, Dudley does so good a job of hiding his love for his daughter that Elsie "never felt that he loved her. . . . fatal recollections and associations had frozen up the springs of natural affection in his breast. There was nothing in the world he would not do for Elsie. He had sacrificed his whole life to her." The only thing he cannot do for her is love her. The words about sacrifice recall Bernard's words to the Doctor: "I would risk my life for her, if it would do her any good, but it would be in cold blood." Such a lack of emotional commitment sends Elsie to her deathbed. She needs to be loved. Bernard's rejection wounds her so deeply because having known only coldness from her father, she has staked everything on winning the love of this substitute father (a role which Bernard as schoolmaster particularly fits); she risks opening herself up, even though she has learned to be cold and withdrawn as a matter of self-preservation. Thus the "blight which fell upon her in the dim period before consciousness," the "accidental principle which . . . so poisoned her childhood and youth," is symbolically the snakebite and psychologically the lack of parental love. Elsie has grown up as what one would today call an autistic child. Helen Darley, who nurses her in her last illness, notices Dudley's "morbid sensitiveness," his "aversion to saying much" about his daughter, "a wish to feel and speak as a parent should, and yet a shrinking, as if there were something about Elsie which he could not bear to dwell upon." Dudley's love for his daughter/wife and Elsie's love for her teacher/father come together at her death. Dudley's first signs of real tenderness bring about Elsie's first ability to weep. Where earlier she has moaned without the solace of tears, "her grief, like her anger . . . a dull ache, longing, like that to finish itself with a fierce paroxysm, but wanting its natural outlet," her father's tender look and tone as he watches by her bedside and tells her how much she reminds him of her mother break "through all the barriers between her heart and her eyes" and with a sudden overflow of feeling Elsie weeps. When Dudley kisses her, although the Doctor warned against allowing her any physical exertion, Elsie rises in a sudden effort, kisses him, and dies.

We have moved, I think, well beyond the traditional interpretation of the dark lady as temptress referred to in the beginning of this chapter. Even—or especially—in this rather crude and simplistic treatment of Elsie Venner as Eve, it is clear that she is more than destructive sexuality. An analysis of her special qualities must take into account her deviation from the norms of the puritanical community whose boundaries exclude her, the aspects of her Eden which make it difficult or impossible for her to develop as part of the community, her resulting sense of alienation, and the responsibility of the male figures in the narrative for her peculiar development.

BEATRICE RAPPACCINI: THE LITERARY CONVENTION AS ALLEGORY

There are a great many similarities between *Elsie Venner* and "Rappaccini's Daughter": the poisoned garden, the snake imagery and of course the dark lady herself, with her dangerous sexuality and her alienation from the human community. But where Holmes finally had to admit that "everything was getting tangled up together, and there would be no chance of disentangling the threads," Hawthorne's tightly woven tale exhibits great skill. Acknowledging (in the guise of M. de l'Aubépine) his love of allegory in the first paragraph and referring to such earlier tales as "The New Adam and Eve" and

"Egotism, or the Bosom Serpent" frees him to use his form without constraint. Because this *is* allegory, however, Beatrice Rappaccini is, like Elsie Venner, a symbol, not a fully realized woman.

Hawthorne was testing the doctrine of Original Sin in "Rappaccini's Daughter" fifteen years before Holmes began to write *Elsie Venner*. Like Elsie, Beatrice is poisonous through no fault of her own, yet her poison, bound up with her very essence, makes her a potential destroyer of any man with whom she comes in close contact. Beatrice, however, is more complex, more ambiguous than Elsie. As Elsie is identified with snakes, Beatrice is linked to the fatal shrub, but the gorgeous poisonous flowers stand for sexuality as well as for intrinsic evil. The names of the lovers in the story are also ambiguous: Giovanni, who is "not unstudied in the great poem of his country," recollects that one of the ancestors of the building in which he lodges "had been pictured by Dante as a partaker of the immortal agonies of the Inferno," [7] but Beatrice is Dante's ideal woman who leads him through the gates of Paradise. It is Giovanni who links her with the *Inferno* rather than with *Paradiso*—probably because *his* name suggests Don Giovanni, or Don Juan, the "hit and run lover" to whom love, the lasting commitment, stands for being swallowed up by a woman, and whose insatiable need to possess one woman after another suggests his own sexual insecurity.[8] Hawthorne's Beatrice will lead, or entice, her young man into Paradise, the poisoned garden of Rappaccini.

In the center of the garden is the ruin of a marble fountain—"so wofully [sic] shattered that it was impossible to trace the original design from the chaos of remaining fragments"—which suggests the chaotic fragments of our own Eden. The garden is planted with magnificently gorgeous flowers, but they seem to Giovanni "fierce, passionate, and even unnatural." He is shocked by "an appearance of artificialness indicating that there had been such commixture, and, as it were, adultery, of various vegetable species, that the production was no longer of God's making, but the monstrous offspring of man's depraved fancy." The gardener turns out to be "no common laborer, but a tall, emaciated, sallow, and sickly-looking man, dressed in a scholar's garb of black . . . beyond the middle term of life, with gray hair, a thin, gray beard, and a face singularly marked with intellect and cultivation, but which could never, even in his more youthful days, have expressed much warmth of heart." * Kin to Aylmer in "The Birthmark" and Chillingworth in *The Scarlet Letter* (and also to Poe's men, whose insatiable quest for knowledge is equivalent to fatal possession, and to Frederic's Dr. Ledsmar), Dr. Rappaccini is the cold-blooded scientist who commits the unpardonable sin of studying human beings as if they were inanimate objects. In this story he is literally father to Beatrice and symbolically the Creator of the Garden. Yet he walks, Giovanni notices, in his own garden with trepidation: ". . . in spite of this deep intelligence on his part, there was no approach to intimacy between himself and these vegetable existences. On the contrary, he avoided their actual touch or the direct inhaling of their odors with a caution that impressed Giovanni most disagreeably; for the man's demeanor was that of one walking among malignant influences, such as savage beasts, or deadly snakes, or evil spirits, which, should he allow them one moment of license, would wreak upon him some terrible fatality." Giovanni is strangely frightened "to see this air of insecurity in a person cultivating a garden, that most simple and innocent of human toils . . . which had been alike the joy and labor of the unfallen parents of the race. Was this garden," he wonders, "the Eden of the present world? And this man, with

---

* I do not want to suggest that the Perfectionists lived in a poisoned community, because I think there were a great many positive things about Oneida—although their doctrine of "free love" was certainly regarded as poisonous by outsiders—but there is something Rappaccini-like about Noyes, the scholar "beyond the middle term of life," experimenting with stirpiculture.

such a perception of harm in what his own hands caused to grow,—was he the Adam?"

The question is on Giovanni's part naive and on Hawthorne's ironic. No innocent, Rappaccini has nurtured his daughter as carefully as the garden vegetation. In fact she *is* one of Rappaccini's flowers. Only Beatrice can tend the purple plant; despite the mask Rappaccini places over his mouth and nostrils, "as if all this beauty did but conceal a deadlier malice," it is too dangerous for him. Giovanni, whom she reminds of "deep hues of purple or crimson and of perfumes heavily delectable," also sees her as "another flower, the human sister of those vegetable ones, as beautiful as they, more beautiful than the richest of them." Beatrice is "arrayed with as much richness of taste as the most splendid of the flowers, beautiful as the day, and with a bloom so deep and vivid that one shade more would have been too much." Soon after this initial impression Giovanni falls asleep and dreams of "a rich flower and beautiful girl. Flower and maiden were different, and yet the same, and fraught with some strange peril in either shape." Later Giovanni watches as a drop of nectar from the gorgeous purple shrub kills "a small orange-colored reptile" and the breath of Beatrice simultaneously makes an insect shrivel up and die. "Beautiful shall I call her, or inexpressibly terrible?" he asks. She is, of course, both. Her voice is "as rich as a tropical sunset." She looks "redundant with life, health, and energy; all of which attributes were bound down and compressed, as it were, and girdled tensely, in their luxuriance, by her virgin zone." Hawthorne could hardly make more clear the association of her beauty and her dangerous sexuality. Giovanni, like Rappaccini with the purple plant, "feels that she is to be touched only with a glove, nor to be approached without a mask." His unconscious identification with Rappaccini here makes *him* the Adam of his question, and Beatrice his Eve.

Beatrice is obviously separated from the larger community by her actual imprisonment within Rappaccini's garden, and beyond that by her poisonousness. But there are other indications of her difference from other women. Like Eve, she stands for knowledge; although she is innocent emotionally and socially, she is brilliant intellectually. Dr. Baglioni, Rappaccini's academic rival, appears to be threatened by her knowledge when he tells Giovanni: "I know little of the Signora Beatrice save that Rappaccini is said to have instructed her deeply in his science, and that, young and beautiful as fame reports her, she is already qualified to fill a professor's chair. Perchance her father destines her for mine!" Rappaccini has deliberately made her different from other women: "Wouldst thou," he asks her, "have preferred the condition of a weak woman, exposed to all evil and capable of none?"

Like Elsie Venner, Beatrice has grown up without a mother and has consequently developed a special relationship with her father. There are similarities and differences between Dr. Rappaccini and Dudley Venner: where Dudley has avoided his daughter, Rappaccini has carefully cultivated Beatrice with as much scientific care as if she were a laboratory experiment, but the end result has been the same—both have done everything for their daughters except love them; where Dudley's lack of closeness to his daughter might be traced to his incestuous fears, Rappaccini lays a trap for Giovanni with his daughter as the bait, wanting, he says, a companion for his lonely daughter, but more likely wanting a male counterpart of Beatrice for the purpose of genetic experimentation. Unlike the kindly Dudley Venner, Rappaccini commits the unpardonable Hawthornian sin of caring "infinitely more for science than for mankind. His patients are interesting to him only as subjects for some new experiment. He would sacrifice human life, his own among the rest, or whatever else was dearest to him, for the sake of adding so much as a grain of mustard seed to the great heap of his accumulated knowledge." Although this testimony comes from Baglioni, and might be uttered more in bitterness than in truth, it is confirmed by Beatrice—"the effect of my father's fatal love of science . . . has estranged me from all society of my kind"—

and by Rappaccini himself. "Pluck one of those precious gems from thy sister shrub and bid thy bridegroom wear it in his bosom," he tells Beatrice. "It will not harm him now. My science and the sympathy between thee and him have so wrought within his system that he now stands apart from common men, as thou dost, daughter of my pride and triumph, from ordinary women. Pass on, then, through the world, most dear to one another and dreadful to all besides!"

Hawthorne, then, in testing the doctrine of Original Sin, does not attribute his heroine's taint to accidental causes, but blames her father for deliberately poisoning her existence, and blames also the Adam in this story. The significance of Giovanni's name, his identification with Rappaccini, his sexual fears have all been mentioned. Like Bernard Langdon, he administers the antidote which kills Beatrice,* but unlike Bernard he cannot stay away from Beatrice and becomes, albeit against his will, as poisonous as she. Unlike Bernard, Giovanni does not have the sympathy of his author. He is, for one thing, a narcissistic and shallow young man. Gazing at himself in the mirror—"a vanity to be expected in a beautiful young man"—he sees "that his features had never before possessed so rich a grace, nor his eyes such vivacity, nor his cheeks so warm a hue of superabundant life." He is sexually excited at this point in anticipation of his meeting with Beatrice in the garden, but the mirror also reveals "a certain shallowness of feeling and insincerity of character." Shallow, too, is his feeling for Beatrice. He realizes that she has "instilled a fierce and subtle poison into his system. It was not love, although her rich beauty was a madness to him; nor horror . . . but a wild offspring of both love and horror." What he feels for her is lust. Like Young Goodman Brown before him, who cannot accept the sexuality and human sinfulness of his wife Faith, Giovanni must obey the law that

---

* The antidote comes, incidentally, from Baglioni, who may be the real serpent in the garden; he sees Rappaccini's experiment as an "insufferable . . . impertinence . . . thus to snatch the lad out of my own hands" and looks for a way to foil his rival.

whirls him onward, yet wonders "whether this intense interest on his part were not delusory; whether it were really of so deep and positive a nature as to justify him in now thrusting himself into an incalculable position; whether it were not merely the fantasy of a young man's brain, only slightly or not at all connected with his heart." More likely, it is connected with his libido. The language which describes his entrance to the garden is clearly sexual, but the actual encounter with Beatrice is just as clearly tinged for Giovanni with horror: he is afraid of passionate sexual contact. He is shown a private entrance to the garden by the mythical old crone of the fairy tales—here old Lisabetta, who smirks and smiles with her withered face, like the serpent who would tempt him. "He paused, hesitated, turned half about, but again went on. His withered guide led him along several obscure passages, and finally undid a door, through which, as it was opened, there came the sight and sound of rustling leaves, with the broken sunshine glimmering among them. Giovanni stepped forth, and forcing himself through the entanglement of a shrub that wreathed its tendrils over the hidden entrance, stood beneath his own window in the open area of Dr. Rappaccini's garden." Once in the garden, however, he becomes coldly intellectual, analyzing the plants with "critical observation." But this is a defense mechanism, for his vanity and insecurity demand a woman who does not present a threat to him. Thus, he responds to Beatrice "as if to an infant"; he converses with her "like a brother." Passionate with her only in his fantasies, he sees her now as "imbued with a tender warmth of girlish womanhood," "endowed with all gentle and feminine qualities," "worthiest to be worshipped." Clearly, Giovanni has a problem distinguishing appearance from reality: "Whatever had looked ugly was now beautiful," but later, what had looked beautiful will become ugly. Giovanni lives in a world of fantasy, and unfortunately we see Beatrice only through his eyes; he wants to see Beatrice "as if they had been playmates from early infancy," but he has a morbid passion for her just because she is poisonous.

Giovanni's confrontation with Beatrice herself creates "a physical barrier between them" that makes his love grow "thin and faint." [9] His difficulty in separating her "God-given spirit" from her "region of unspeakable horror" becomes the reader's difficulty.

Indeed this dark lady stands apart from ordinary women; indeed she is as beautiful as she is dangerous. "Half-childish and half womanlike" as Eve, she has sexually tempted Giovanni, but she is as much seduced as seducer, and finally less sinful than Giovanni (or Rappaccini), as she recognizes. Dying, she asks Giovanni, "Oh, was there not, from the first, more poison in thy nature than in mine?" She and Giovanni stand, in lines reminiscent of the closing lines of *Paradise Lost*, "in utter solitude," but they cannot leave the Garden together because Giovanni has condemned her with "fiendish scorn." She "must pass heavily, with that broken heart, across the borders of Time" alone. Beautiful, dangerous, estranged, Beatrice Rappaccini will serve as a model for Hawthorne's other dark ladies.

IN WHICH THE AMBIGUITIES OF THE DARK LADY
ARE COMPOUNDED BY THE APPEARANCE OF
THE PALE MAIDEN: MELVILLE'S ISABEL

Melville, like Hawthorne and Holmes, was fascinated with the story of the Fall, underlining, for example, in his copy of *Richard II* the Queen's agonized question to the old gardener who had reported the evil news of her Richard's deposition: "What Eve, what serpent, hath suggested thee/To make a second fall of cursed man?" [10] His dark lady in *Pierre*, however, is identified neither with snakes nor with poison, but with wild Nature. Isabel Banford's first memories are of the somewhat threatening and isolated "deep stunted pine woods": [11]

47

"In summer the forest unceasingly hummed with unconjecturable voices of unknown birds and beasts. In winter its deep snows were traced like any paper map, with dotting night-tracks of four-footed creatures, that even to the sun, were never visible, and never were seen by man at all." Pierre is a country lad, but civilized; he is engaged to a pale maiden from the city—until he sees the haunting face of Isabel.

> Encircled by bandelets of light, it had still beamed upon him; vaguely historic and prophetic; backward, hinting of some irrevocable sin; forward, pointing to some inevitable ill. One of those faces, which now and then appear to man, and without one word of speech, still reveal glimpses of some fearful gospel. In natural guise, but lit by supernatural light; palpable to the senses, but inscrutable to the soul; in their perfectest impression on us, ever hovering between Tartarean misery and Paradisiac beauty; such faces, compounded so of hell and heaven, overthrow in us all foregone persuasions, and make us wondering children in this world again.

Isabel's theme song is "Isabel and Mystery." When she first plays it for Pierre on her guitar, he feels a strange wild heat burn upon his brow and rushes from the room, all thought of what he had come to tell her driven from his mind. He feels bewitched, enchanted, "as a tree-transformed and mystery-laden visitant, caught and fast bound in some necromancer's garden." The attraction which Isabel has for Pierre is much like that of Beatrice for Giovanni: he is magnetically drawn to her by forces he cannot control, and the attraction is both a need to penetrate her mystery and an inability to resist her vibrant sexuality. Physically, Isabel resembles both the earlier Beatrice Rappaccini and the later Elsie Venner. She is a wild beauty with long dark cascading hair and mournful, unfathomable, all-ravishing eyes. She resembles them further in having no mother and a father who has neglected to give her the nourishing love which any child needs—Isbael's father, for all practical purposes, has deserted her. Like Elsie and Beatrice, moreover, she is a deviant: she is a foreigner, an illegitimate child, an orphan, an impover-ished, uneducated, homeless, half-mad outcast.

In this book subtitled *The Ambiguities,* Isabel figures as the central ambiguity. Is she, for example, the good angel or the bad angel? When Pierre gets her letter toward the beginning of the book, he imagines the good angel saying to him, "Read, Pierre, though by reading thou may'st entangle thy-self, yet may'st thou thereby disentangle others," while the bad angel "insinuatingly breathed—Read it not, dearest Pierre; but destroy it, and be happy." But at the end of the book when Lucy has announced her impending arrival to Pierre and Isabel, Isabel names herself the bad angel. "Me-thought she was that good angel," Isabel says of her vision of Lucy, "which some say hovers over every human soul; and methought—oh, methought that I was thy other,—thy other angel, Pierre. Look: see these eyes,—this hair—nay, this cheek;—all dark, dark, dark,—and she—the blue-eyed—the fair-haired." Tormented, she asks him, "Doth not a fu-nerealness invest me? Was ever a hearse so plumed?—oh, God! that I had been born with blue eyes, and fair hair! Those make the livery of heaven! Heard ye ever yet of a good angel with dark eyes, Pierre?—no, no, no—all blue, blue, blue—heaven's own blue—the clear, vivid, unspeakable blue, which we see in June skies, when all the clouds are swept by.—But the good angel shall come to thee, Pierre. Then both will be close by thee, my brother; and thou mayst perhaps elect,—elect!" If Isabel stands clearly neither for good nor for bad, can we say that she stands for the heart as opposed to the head? Her juxtaposition with Lucy certainly points up her vibrant life in general and her sexuality in par-ticular in contrast to Lucy's saintly, virginal and ethereal qual-ities. Yet, Pierre chooses to claim her as his sister out of a sense of duty—with his head, in other words, as opposed to all the hedonistic promptings of his heart. Moreover, while Melville identified himself with the heart,[12] choosing Isabel brings about Pierre's downfall and death—and not only his own but that of Isabel, Lucy, his mother, and the house of

Glendinning as well. If the face of Isabel is "vaguely historic and prophetic," reminding the reader of the Original Sin and Fall and of the sin and fall to come, is it certain that her relationship with Pierre is sinful? *Is* she his sister? Not even Pierre can say, for although she resembles the "chair-portrait" of his youthful father, so does she resemble the portrait of an unknown European man. If she is his sister, then Pierre lives with her in what is probably an incestuous relationship; if she is not his sister, then he lives with her in sin as his common-law wife.

One thing that seems clear in this novel so fraught with ambiguities that not even its author had control of his materials, is Melville's concern with incest. We have seen the theme of incest associated with the dark lady in both *Elsie Venner* and "Rappaccini's Daughter," but where Holmes and Hawthorne merely hint at this theme, Melville states his interest—probably because he uses incest as a symbol. All of Pierre's sexual relationships—with his mother, his fiancée, his "sister" and his male cousin Glendinning Stanly (with whom he has "cherished a much more than cousinly attachment," knowing in his "boy-love" "occasional fillips and spicinesses")—are perverted. The syrupy narrative which occupies the first hundred and fifty pages of the novel is about Pierre's proposed exchange of sister-mother for sister-wife. Pierre behaves toward his "pedestalled mother" as a courtly lover. Addressing her as "Sister Mary," he calls for her mornings at her chamber door, superintends the finishing touches of her toilet, and helps her to the choicest morsels at the breakfast table. While she is made of "the very virtue of exquisite marble," Pierre's homage arouses "all the proudest delights and witcheries of self-complacency which it is possible for the most conquering virgin to feel."

> That nameless and infinitely delicate aroma of inexpressible tenderness and attentiveness which, in every refined and honorable attachment, is contemporary with the courtship and precedes the final banns and the rite; but which, like the *bouquet* of the costliest German wines, too often evaporates upon pouring

love out to drink, in the disenchanting glasses of the matrimonial days and nights; this highest and airiest thing in the whole compass of the experience of our mortal life; this heavenly evanescence—still further etherealised in the filial breast—was for Mary Glendinning, now not very far from her grand climacteric, miraculously revived in the courteous lover-like adoration of Pierre.

Mary Glendinning's choice of a bride for Pierre is the girl who is no sexual rival for herself. Lucy "will not estrange him from me; for she too is docile—beautiful, and reverential, and most docile," she reflects. "How glad am I that Pierre loves her so, and not some dark-eyed haughtiness, with whom I could never live in peace." She compares her own sexuality with that of Lucy in terms of wine; where Lucy is "a very pretty little Pale Sherry pint-decanter of a girl," she herself is "a quart-decanter of . . . Port—potent Port. Now, Sherry for boys, and Port for men."

Lucy is the girl Pierre would take to be his wife and treats like his sister: Isabel is the girl he takes to be his sister and treats like his wife. No such scruples as trouble him with Lucy bother him when he embraces Isabel.[13] He knows that "never, never would he be able to embrace Isabel with the mere brotherly embrace; while the thought of any other caress, which took hold of any domesticness, was entirely vacant from his uncontaminated soul, for it had never consciously intruded there." Subsequent embraces are certainly more than brotherly; for example: "He held her tremblingly; she bent over toward him: his mouth wet her ear. . . . Over the face of Pierre there shot a terrible self-revelation; he imprinted repeated burning kisses upon her; pressed hard her hand; would not let go her sweet and awful passiveness. They changed; they coiled together, and entangledly stood mute." The coiling together suggests that this is the beginning of Pierre's downfall, but whether because the embrace is brotherly or because it is more than brotherly remains ambiguous. Certainly, Isabel's "passiveness" suggests that Pierre has as much to do with the tempting as the "temptress." The rationale Pierre later offers for his incestuous love for Isabel is reminiscent of the logic of Mark Twain's Satan in *The Mysterious Stranger:* "It is all a dream—we dream that we dreamed that we dream," he tells Isabel. And in that dream virtue and vice are nothing: "a nothing is the substance, it casts one shadow one way, and another the other way; and these two shadows cast from one nothing; these, seems to me, are Virtue and Vice. . . . From nothing proceeds nothing, Isabel! How can one sin in a dream?" She tells him that now that he would be "lunatic to wise men" she understands him.

Pierre has a dream within a dream, in which Melville attempts to probe incest as a symbol. In that dream Pierre sees the Mount of the Titans, known in Saddle Meadows from a distance as the Delectable Mountain, but close up "stark desolation; ruin, merciless and ceaseless; chills and gloom—all here lived a hidden life, curtained by that cunning purpleness, which, from the piazza of the manor-house, so beautifully invested the mountain once called Delectable, but now styled Titanic." The mountain changes in the dream to the mighty Enceladus (the giant overcome by Dionysus in the battle between the giants and the gods): "a moss-turbaned, armless giant, who despairing of any other mode of wreaking his immitigable hate, turned his vast trunk into a battering ram, and hurled his own arched-out ribs again and yet again against the invulnerable steep." Enceladus is vulnerable not only because he is armless, but because he is castrated: "Nature . . . performed an amputation, and left the impotent Titan without one serviceable ball-and-socket above the thigh." And Nature in the dream is both the small white amaranthine flower which overspreads the land with sterility because the cattle will not eat it, and the life-supplying catnip, that dear farmhouse herb choked off by the intractable snow-white celestial flower. Suddenly Pierre sees his own features gleam upon him with "prophetic discomfiture and woe" on the armless trunk of Enceladus. Waking from that ideal horror to his actual grief, Pierre reflects:

Old Titan's self was the son of incestuous Coelus and Terra, the son of incestuous Heaven and Earth. And Titan married his mother Terra, another and accumulatively incestuous match. And thereof Enceladus was one issue. So Enceladus was both the son and grandson of an incest; and even thus, there had been born from the organic blended heavenliness and earthliness of Pierre, another mixed, uncertain, heaven-aspiring, but still not wholly earth-emancipated mood; which again, by its terrestrial taint held down to its terrestrial mother, generated there the present doubly incestuous Enceladus within him.

This is Melville's not very clear explanation of his symbol. What he seems to be saying is that the Transcendental doctrine of "correspondence," or the marriage of opposites (expressed for example in Emerson's "Uriel": "Evil will bless and ice will burn"), is an incestuous marriage. This is the meaning of Plotinus Plinlimmon's essay on "Chronometricals and Horologicals" which has such a profound effect on Pierre: God operates on chronometrical time and man on horological time, "And thus, though the earthly wisdom of man be heavenly folly to God; so also, conversely, is the heavenly wisdom of God an earthly folly to man."* If heavenly wisdom is earthly folly, then the only way God's truth and man's truth correspond is through their contradictions.

Pierre, then, no selfish Giovanni, follows what he thinks are his Christ-like impulses in denying the wisdom of the world and devoting his life to the protection of Isabel. This is his folly, for "he who finding himself a chronometrical soul, seeks practically to force that heavenly time upon the earth; in such an attempt he can never succeed, . . . and . . . if he seek to regulate his own daily conduct by it, he will but array all men's earthly time-keepers against him." But it is not clear whether Isabel corresponds to chronometrical or to horological time. More than farmhouse herb, she is consciously made by Melville to be both life-giving, as opposed

* So much for the heavens on earth which utopians attempted in America, beginning with the Massachusetts Bay Colony and including those contemporary with *Pierre*.

to the sterility of the celestial amaranthine flower, and death-bringing, both innocent in the ways of the world and wise in her witchery, both unfortunate lonely orphan and fiendish outcast. In the final scene, where Pierre tears "her bosom loose" and seizes the secret vial of poison, he names her in all her ambiguity: "Girl—wife or sister, saint or fiend! . . . in thy breasts, life for infants lodgeth not, but death-milk for thee and me!"

Melville has endowed Isabel Banford with all of the conventional trappings of the dark lady, of Eve the temptress. She is beautiful, witchlike in her magnetism, sexually alluring yet full of danger, physically and spiritually alienated from the community outside of whose boundaries she exists as orphan, foreigner and half-mad, strange creature, with haunting eyes that will lure the Adamic hero to his destruction, and yet redolent with life-giving vitality. Isabel is the most complicated of the dark ladies analyzed so far because Melville incestuously unites in her the opposites of life and death, of heaven and hell. Despite her ambiguity, however, Isabel is still a symbol, not a woman—the symbol of Melville's art. His Bad Angel is the source of his creativity, but it is also his despair.

CELIA MADDEN: THE TEMPTRESS AS "GREEK"

Celia occupies a place midway between the flatness of an Elsie Venner and the fullness of Hawthorne's most artfully achieved dark lady. She shares with these heroines great beauty, irresistible yet dangerous sexuality, qualities which set her apart from those around her. Not a dark lady, Celia has remarkable red hair, but red, in its ostentatiousness and foreignness, is just as bad as black.[14] (Alice, with whom Celia is juxtaposed, has hair of the light brown sort.) Her red hair and her name, Celia, link her to her Irish-Catholic ancestors, as opposed to the community of Octavian Methodists to which Theron belongs, and also separate her from those dark ladies whose exotic qualities can often be traced to Jewish ancestry (like Hawthorne's Miriam with her "Jewish hair" and threatening Biblical women such as Delilah, Judith, Jael), for Celia makes a great point of being not "Hebrew," but "Greek."

Harold Frederic, then, despite his attempt to portray realistically religious revivalism, the influence of social Darwinism, the theme of America versus Europe (represented by Protestant revivalism and Irish Catholicism)—all of great importance in the latter part of the nineteenth century—is primarily writing allegory; one need go no further than the title to see that his concern is the myth of the Fall of Man. The familiar symbols are all present: the garden, complete with snakes, the Adamic hero, and the temptress.

All of the gardens of this novel exclude Celia. Alice, Theron's wife, transforms a muddy wasteland into a place of "huge, imbricated flowering masses, . . . tall, overladen flower-spikes of gladioli, . . . hollyhocks and flaming alvias [sic] . . . clustered blossoms on the standard roses, . . . delicately painted lilies on their stilt-like stems." [15] Theron's progression, on the other hand, is from bloom to blight. Early in the novel, with his "innocent candor and guileless mind," he sees the trees as "lofty and beautiful in the morning sunlight, and with what matchless charm came the song of the robins, freshly installed in their haunts among the new pale-green leaves! Above them, in the fresh, scented air, glowed the great blue dome, radiant with light and the purification of spring." Later, after his fall, Theron has "no ears for these noises of the woodland," and his casual glance through the window catches "a desolate picture of blackened dahlia stalks and shrivelled blooms. The gayety and color of the garden were gone, and in their place was shabby and dishevelled ruin."

Dr. Ledsmar's is a Rappaccini-like "adultery of various vegetable species" where he tests "the probabilities for or against Darwin's theory that hermaphroditism in plants is a late by-product of these earlier forms." Not only does Ledsmar experiment with plants in his unnatural garden; he experiments with human beings as well. Dr. Ledsmar stands for Satan in this allegory. His real interest, appropriately, is snakes; he has written a book on serpent worship and established a reptile collection. His evil intentions are revealed when he addresses one of his evil-headed, fork-tongued lizards as "the Rev. Theron Ware."

Finally, there is the conservatory garden of Michael Madden, Celia's tubercular brother. This young man who "should have been a priest" and who stands "waiting at the gate" for Celia is clearly the Archangel. "You are much changed, Mr. Ware, since you came to Octavius, and it is not a change for the good," he tells Theron in his conservatory where "the air was moist and close, and heavy with the smell of verdure and wet earth." "If it [your face] seemed to me like the face of a saint before, it is more like the face of a barkeeper now!" And then he expels him from the Garden: "Go back to the way you were brought up in, and leave alone the people whose ways are different from yours."

Celia belongs to no garden; rather, she leads Theron *from* the garden to her private chamber. Madame Merle's comment in *The Portrait of a Lady* that one learns about human beings from their surroundings (their shells) is pertinent here. Celia's boudoir is Celia personified: the color scheme is amber, straw, primrose and varying shades of blue. It is a sensuous temple which is both "Greek" and Catholic: its walls are "flat upright wooden columns, terminating high above in simple capitals," lamps are placed so as to illuminate statues of naked men and women and paintings of the Virgin Mary and the Child. The sensuous quality of the room is captured in the draperies and huge cushions and pillows which encompass three sides of the room. The fourth side, filled with candles, seems to be an altar for Celia's piano— which Theron takes for a casket. Celia herself dons a robe of "shapeless, clinging drapery, lustrous and creamy and exquisitely soft, like the curtains." Her wonderful hair hangs free and luxuriant about her neck and shoulders, and the inten-

sity of its fiery color makes all the other hues of the room pale
and vague. Her posture reminds Theron of the statue of "that
armless woman in marble he had been studying"—Venus.
Celia also reminds him of the Madonna. At first the incon-
gruity of "the unashamed statues and this serene incarnation
of holy womanhood" jars him, but then he looks at Celia as
she plays her piano and decides, "In the presence of such a
face, of such music, there ceased to be any such thing as
nudity, and statues no more needed clothes than did those
slow, deep magnificent chords which came now, gravely ac-
cumulating their spell upon him."

Celia tells Theron on that fatal evening, "I divide people
up into two classes . . .—Greeks and Jews." "Greek," she
explains, is "absolute freedom from moral bugbears, . . . the
recognition that beauty is the only thing in life that is worth
while." The music of Chopin is for her "the Greekiest of the
Greeks" and for Theron "a rich, bold confusion," an "erratic,
rippling jangle," "dreamy, wistful meditative beauty," "the
wooing sense of roses and moonlight, of perfumes, white
skins, alluring languorous eyes." The propelling motion of
the music makes Theron dizzy; he begins to breathe hard,
and then becomes giddy and faint. He is deeply shaken, but
he tells her, "I want to be a Greek myself, if you're one, . . .
I want to get as close to you—to your ideal, that is, as I can."
It is important that at this point Celia yawns. She is purely a
temptress. What he perceives about her reciprocated feeling
for him is misperception: *"He read* unsuspected tendernesses
and tolerances of friendship in the depths of her eyes, which
emboldened him to stir the fingers of that audacious hand in
a lingering, caressing trill upon her shoulder" (emphasis
added), but she is only playing with him. The whole
scene—introducing him to the sins of tobacco and liquor, the
sensuous music, Celia's loose, flowing Grecian robes and
loosened hair—is a pastime, not so different from Ledsmar's
feeding his Oriental servant lethal doses of opium to see how
much he can tolerate. Her yawn foreshadows the final scene
when she will tell him, "We find that you are a bore." But by

that time, unfortunately for Theron, he is completely snared. Celia—"clearly not the sort of girl to take a Protestant husband," but one who is the sort of girl to inflame a married Protestant minister—has kissed him, and poor Theron takes her kiss to mean that she loves him. "Even as he strode back through the woods to the camp meeting, it was the kiss that kept his feet in motion, and guided their automatic course. All along the watches of the restless night, it was the kiss that bore him sweet company, and wandered with him from one broken dream of bliss to another. Next day, it was the kiss that made of life for him a sort of sunlit wonderland." For Celia, as she will later tell Theron, that kiss "was of the good-bye order."

Celia is tempting not only because she is beautiful, not only because she knows how to entice and play with men, but also because like Eve she represents knowledge. There is her knowledge of music, which in a broader sense is linked to "culture"—the European sophistication that Christopher Newman goes to Europe to discover. Celia, too, has been to Europe; she returns as "a confident young woman, swift of tongue and apprehension, appearing to know everything there was to be known by the most learned, able to paint pictures, carve wood, speak in diverse languages, and make music for the gods, yet with it all a very proud lady, one might say a queen." [16] The language which describes Celia's artistic knowledge suggests her sexual knowledge; one has already seen this juxtaposition in the sensual quality of her altar to art, her chamber. Octavians are equally fascinated by "the bold, luxuriant quality of her beauty, the original and piquant freedom of her manners, the stories told in gossip about her lawlessness at home" and "her intellectual attainments and artistic vagaries." Both kinds of knowledge are inherent in Celia's relationship to Father Forbes and Dr. Ledsmar; she and Dr. Ledsmar have a sort of running heart-head battle over Father Forbes, for one thing, and there is more than a suggestion of a love affair between Celia and the urbane priest. The knowledge of these Catholics—their knowing, for example, thousands of books by heart—makes Theron tremble at the very thought of his being on the way to knowing them, too. His Catholic friends represent "an intellectual world, a world of culture and grace, of lofty thoughts and the inspiring communion of real knowledge, where creeds were not of importance, and where men asked one another, not 'Is your soul saved?' but 'Is your mind well furnished?' " Theirs is the wisdom of the serpent. Their "culture" includes lolling about like gorged snakes after a meal, for example, while their intellectual ideas ferment.

Celia's own Catholicism is close to the spirit of the Greeks, largely, as she explains, because of the adoration of the Virgin. Women stand for "art and poetry and the love of beauty, and the gentle, spiritual, soulful life. The Greeks had it; and Christianity would have had it too, if it hadn't been for those brutes they call the Fathers. They loved ugliness and dirt and the thought of hell-fire. They hated women." The Greek spirit has kept alive Jesus's appreciation of women. It is only "epileptic Jews who could imagine a religion without sex in it." All of the pictures and statues in Celia's room are maternal representations—not only the Virgin Mary to whom Theron has likened her, but Isis with the infant Horus in her arms, Nahamie, bearing the miraculously born Buddha, Olympias with her child Alexander, Perictione holding her babe Pluto. Celia believes, in other words, in a matriarchal society—not because she is maternal, but because of the power mothers have, especially over male children. "Almost every religion had its Immaculate Conception," she tells Theron." . . . man turns naturally toward the worship of the maternal idea. That is the deepest of all our instincts,—love of woman, who is at once daughter and wife and mother." Every religion, Celia might have added, except Protestantism; the Protestants of Octavius are in a metaphorical sense the same as the Jews—they have taken the emphasis away from a matriarchal in favor of a patriarchal religion. It is worship of God the Father and the creation of a lowered sphere for women within that patriarchal system that Celia resents. Significantly, she likes Theron best when he sees her in a maternal context. When he tells her, ". . . the strangest sensation seized upon me. It was absolutely as if I were a boy again, a good, pure-minded fond little child, and you were the mother that I idolized," she responds, "I find myself liking you better at this moment . . . than I have ever liked you before." Similarly, when she earlier led him to her house to play the piano for him, there was "a helpful, nurse-like way in which she drew his arm through hers."

Theron's own theology is patriarchal, as is the hierachy of his church. Were Theron to spell it out, his idea of woman's place might not be so very different from Dr. Ledsmar's. A woman, he tells Theron, "is infinitely more precocious as a girl. At an age when her slow brother is still stubbing along somewhere in the neolithic period, she has flown way ahead to a kind of medieval stage, or dawn of medievalism, which is peculiarly her own. Having got there, she stays there; she dies there. The boy passes her, as the tortoise did the hare. He goes on, if he is a philosopher, and lets her remain in the dark ages, where she belongs. If he happens to be a fool, which is customary, he stops and hangs around in her vicinity." Women are not learned, he insists; rather they are attracted by the "pagan sensuality and lascivious mysticism which enveloped the priesthood in Greek and Roman days." Although Ledsmar never tires of downgrading women, he subscribes to the cliché about woman's mysteries: "We have been studying the female of our own species for some hundreds of thousands of years, and we haven't arrived at the most elementary rules governing her actions. " His degradation of women, of course, reflects his rivalry with Celia. He chooses to be a "Jew" for the same reason that Theron chooses to be a "Greek"—because of his feeling for Celia.

Theron, however, who thinks he loves Celia, is shocked by her unconventional ideas about the rights of women, or more precisely about her rights to her individual personhood. At first Theron takes Celia's unusual ideas to be the whims of a rich woman. When she tells her theory of life, "The instant a

wish occurs to me, I rush to gratify it," he looks at her with
humility and awe: "The glamour of a separate banking account shone upon her." He suggests naively, "One reads
. . . of American heiresses going to Europe and marrying
dukes and noblemen. I suppose you will do that too. Princes
would fight one another for *you*." "That is the old-fashioned
idea," she answers him,

> that women must belong to somebody, as if they were curios,
> or statues, or race-horses. You don't understand, my friend,
> that I have a different view. I am myself, and I belong to myself,
> exactly as much as any man. The notion that any other human
> being could conceivably obtain the slightest property rights in
> me is as preposterous, as ridiculous, as—what shall I say?—as
> the notion of your being taken out with a chain on your neck
> and sold by auction as a slave, down on the canal bridge. I
> should be ashamed to be alive for another day, if any other
> thought were possible to me. . . . What on earth is it to me that
> other women crawl about on all-fours, and fawn like dogs on
> any hand that will buckle a collar onto them, and toss them the
> leavings of the table? I am not related to them. I have nothing to
> do with them. They cannot make any rules for me. If pride and
> dignity and independence are dead in them, why, so much the
> worse for them! It is no affair of mine. Certainly it is no reason
> why I should get down and grovel also. No; I at least stand erect
> on my legs.

This is more than Theron can do. At first he only falters,
"That is not the generally accepted view, I should think."
And then he thinks of Dr. Ledsmar's epithets: "mad ass, a
mere bundle of egotism, ignorance, and red-headed lewd-
ness." But the presence of the physical Celia makes him
drive away his "Jewish" thoughts. He plays instead with the
ribbons of her dress and reflects, "It was nothing less than
another Declaration of Independence he had been listening
to."

Independent as well as rich, beautiful, talented and sophisticated, Celia clearly exists outside the moral structure of the
Octavian Protestants. Not only does she articulate her own

"Declaration of Independence"; she goes so far as to express the superiority of the matriarchal over the patriarchal culture. Thus she has ties not only to the more simple version of the dark lady, as investigated so far, but also to the "new woman." Her deviance, like that of Elsie Venner, Beatrice Rappaccini and Isabel Banford, can be traced to her having no mother for a model and a minimal sort of father, a kindly, perfunctory man who gives Celia everything in the world in a material sense, but very little in a personal sense. Of course Celia's self-knowledge comes, too, from her European travel and her connection with the worldly priest and the scientist Ledsmar. Frederic has used all of the stock literary conventions, but with a twist. Celia's magnificent red hair, her independence, her passion, her artistry should make for a vivid, lively woman. Unfortunately, she has little more life to her than the temptresses so far studied. One cannot really believe in her "declaration"; this rich and outspoken hedonist who has never known what it is to suffer is as one-dimensional in her way as the crudely symbolic Elsie Venner.

HAWTHORNE'S MIRIAM: THE TEMPTRESS AS JEW

It is an interesting footnote to *The Damnation of Theron Ware* that it was published in Britain as *The Illumination,* suggesting Frederic's awareness of the value of innocence and experience to the New and Old Worlds. Hawthorne's *The Marble Faun* also had an English title, *The Transformation,* which likewise implies a fortunate Fall. In that book, Miriam asks (like Milton's Eve rationalizing her deed to Adam—"This happy trial of thy love, which else/ So eminently never had been known . . . "):

> Was the crime—in which he and I were wedded—was it a blessing, in that strange disguise? Was it a means of education, bringing a simple and imperfect nature to a point of feeling and intelligence which it could have reached under no other discipline? . . . The story of the fall of man! Is it not repeated in

our romance of Monte Beni? And may we follow the analogy yet further? Was that very sin—into which Adam precipitated himself and all his race—was it the destined means by which, over a long pathway of toil and sorrow, we are to attain a higher, brighter, and profounder happiness than our lost birthright gave? Will not this idea account for the permitted existence of sin, as no other theory can? [17]

But unlike Celia's Jamesian sin of using people ("We thought you were going to be a real acquisition," she tells Theron), the crime which Miriam precipitates is murder. Miriam, like Eve, brings death into the world. Moreover, while Celia is the instrument of Theron's fall, that fall—or illumination—is not irremediable: "Nothing essential had been taken away," Sister Soulsby finds; "the face underneath was still all right." And Celia herself, who can seek absolution through the Catholic vehicle of confession, is not hopelessly sinful. In fact, Celia does not seem to feel any guilt; she maintains her stance of aloofness and superior self-righteousness to the end of the novel. Miriam, on the contrary, does realize her own part in the fall of Donatello—which is not temporary. He is permanently changed and is to spend the rest of his life in a dungeon, while Miriam, in her suffering awareness of the need to live with the consequences of their crime, will spend the rest of her life in lonely penitence. The greater reality of Miriam's sin and Miriam's own self-awareness and suffering not only make her more believable than the hedonistic Celia, but make her the most convincing figure in this romance peopled otherwise with stiff allegorical representations.

It is fitting that it be Miriam who challenges orthodox theology with her question about the Fortunate Fall, for her name is a composite of the Greek "Mariam" (or Mary) and the Hebrew "Miryam" (rebellion); she is both a vehicle of guilt and a vessel of redemption. Physically, Miriam is a full-blown sister of the more linear Beatrice Rappaccini:

She was very youthful, and had what was usually thought to be a Jewish aspect; a complexion in which there was no roseate bloom; yet neither was it pale; dark eyes . . . black, abundant hair. . . . if she were really of Jewish blood, then this was Jewish hair, and a dark glory such as crowns no Christian maiden's head. . . . She might ripen to be what Judith was, when she vanquished Holofernes with her beauty, and slew him for too much admiring it. [18]

She is linked to Beatrice, too, by her resemblance to Guido's portrait of Beatrice Cenci, who was accused of the crimes of patricide and incest (and who also fascinated Isabel in *Pierre*). Miriam says of her: "Beatrice's sin may not have been so great: perhaps it was no sin at all, but the best virtue possible in the circumstances. If she viewed it as a sin, it may have been because her nature was too feeble for the fate imposed upon her. . . . I would give my life to know whether she thought herself innocent, or that one great criminal since time began." Miriam sees Beatrice Cenci, in other words, as a real woman caught up in a world not of her own making. Hilda, on the other hand, sees her as "a fallen angel—fallen, and yet sinless." But Hilda, like Pierre's Lucy, has no perception of sin; she is ethereal, inhuman, residing in her dovecote far above the profane world.

Paradoxically, although Miriam is the one "real" character in the novel, she is surrounded by mystery, as the other characters are not (except Donatello, whose mystery—is he faun or human?—is as simple as Donatello himself, compared to Miriam's). "There was an ambiguity about this young lady," Hawthorne writes; ". . . nobody knew anything about Miriam, either for good or evil." Not even Miriam's friends know who she is, but they take her good qualities "as evident and genuine, . . . never imagining that what was hidden must be therefore evil." They are not aware that her very name and occupation—"Miriam Schaefer, artist in oils"—is a disguise. The rumors that circulate about her are exotic: one has it that she is the daughter and heiress of a rich Jewish banker who fled from her home to escape a union with a cousin; another that she was a German princess who was supposed to marry, for reasons of state, either a decrepit sovereign or a prince still in his cradle; another that she was the offspring of a Southern American planter who had given her an elaborate education and endowed her with great wealth, "but the one burning drop of African blood in her veins so affected her with a sense of ignominy that she relinquished all and fled her country"; and still another held that she was the lady of an English nobleman and out of love for her art had thrown over her rank. All of these rumors (as well as the portrait of Beatrice Cenci) suggest an estranged father, but no mother in the background. In actuality, however, Miriam is linked through her father to the corrupt hierarchy of Rome and through her mother to the Jews who occupy "the foulest and ugliest part of Rome. In that vicinity lies the Ghetto," Hawthorne writes, "where thousands of Jews are crowded within a narrow compass, and lead a close, unclean, and multitudinous life, resembling that of maggots when they overpopulate a decaying cheese." [19]

Only one man knows who "Miriam" is, and that is her "Shadow," who poses as Miriam's model and passes himself off as Brother Antonio, a Capuchin monk. This "dark, bushy-bearded, wild" man is recognized by Donatello, the creature of pure instinct, as the Devil in Guido's portrait of the Archangel Michael setting his foot upon the demon. He is first encountered in the hellish catacombs of Rome, where, like the Biblical Satan, he is a heretic, hoping to lead some straggler astray. "What this lost wretch pines for," almost as much as for the blessed sunshine, the guide to the catacombs tells the party of artists, "is a companion to be miserable with him." From that moment on he dogs Miriam's steps, reminding her at every opportunity of their common link to some horror in the past—except, as in a romantic opera when a cross is brandished in the face of Mephistopheles, when Miriam mentions the word "prayer"; then "a tremor and horror appeared to seize upon her persecutor." Of this common link, we are told no more than "that there seemed to be a sadly mysterious fascination in the influence of this ill-omened person over Miriam; it was such as beasts and reptiles of subtle and evil nature sometimes exercise upon their victims." Her "doom," as she calls him, will settle for nothing less than complete possession: "You must throw off your present mask and assume another. You must vanish out of the scene; quit Rome with me, and leave no trace whereby to follow you. It is in my power, as you well know, to compel your acquiescence in my bidding." We learn that he has known her since her girlhood, that he knows her real name, that he was involved in a terrible crime in which suspicion of being an accomplice fell upon Miriam, and that he was probably her destined husband through a prearranged contract with a character "so vile, and yet so strangely subtle, as could only be accounted for by the insanity which often develops itself in old, close-kept races of men, when long unmixed with newer blood." What this horrible crime was and what has been Miriam's part in it is, in true Gothic tradition, never revealed.

Miriam's "mystery" links her to Isabel and to Zenobia (also an assumed name). But instead of coping with her mysterious misfortune by proclaiming her own helplessness and dependency upon male protection as does Isabel, Miriam, caught up in and pursued by a corrupt patriarchal order, like Zenobia "speedily created a new sphere" for herself. The sphere which she chooses is the only one in which a nineteenth-century woman could move freely—that of art. "The customs of artist life," Hawthorne explains, "bestow such liberty upon the sex, which is elsewhere restricted within so much narrower limits; and it is perhaps an indication that, whenever we admit women to a wider scope of pursuits and professions, we must also remove the shackles of our present conventional rules." [20] In choosing such a life, however, "We artists . . . think it necessary to put ourselves at odds with Nature," Miriam tells Donatello. The consequences of disguise, of assumed identity, of choosing an unconventional "sphere," are loss of identity, loneliness and alienation.

The prominent traits of Miriam's character—her threatening sexuality and her deviance from Nature, from the conventional feminine sphere, from the human community—are to be seen in her art. Terrible Jewish heroines "acting the part of a revengeful mischief towards man"—Jael driving the nail through the temples of Sisera, Judith beheading Holofernes, the daughter of Herodias receiving the head of John the Baptist on a charger—constitute one subject. The other is "domestic and common scenes"—courtship, the various stages of wedded life, a drawing of an infant's shoe. But in all of these sketches "a figure was portrayed apart. . . . Always it was the same figure, and always depicted with an expression of deep sadness; and in every instance, slightly as they were brought out, the face and form had the traits of Miriam's own."

Like Beatrice Cenci (and like all of the dark ladies in this chapter), Miriam's sorrow removes her "out of the sphere of humanity." Both at the beginning and at the end of the novel Miriam's separation from other human beings is emphasized, as, for example, in this early passage: "It was to little purpose that she approached the edge of the voiceless gulf between herself and them. Standing on the utmost verge of that dark chasm, she might strive to call out, 'Help, friends! Help!' but, as with dreamers when they shout, her voice would perish inaudibly. This perception of an infinite, shivering solitude . . . is one of the most forlorn results of any . . . peculiarity of character that puts an individual ajar with the world." True, Miriam belongs to the little community of artists comprised of Kenyon and Hilda, and to which Donatello is attracted, but Kenyon is as cold as his marble; Miriam cannot tell him her terrible secret, and Hilda, Miriam's closest friend, possesses a "subtile attribute of reserve that insensibly kept those at a distance who were not suited to her sphere." "I am a poor, lonely girl," she tells Miriam, "whom God has set here in an evil world, and given her only a white robe, and bid her wear it back to Him, as white as when she put it on. Your powerful magnetism would be too much for me. The pure, white atmosphere, in which I try to discern what things are good and true, would be discolored. And, therefore, Miriam, before it is too late, I mean to put faith in this awful heart-quake, which warns me henceforth to avoid you." Only Donatello does not forsake her. He is her Adam.

Like the Faun of Praxiteles with whom he is compared, Donatello "is endowed with no principle of virtue, and would be incapable of comprehending such; but he would be true and honest by dint of his simplicity. . . . he has a capacity for strong and warm attachment, and might act devotedly through its impulse." He could be educated, "so that the coarser animal portion of his nature might eventually be thrown into the background, though never utterly expelled." The Faun represents "all the genial and happy characteristics of creatures that dwell in woods and fields, . . . Trees, grass, flowers, woodland streamlets, cattle, deer, and unsophisticated man." Donatello has an indefinable characteristic "that set him outside of the rules." * Unlike Miriam, who is linked to the past and to the future, Donatello "has nothing to do with time." Unlike Miriam, too, Donatello has no shadow. She sees him as "enjoying the warm, sensuous, earthy side of nature; reveling in the merriment of woods and streams; living as our four-footed kindred do—as mankind did in its innocent childhood, before sin, sorrow, or morality itself had ever been thought of . . . with no conscience, no remorse, no burden on the heart, no troublesome recollections of any sort; no dark future either." These words are not so very different from Hawthorne's (ironic) description of America in his preface to *The Marble Faun:* "No author, without a trial, can conceive of the difficulty of writing a romance about a country where there is no shadow, no antiquity, no mystery, no picturesque and gloomy wrong, nor anything but a commonplace prosperity, in broad and simple daylight, as is happily the case with my dear native land." Hawthorne sets this story of the Fall of Man, therefore, in Rome, "the native soil of ruin":

---

* This is evidently all right for the American Adam; it is a plus; it makes him a hero—but this same quality makes the American Eve a deviant.

The final charm is bestowed by the malaria. There is a piercing, thrilling, delicious kind of regret in the idea of so much beauty thrown away, or only enjoyable at its half-developments, in winter and early spring, and never to be dwelt amongst, as the home scenery of any human being. For if you come hither in summer, and stray through these glades in golden sunset, fever walks arm in arm with you, and death awaits you at the end of the dim vista. Thus the scene is like Eden in its loveliness; like Eden, too, in the fatal spell that removes it beyond the scope of man's actual possession.

Donatello, however, feels nothing melancholy as he waits for Miriam in the sylvan freshness of the Borghese gardens with the green and blue lizards as playmates. He does not yet see the lizards as evil omens; nor is he yet saddened when the "venomous reptile" responds to his call, like the "coil of the serpent" which will knot him together with Miriam "for time and eternity." Donatello is unaware, as he waits for her in the garden, that his relationship with Miriam will drag him out of his leafy nook down to her dungeon, literally and symbolically. She warns him: "If you were wise, Donatello, you would think me a dangerous person. . . . If you follow my footsteps, they will lead you to no good. You ought to be afraid of me." But he replies, "I would as soon think of fearing the air we breathe." So Miriam steps outside of time, as it were, to join Donatello. This is the first of two Edenic escapes which frame Donatello's fall, linking him to Miriam, to Time. ". . . for this one hour let me be such as he imagines me," Miriam says to herself in the early scene.

"Tomorrow will be time enough to come back to my reality. My reality! What is it? Is the past so indestructible—the future so immitigable? Is the dark dream in which I walk of such solid, stony substance that there can be no escape out of its dungeon? Be it so! There is, at least, that ethereal quality in my spirit that it can make me as gay as Donatello himself—for this one hour!" . . . So the shadowy Miriam almost outdid Donatello on his own ground. They ran races with each other, side by side, with shouts of laughter; they pelted one another with early flowers, and gathering them up twined them with green leaves into garlands for both their heads. They played together like children, or creatures of immortal youth. So much had they flung aside the somber habitudes of daily life that they seemed to be sportive forever, and endowed with eternal mirthfulness instead of any deeper joy. It was a glimpse far backward into Arcadian life, or, further still, into the Golden Age, before mankind was burdened with sin and sorrow.

In the later escape, Miriam is disguised as a contadina, Donatello as a peasant. Now they step outside of Time only for a brief respite before their eternal punishment; there is a greater awareness of the temporary quality of Miriam and Donatello's "sacred hour," and Kenyon perceives a tear-stained face behind Miriam's mask. Their frivolity is "not in the simplicity of real mirth."

In between these two episodes occurs Donatello's fall. Miriam again warns him—"flee from me. Look not behind you! Get you gone without another word. . . . Cast me off, or you are lost forever"—but what he sees in her eyes is different from what he hears her say. And so he hurls Miriam's persecutor from the Tarpeian Rock, the "Traitor's Leap," which "symbolizes how sudden was the fall . . . from the utmost height of ambition to its profoundest ruin." Just as suddenly, the simple and joyous creature is gone forever; Miriam and Donatello are part of the sinful brotherhood of mankind. Their "individual wrongdoing melts into the great mass of human crime," and makes them "guilty of the whole, . . . members of an innumerable confraternity of guilty ones, all shuddering at each other." The link to Miriam, to Time, is cemented by an embrace "closer than a marriage bond": "She pressed him close, close to her bosom, with a clinging embrace that brought their two hearts together, till the horror and agony of each was combined into one emotion, and that a kind of rapture." It is the rapture that Adam and Eve felt immediately after their crime in *Paradise Lost:*

Carnal desire inflaming, hee on Eve
Began to cast lascivious Eyes, she him
As wantonly repaid; in Lust they burn:
Till Adam thus 'gan Eve to dalliance more.

And "the moral seclusion that . . . suddenly extended itself around them" recalls the last line of *Paradise Lost:* "Through Eden took their solitary way."

Their way will indeed be solitary. Neither marble nor faun, Donatello has become, in descending to Miriam's depths, a man: "My secret is not a pearl," she had warned, "yet a man might drown himself in plunging after it." And Miriam? If Hawthorne has attempted to transform Donatello from a work of Art and Nature into a man, he has tried to transform Miriam into a work of Art. Not content with the allegorical references to Eve, he attempts to portray her as the archetypal temptress by comparing her tò Beatrice Cenci and Cleopatra, to Judith, Jael and Salome. He even has her express a wish to be transformed into marble. In this insistent didacticism, Hawthorne has violated his own principles: "Nobody, I think, ought to read poetry, or look at pictures or statues, who cannot find a great deal more in them than the poet or the artist has actually expressed. Their highest merit is suggestiveness." While Miriam's "original sin" is an artistic triumph—"its highest merit is suggestiveness," leaving the reader to imagine the horror—Miriam herself is a failure as an artistic creation. Hawthorne has brushed in too many strokes. Miriam, for all of her early vividness and bloom, finally fades away like a phantom. The last glimpse of her is as a penitent kneeling beneath the "central eye" of the Pantheon: "The upturned face was invisible, behind a veil or a mask, which formed a part of the garb." The author designed the story and the characters "to bear," writes Hawthorne, "a certain relation to human nature and human life, but still to be . . . artfully and airily removed from our mundane sphere." Donatello, Hilda and Kenyon he airily removed; Miriam he artfully removed.

HESTER PRYNNE: THE DARK LADY AS "DEVIANT"

Beatrice and Miriam lack that "certain relation to human nature and human life," as do Elsie Venner, Isabel Banford and Celia Madden. But Hester Prynne is warm, alive, human—so much so that it is difficult to determine just where Hawthorne's sympathies lie. In making her the best—the most "human"—character in the book he is at his most ambiguous in his valuation of both community mores and individual deviance, with Hester's life-giving but threatening sexuality once again standing for the hazard which individuality poses to the very survival of the community. I do not use the word "ambiguous" lightly here; I believe that Hawthorne was not able finally to resolve his own dilemma. He, as his own marriage to the "safe" Sophia demonstrates, needed the security of community; but as alienated artist he felt estranged from that community which defined "masculinity" in terms of success in the commercial world. His profound sense of alienation led him in 1825 to seclude himself in his "owl's nest" from a world in which he perceived no way to acknowledge the "femininity" of his own artistic nature. In an attempt to reestablish contact with the human community, he wrote to Longfellow on June 4, 1837: "By some witchcraft or other—for I really cannot assign any reasonable why and wherefore—I have been carried apart from the main current of life, and find it impossible to get back again. Since we last met . . . I have secluded myself from society; and yet I never meant any such thing, nor dreamed what sort of life I was going to lead. I have made a captive of myself and put me into a dungeon; and now I cannot find the key to let myself out—and if the door were open, I should be almost afraid to come out. . . . For the last ten years I have not lived, but only dreamed about living." [21] His few attempts to find his "place" in the world were futile. He sees himself, in "The Custom House" preface to *The Scarlet Letter*, as an "idler," an oddity to have sprung from "the old trunk of the family tree, with so much venerable moss upon it," and never regards his sojourn there as anything other than "a transitory life" because in the quest for "Uncle Sam's gold" all "imaginative delight . . . passed away out of my mind." [22] His sojourn at Brook Farm proved no more successful. As he wrote to Sophia in the fall of 1841, "A man's soul may be buried and perish under a dung-heap or in the furrow of a field, just as well as under a pile of money." His salvation was his marriage to Sophia; she provided him with both a link to society and protective solitude—the combination necessary for his creativity. "Thou only hast revealed me to myself," he wrote to her in 1840, "for without thy aid, my best knowledge of myself would have been merely to know my own shadow— to watch it flickering on the wall, and mistake its fantasies for my own real actions. Indeed, we are but shadows—we are not endowed with real life, and all that seems most real about us is but the thinnest substance of a dream—till the heart is touched. That touch creates us—then we begin to be—. . . ." But Sophia was no richly vital, fully sexual Hester Prynne. She is, in the same letter, his "Dove": "I begin to understand why I was imprisoned so many years in this lonely chamber, and why I could never break through the viewless bolts and bars; for if I had sooner made my escape into the world, I should have grown hard and rough, and been covered with earthly dust, and my heart would have become callous by rude encounters with the multitude; so that I should have been all unfit to shelter a heavenly Dove in my arms." [23]

Hawthorne, then, places great value on belonging to the society *through* Sophia, his dove, the preserver of society's standards; yet at the same time, as an artist he is at odds with that very society. Whoever touches Uncle Sam's gold, he warns in "The Custom House," "should look well to himself, or he may find the bargain to go hard against him, involving, if not his soul, yet many of its better attributes; its sturdy force, its courage and constancy, its truth, its self-reliance, and all that gives emphasis to manly character." His use of the word "manly" here is different from his perception of society's definition of that term elsewhere in "The Custom

House." It suggests the difficulty he has accepting what he feels to be the "unmanly" qualities of his artistic self, and is therefore a clue to his own sexual insecurity. Those "manly" attributes are also the very qualities which both make Hester Prynne attractive and condemn her: "sturdy force," "courage and constancy," "truth," "selfreliance,"—attributes diametrically opposed to those of Sophia, qualities which in a woman cannot preserve the community, but would destroy it.

Hawthorne's ambiguity about Hester, then, is an attempt to work out his ambiguity toward himself, as artist, as man, as member of the human community. When he places her scarlet letter on his own breast in "The Custom House," he experiences "a sensation not altogether physical, yet almost so, as of burning heat; and as if the letter were not of red cloth, but red-hot iron." The "A" of the alienated artist is *the* subject of most of Hawthorne's tales. This warning from "Wakefield," for example (later echoed by Zenobia in *The Blithedale Romance*), is a warning for Hawthorne the artist and Hester the woman alike: "Amid the seeming confusion of our mysterious world, individuals are so nicely adjusted to a system, and systems to one another and to a whole, that, by stepping aside for a moment a man exposes himself to a fearful risk of losing his place forever."

The importance of "place" must not be discounted by twentieth-century readers who would see Hester Prynne as "androgynous" and Hawthorne as a writer with "feminist" sympathies.[24] If Hawthorne the artist was not sure which values—those of Uncle Sam or those of "truth" and "selfreliance"—were manly, how much less did Hester Prynne lack a context for her androgynous qualities. Hawthorne himself would deny women such a context. He wrote, for example, in his biography of "Mrs. Hutchinson":

> Woman's intellect should never give the tone to that of man; and even her morality is not exactly the material for masculine virtue. [It is] a false liberality, which mistakes the strong division-lines of Nature for arbitrary distinctions. . . . As yet, the great body of American women are a domestic race; but when a

continuance of ill-judged incitements shall have turned their hearts away from the fireside, there are obvious circumstances which will render female pens more numerous and more prolific than those of men . . . and the ink-stained Amazons will expel their rivals by actual pressure, and petticoats wave triumphantly over all the field. Fame does not increase the peculiar respect which men pay to female excellence, and there is a delicacy . . . that perceives, or fancies, a sort of impropriety in the display of woman's natal mind to the gaze of the world. . . . In fine, criticism should examine with a stricter, instead of a more indulgent eye, the merits of females at its bar, because they are to justify themselves for an irregularity which men do not commit in appearing there; and woman, when she feels the impulse of genius like a command of Heaven within her, should be aware that she is relinquishing a part of the loveliness of her sex, and obey the inward voice with sorrowing reluctance, like the Arabian maid who bewailed the gift of prophecy.[25]

I have quoted this long passage on Anne Hutchinson because it is necessary to understand Hawthorne's attitude toward strong women in any attempt to decide upon his sympathies for Hester Prynne, and because *The Scarlet Letter* is set in Anne Hutchinson's Boston. There are two deliberate references linking Anne Hutchinson to Hester Prynne. In the initial chapter a wild rose-bush blooms by the prison door from which Hester emerges; it is said to have "sprung up under the footsteps of the sainted Anne Hutchinson." And in the chapter called "Another View of Hester" we are told that had little Pearl not come to her from the spiritual world, then "she might have come down to us in history, hand in hand with Anne Hutchinson as the foundress of a religious sect. She might . . . have been a prophetess. She might, and not improbably would, have suffered death from the stern tribunals of the period, for attempting to undermine the foundations of the Puritan establishment." This is a clue to the whole questions of Hester and of Hawthorne's ambiguity in posing her against a group of grim, intolerant and even un-Christian Puritans, who do, nevertheless, comprise a community. Hester's deviance from its norms represents not an alternative community, not the Garden, but the wildness of the forest.

The Scarlet Letter is a novel about a failed community. Like *The Blithedale Romance,* the novel specifically about Hawthorne's involvement in a (failed) utopian community, the earlier *Scarlet Letter* is contemporaneous with that experience. As he saw the attempt to re-create Eden at Brook Farm as a doomed attempt in *Blithedale,* so he perceived the vision of the founders of the Massachusetts Bay Colony as doomed from the beginning. He believed the roots of evil to exist in the individual, not in social institutions; he was more interested in psychology than in social change. One is prepared by the remark in the preface that "Neither the front nor the back entrance of the Custom House opens on the road to Paradise" for the opening of *The Scarlet Letter:* "The founders of a new colony, whatever Utopia of human virtue and happiness they might originally project, have invariably recognized it among their earliest practical necessities to allot a portion of the virgin soil as a cemetery, and another portion as the site of a prison." There is not only death in this New World Garden of Eden; there are deviants who are so obnoxious or dangerous to the community that they must be locked up. Such malefactors might be Antinomians, Quakers or other "heterodox religionists," Indians, or witches, among them Anne Hutchinson and Hester Prynne—the one represented by the wild rose-bush, and the other, in contrast to the "sad-colored garments" of the Puritans, by the "fantastic flourishes of gold thread" of the letter A, embroidered with "much fertility and gorgeous luxuriance of fancy." The community *is* grim, but it is lawful; the rose-bush is beautiful, but it is wild; and the fantastically embroidered scarlet letter has the effect of taking Hester "out of the ordinary relations with humanity, and enclosing her in a sphere by herself."

Hester's prideful stance upon the scaffold as she faces her judges, then, is deliberately modeled upon Anne Hutchinson's; they pose the same threat to the community. "In the midst, and in the centre of all eyes, we see the woman,"

Hawthorne wrote in his portrait of Anne Hutchinson. "She stands loftily before her judges with a determined brow; and unknown to herself, there is a flash of carnal pride half hidden in her eye." [26] The members of this "community," in the words of John Winthrop's "A Modell of Christian Charity" of 1629, the written compact for the Massachusetts Bay Colony, entered into a "covenant" with God to do His will, literally to found "a city upon a hill," a New World Garden of Eden. Winthrop himself, in this document, is the Moses who will lead his people to the promised land.[27] As Erikson points out in *Wayward Puritans,* cited above, every community has its own set of boundaries, and its boundaries are determined by the behavior of its members. The boundaries of the Massachusetts Bay Colony were clear; Winthrop defined them in his "Little Speech on Liberty," where "civil" or "federal" liberty is a covenant between God and man, represented politically by the subjection of citizens to those in authority as God's representatives. It is this same kind of "liberty" which makes a wife, after she has chosen her husband through her own free will, subject to him: "a true wife accounts her subjection her honor and freedom." [28] Ostensibly punished for her Antinomian (literally, against the law) beliefs, Anne Hutchinson was a woman who did not keep "in the place God had set her." [29] Witch or feminist, depending on one's point of view—her skills as nurse and midwife indicating her knowledge of the secrets of birth and healing outside the realm of men, and her theological discussion groups our first women's consciousness-raising sessions—she opposed the church fathers, among them the same John Wilson who takes part in condemning and punishing Hester.

Hester, too, has perpetrated a crime against church and state: she has committed adultery and borne an illegitimate child. But her refusal as a woman to keep to her appointed place would have placed her outside the boundaries of the self-righteous community had her conduct been otherwise irreproachable. And Hester is a real, not an imagined threat to the community, as her "natural dignity and force of character"—unusual in a person just emerging from a long prison confinement to face a public humiliation—make clear. Had no stigma attached itself to her, she would have attempted nothing less than revolution. Hester often broods upon the "dark question" of "the whole race of womanhood," and her conclusions—that the "system of society is to be torn down, and built up anew"—are bothersome to Hawthorne because it would mean a modification of "the very nature of the opposite sex" necessary to woman's being "allowed to assume what seems a fair and suitable position." There can be no reforms, he says, until woman shall have undergone a mighty change "in which, perhaps, the ethereal essence, wherein she has her truest life, will be found to have evaporated." A man who himself married a pale maiden can only be at best ambivalent in his admiration for Hester. He calls the "ethereal essence" her "truest life." And he cannot help adding, "A woman never overcomes these problems by any exercise of thought. They are not to be solved, or only in one way. If her heart chance to come uppermost, they vanish."

In Hawthorne's later books the "ethereal essence" of the dark lady will have evaporated; it will belong to the pale maiden, the blonde or brown-haired New England girl. Because Hester is not split into schizophrenic segments, she comes across as a whole person, one who elicits the reader's sympathy and admiration. She is his most perfect Eve, combining sensuality with an "ethereal essence." Like Eve's, Hester's crime was not really in tempting Adam, but in disobeying God the Father. Her exotic beauty, then, is an emblem of her spiritual deviance. She is tall, "with a figure of perfect elegance." Her dark and abundant hair is "so glossy that it threw off the sunshine with a gleam," and her face, "besides being beautiful from regularity of feature and richness of complexion, had the impressiveness belonging to a marked brow and deep black eyes." Her physical appearance "seemed to express the attitude of her spirit, the desperate recklessness of her mood, by its wild and picturesque peculiarity." Most significant, of course, is the fantastically embroidered scarlet letter, an emblem of Hester's extravagant beauty, deviance and alienation.

Physically and spiritually, Hester resembles the other dark ladies of this chapter. But Elsie and Beatrice are poisoned, Isabel is weak and dependent, Miriam is haunted by some past crime. Each, through no fault of her own, is a woman caught in a world not of her own making, corrupted offstage as it were, through some "original sin." What makes Hester so interesting is that she has chosen both her act of illicit love and her feminist philosophy. She is a woman who acts, not a woman who is acted upon. Hester's emergence from prison into the open air "as if by her own free will" is an act of self-reliance both literally and symbolically. "Shame, Despair, Solitude" will make a weak person—like Dimmesdale—weaker, but they have only served to harden Hester's strength. Although the shame of the scarlet letter burns, "the tendency of her fate and fortunes had been to set her free. The scarlet letter was her passport into regions where other women dared not tread."

Hester's self-reliance sets her apart from every other character in the book—with the exception of Pearl, who is a law unto herself. This "infant worthy to have been brought forth in Eden" is part preternaturally wise child, part elfin spirit, but primarily a symbol—"the scarlet letter in another form; the scarlet letter endowed with life." Hester makes deliberate use of this parallel by dressing Pearl in a gorgeous crimson velvet tunic "abundantly embroidered with fantasies and flourishes of gold thread" when they visit Governor Bellingham's house. The beauty of the child so dressed cannot help reminding those present "of the token which Hester Prynne was doomed to wear on her bosom." And just as that token is both Hester's shame and her passport to freedom, so Pearl's illegitimacy is balanced by her "moods of perverse merriment which . . . seemed to remove her entirely out of the sphere of sympathy or human contact."

Chillingworth, the Satan in this Garden of Eden—

Hawthorne labels him literally as such and associates him both with snakes and savage Indians, is motivated only by revenge. He feeds off Dimmesdale like a parasite, and when the minister finally escapes the old man's clutches by confessing, Chillingworth's countenance becomes blank and dull, lifeless: "All his strength and energy—all his vital and intellectual force—seemed at once to desert him: insomuch that he positively withered up, shrivelled away, and almost vanished from mortal sight, like an uprooted weed that lies wilting in the sun."

Dimmesdale, Hester's Adam, declines from a "simple and childlike" person, one of "freshness and fragrance, and dewy purity of thought" who "could only be at ease in some seclusion of his own," to a weak and helpless person, one who is dependent on the esteem of his parishoners or, masochistically, on punishment by his evil enemy for his self-concept. Hester is shocked, after their midnight interview, at his disintegration: "His nerve seemed absolutely destroyed. His moral force was abased into more than a childish weakness. It grovelled helpless on the ground." During their forest meeting, she confronts him with his weakness, and he answers her, "Be thou strong for me! . . . Advise me what to do." At first Hester attempts to revive in him the inner strength for which she first loved him: "And what hast thou to do with all these iron men and their opinions? . . . Preach! Write! Act! Do anything, save to lie down and die!" But Dimmesdale has no self-reliance left; he is by this time only half a man, as his eyes indicate, their "fitful light" kindled by *her* enthusiasm, flashing up and dying away. "Thou tellest of running a race to a man whose knees are tottering beneath him," he tells her. "There is not the strength or courage left me to venture into the wide, strange, difficult world, alone!" The minister agrees to leave the community only when Hester, maternally, promises to go with him and arrange all the details of their escape, but he dares defy the universe only in Hester's presence. Away from her, he is afraid. Where he once loved her, he is now threatened by her sexuality; like

Young Goodman Brown, he prefers her in fantasy. He would prefer even to see her as an image of "sinless motherhood"; he can no longer accept her as a real woman, nor himself as a real man.

As for the other characters in the book, the townsfolk and officials of the church and state, they are too shadowy to merit much consideration, but unlike Hester, they rely for their self-concepts upon the mores of the community. They judge and scorn Hester because she violates the mores; thus her act of individuality threatens their very identity.

Hester's difference is pointed up in a number of ways. Her physical beauty, obviously, sets her immediately apart, but she is not simply beautiful; her beauty is of "a rich, voluptuous, Oriental characteristic." In Miriam this "Oriental" characteristic becomes "Jewish" hair, and the point that like Miriam, Hester is not typically Protestant American is emphasized by linking her to the hated (and exotic) Catholics: "Had there been a Papist among the crowd of Puritans, he might have seen in this beautiful woman, so picturesque in her attire and mien, and with the infant at her bosom, an object to remind him of the image of Divine Maternity, . . . something which should remind, indeed, but only by contrast, of that sacred image of sinless motherhood." There is no Papist, of course, and Hester is *not* sinless. Her "taint of deepest sin in the most sacred quality of human life" is exactly what Dimmesdale cannot and the Puritan community will not accept; it makes Hester Eve, not Mary. As Chillingworth says, "By thy first step awry thou didst plant the germ of evil; but since that moment, it has all been a dark necessity."

Like her beauty, Hester's house, her shell, physically and symbolically separates her from the rest of the community. It is on the outskirts of the town, not in close vicinity to any other habitation, and "its comparative remoteness put it out of the sphere of that social activity which already marked the habits of the emigrants." Standing for Hester's own self-reliance as well as her isolation, her house looks "across a basin of the sea at the forest-covered hills, towards the *west*" (emphasis added). In fact, she is more at home in the nearby forest than she is in the town; it is there that she removes the scarlet letter and the cap which confines her luxuriant hair. Hester's familiarity with the forest stands for the unrestrained quality of her nature, her "long seclusion from society" which has taught her "to measure her ideas of right and wrong" by no standard "external to herself." Her standards are by no means wrong: her isolation has taught her, unlike her "Christian" neighbors, to be kind. Clearly she is deeply and uniquely human in feeding and clothing the poor, in caring for the sick, in sympathizing with the sufferer. Her nature is "warm and rich; a well-spring of human tenderness, unfailing to every real demand, and inexhaustible by the largest." A "self-ordained Sister of Mercy," her scarlet A comes to mean "Able," to have the effect of a cross on a nun's bosom. Still, she is "not merely estranged, but outlawed from society," largely through her own choice by the end of the book. In her courage and independence, her "latitude of speculation," Hester becomes "altogether foreign" to the rest of the community. She has wandered "without rule or guidance, in a moral wilderness; as vast, as intricate and shadowy, as the untamed forest." For years she has looked "from this estranged point of view at human institutions, and whatever priests or legislators had established; criticising all with hardly more reverence than the Indian would feel for the clerical band, the judicial robe, the pillory, the gallows, the fireside, or the church."

It is the forest, finally, that points up the difference not only between Hester and the rest of the townspeople, who regard it as the province of the Devil, but between Hester and Dimmesdale as well. If the forest is *her* home, it is not his. He, like Sophia, is society's representative; he stands for culture and civilization as the estranged Hester does not. The minister, Hawthorne is careful to point out, has "never gone through an experience calculated to lead him beyond the scope of generally received laws." He stands at "the head of a social system" which upholds the judicial robe, the pillory, the gallows, the fireside, the church. Hester, on the other hand, has been taught by "Shame, Despair, Solitude"; these "stern and wild" influences have "made her strong, but taught her much amiss." He is "the sainted minister in the church"; she is "the woman of the scarlet letter" in "that magic circle of ignominy." His "sin" with her in the forest, then, is a sin of "principle," committed in weakness, not a "sin of passion" like their first adulterous love. That love, they tell each other, "had a consecration of its own"; it was not a crime like Roger Chillingworth's violation "in cold blood [of] the sanctity of a human heart." But in the forest Hester persuades Dimmesdale to leave the community where he is a leader and become an outlaw, to breathe the "wild, free atmosphere of an unredeemed, unchristianized, lawless region," even to take on another name—to give up his very identity. And "tempted by a dream of happiness, he . . . yielded himself, with deliberate choice, as he had never done before, to what he knew was deadly sin." What may be right for Hester is not right for Dimmesdale. What happens to him after he and Hester decide to flee is that he becomes quite literally mad. At every step he takes homeward, in the chapter called "The Minister in a Maze," he feels "incited to do some strange, wild, wicked thing"; he can barely restrain himself from uttering blasphemies, insulting deacons and parishioners, teaching wicked words to children. When he reaches home, he stays up all night writing his Election Sermon, a masterpiece inspired by a maniacal frenzy, which is the triumph of his career. Once he delivers the sermon, however, his strength is gone; he resembles "the wavering effort of an infant with its mother's arms in view"—Hester, the agent of his destruction and of his salvation.

Hester is both. Hawthorne means seriously the last line of the book, the inscription on the common tombstone of Dimmesdale and Hester: "On a field, Sable, the Letter A, Gules." The red A on a black background: individual passion against the restraints of the community. He deliberately set out to create the kind of balance Whitman achieves in equating the "I" with the "en Masse," and in a way the balance works because one senses he is exactly divided between the attraction and the repulsion he feels for his wonderfully individualistic heroine. Surely Hawthorne intends Hester to stand for a contrast to the sinful Puritan community which represses all human emotions; but when he is confronted with the choice of alienated individualism or communal repression, his final sympathies are ambiguous. Hawthorne *might* have created our first androgynous heroine, but within the context of *The Scarlet Letter* and of his own nineteenth century there is no place for all that energy of Hester Prynne's, and when she tempts others to her own brand of lawlessness, she threatens with destruction the society in which the Dimmesdales and the Hawthornes do live and serve.

"White Girl (Symphony in White)," by James Abbott McNeill Whistler, 1862. Courtesy, National Gallery of Art, Harris Whittemore Collection, Washington, D.C.

III
The American Princess

Only since about 1840 have blondeness and darkness
come to connote distinct types of character. . . .
Usually the moral is clear, but often the reader
doubts the justice of this moral—and even feels
that the author, also, doubted in his heart of
hearts. This doubt is, perhaps, the most significant thing of all.

—Frederick I. Carpenter,
"Puritans Preferred Blondes" [1]

A creature of the same culture, an invention of the same
imagination as the dark lady, the pale maiden represents the
traditional espoused values of the community. She is a descendant of the sentimental heroine, whose story nineteenth-
century ladies read over and over,[2] but as the American Eve
before the Fall, she is something more. I call her the American Princess because she has indigenous qualities that distinguish her from the sentimental heroine, regal qualities
that will eventually take her to Europe in search of old worlds
to conquer.

In her most complete and complex characterization, the
American Princess possesses a unique combination of innocence *and* self-reliance: Isabel Archer embodies the spirit

of Transcendentalism—another name for "Idealism," according to Emerson who writes in his essay "The Transcendentalist":

> Society is good when it does not violate me . . . You think me the child of my circumstances: I make my circumstance. Let any thought or motive of mine be different from that they are, the difference will transform my condition and economy. I—this thought which I called I—is the mold into which the world betrays the shape of the mold. You call it the power of circumstance, but it is the power of me.[3]

And here is Isabel Archer, replying to Madame Merle's observation that "every human being has his shell, . . . the whole envelope of circumstances" that together make up a man or a woman: "I know that nothing else expresses me. Nothing that belongs to me is any measure of me; everything's on the contrary a limit, a barrier, and a perfectly arbitrary one." But this is 1881. 1852 finds the American Princess cast as "a rural bowl of milk" in *Pierre* or "a shadowy snow maiden" in *The Blithedale Romance.* In 1852 her hair is "bright blonde"; in 1881 it is "dark even to blackness"—yet of a very different darkness from Hester Prynne's. As her hair darkens, so does the quality of her spirit deepen. From simplicity to complexity, then, this chapter will trace her development from the ethereal Lucy in Melville's *Pierre* through Hawthorne's Priscilla and Hilda, James's Daisy Miller, Milly Theale and Maggie Verver to Isabel Archer.

Unlike the American Adam, Eve as American Princess is never given a chance by the male novelists who create her to be truly self-reliant—a Huckleberry Finn, for example. She is always attached to a Prince. Thus, Lucy is seen in relation to Pierre, Priscilla to Hollingsworth (and Coverdale), Hilda to Kenyon, Daisy to Giovanelli (and Winterbourne), Milly to Densher, Maggie to Amerigo, and Isabel to Osmond (as well as Goodwood, Warburton and Ralph Touchett). This list suggests that her ability to distinguish the prince from the fortune hunter is not very great, but a somewhat dingy prince makes her own qualities as princess shine all the brighter—especially in the case of Maggie Verver. It also suggests that the idea of innocence and self-reliance is tested in the portrayal of the American Princess only within prescribed conventional limits.

THE PALE MAIDEN

Lucy

The "bright blonde" Lucy is little more than stereotype. The thickly sweet verbiage which describes her reads like Marvell's deliberately exaggerated seduction proposal to his coy mistress, for example: " . . . there will always be beautiful women in the world; yet the world will never see another Lucy Tartan. Her cheeks were tinted with the most delicate white and red, the white predominating. Her eyes some god brought down from heaven; her hair was Danae's, spangled with Jove's shower; her teeth were dived for in the Persian Sea." If, as I have maintained in my discussion of Isabel, everything in this book is symbolic, then Isabel and Lucy are the two contrasting poles, which Pierre, the Transcendentalist, tries to marry. Unfortunately, this "correspondence" does not work; it is incestuous and leads to the death of all three participants in this unholy union.

Pierre's love for Lucy is "profane, since it mortally reaches toward the heaven in ye." He worships her as he worships his "pedestalled mother," addressing her as an idealized sister and telling her, "By heaven, thou belong'st to the regions of an infinite day" (in contrast to Isabel, whom he sees only at night). It is she to whom that "Grand Master, Adam, first knelt." If the love of Lucy and Pierre is that "first begot by Mirth and Peace, in Eden," it is never to be consummated on this earth, as Pierre realizes. "This to be my wife?" he asks himself. "I that but the other day weighed an hundred and fifty pounds of solid avoirdupois;—I to wed this heavenly fleece? Methinks one husbandly embrace would break her airy zone."

Appropriately, the "wondrous fair of face, blue-eyed, and golded-haired" Lucy is "arrayed in colors harmonious with the heavens" and associated with fleecy whiteness. The first reference to her is of the "snow-white glossy pillow," which Pierre glimpses through her open window. Later, he enters her chamber and sees her "snow-white bed" with its "snow-white roll that lay beside the pillow" and longs to "unroll the sacred secrets of that snow-white, ruffled thing," but dares not because it belongs to the "holy angel, Lucy!" The vivid transparency of Lucy's clear Welsh complexion glows like "rosy snow" as she stands bathed by the sun "in golden loveliness and light, . . . fleecily invested" by her flowing, white, blue-ribboned dress. It seems to Pierre that she can only depart the house by floating out of the open window, so touched is she "with an indescribable gaiety, buoyancy, fragility, and an unearthly evanescence."

Lucy never changes; she never loses her snow-whiteness, her fleeciness, her evanescence, her angelic qualities. When Pierre deserts her, she merely swoons and then takes to her bed, but she never judges him; in fact, she forgives him and comes to his aid as ministering angel when she divines that he is in trouble. When she hears Isabel in the final scene call herself Pierre's sister, she dies of the shock; like a true sentimental heroine "Lucy shrunk up like a scroll, and noiselessly fell at the feet of Pierre." By the end of the book, however, Lucy's is no longer the natural innocence of Saddle Meadows. Her country bloom is gone, but it has not been replaced by the usual sallowness: " . . . as if her body indeed were the temple of God, and marble indeed were the only fit material for so holy a shrine, a brilliant, supernatural whiteness now gleamed in her cheek. Her head sat on her shoulders as a chiseled statue's head; and the soft, firm light in her eye seemed as much a prodigy, as though a chiseled statue should give token of vision and intelligence." Her whiteness becomes in Pierre's dream the sterility of the "small white amaranthine flower" which is "irreconcilably distasteful to the cattle." This "multiple and most sterile inodorous immortalness of the small white flower" crowds out that "dear farm-house herb," the life-sustaining catnip. Isabel and Lucy have become in Pierre's dream "the catnip and the amaranth!—man's earthly household peace, and the ever-encroaching appetite for God."

Pierre's dream reflects Lucy's own perception of their relationship when she comes to him in town. "Let it seem," she writes to him, "as though I were some nun-like cousin immovably vowed to dwell with thee in thy strange exile. Show not to me,—never show more any visible conscious token of love. . . . Our mortal lives, oh, my heavenly Pierre, shall henceforth be one mute wooing of each other; with no declaration; no bridal; till we meet in the pure realm of God's final blessedness for us;—till we meet where the ever-interrupting and ever-marring world cannot and shall not come; where all thy hidden, glorious unselfishness shall be gloriously revealed in the full splendour of that heavenly light." Despite the strange cohabitation of Lucy, Pierre and Isabel in the eyes of the world, Lucy "in her own virgin heart" remains "transparently immaculate without shadow of flaw or vein."

Priscilla

Priscilla is neither so perfect nor so ethereal as Lucy. Although Priscilla is described as a "shadowy snow-maiden," [4] there is a taint of the world about her. But this is one of the interesting (and disturbing) things about *The Blithedale Romance:* everything is seen through a veil and it is impossible to distinguish appearance from reality. Priscilla remains a woman of mystery.

What or who Priscilla is cannot be learned from Miles Coverdale, the narrator of the romance. As his name indicates and his statements throughout the book reveal, he has very little sympathy for or understanding of his fellow human beings and his perceptions are not to be trusted. Since all of the characters are perceived through the veil of Coverdale's observations and insinuations, everything he says must be regarded with suspicion. His "pure influences" of Blithedale, for example, are not so wholesome for Zenobia or Hollingsworth, leading to death in the one case and helpless dependency in the other. They are fruitful only for Coverdale himself; he can turn the whole affair into a ballad. If his confession of love for Priscilla at the end of the book rings false, so too does his estimate of Priscilla as a "spiritual" being. Zenobia perceives this and tells Coverdale what she thinks of his conception of Priscilla as "shadowy snow-maiden, who, precisely at the stroke of midnight, shall melt away at my feet in a pool of ice-cold water": "Since you see the young woman in so poetical a light, . . . you had better turn the affair into a ballad." She herself sees Priscilla, on the other hand, as "neither more nor less . . . than a seamstress from the city." Women judge one another, she tells Coverdale, "by tokens that escape the obtuseness of masculine perceptions." The needle marks on Priscilla's forefinger, "her paleness, her nervousness, and her wretched fragility" lead Zenobia to conclude that "she has been stifled with the heat of a salamander-stove, in a small, close room, and has drunk coffee, and fed upon dough-nuts, raisins, candy, and all such trash, till she is scarcely half alive; and so, as she has hardly any physique, a poet, like Mr. Miles Coverdale, may be allowed to think her spiritual." Priscilla may be more than spiritual being, but how much more is hard to say. Unlikely as it seems that Hawthorne would portray the pale maiden, of which his future wife was a kind of prototype, as the degraded woman, there are enough hints to suggest on either a conscious or unconscious level that Priscilla may be a prostitute.[5]

Hawthorne's characters are always revealed most clearly through special symbols—Hester's "A," Zenobia's flower, Hilda's doves. Priscilla's symbol is her little purses: "Their peculiar excellence, besides the great delicacy and beauty of manufacture, lay in the almost impossibility that any uninitiated person should discover the aperture; although, to a practised touch, they would open as wide as charity or prodigality might wish." Coverdale wonders if they are not "a symbol of Priscilla's own mystery." Priscilla's "mystery" seems not so mysterious if one reads this passage closely. Hawthorne supplies several more clues as to what "the particular peril or irksomeness of position" from which Priscilla has recently escaped might be. She has been brought to Blithedale by Hollingsworth, the reformer of criminals; Coverdale deems it possible that "he might have brought one of his guilty patients, to be wrought upon, and restored to spiritual health by the pure influences which our mode of life would create." Old Moodie, her father, slinks about furtively in order to insinuate Priscilla's "little purses" upon willing customers. When Moodie comes to Blithedale to check on his daughter, he asks Hollingsworth if there has been any call for Priscilla. "You know, I think, sir, what I mean," he says; "and though his face was hidden from us," Coverdale reports, "his tone gave a sure indication of the mysterious nod and wink with which he put the question." Priscilla's occupations in the city further link her with prostitution: seamstresses were associated in the nineteenth century with that trade,[6] and as the Veiled Lady, Coverdale remarks that "her sisterhood have grown too numerous to attract much individual notice."

In defense of this view, I would remind the reader that pale maidens deprive men, who enshrine them and declare them as objects of their affection, of a necessary vitality (like the amaranthine flower). If there are just as many hints that Priscilla really is a spiritual being, literally the half-sister of Zenobia, her psychosexual opposite, then a squeamish minor poet and his creator might well unconsciously wish to degrade her. Like Hilda and Sophia, Priscilla is associated with doves—one dove, in this case, which keeps a desolate vigil perched outside Priscilla's window in the city, as if to protect the girl, unlike its fellows who nestle in their warm dovecote. Like Zenobia she is associated with flowers, but where Zenobia's are tropical hothouse flowers at Blithedale and a jeweled artificial flower in the city, Priscilla's are "rural buds and leaflets." Although "among those fragrant blossoms, and conspicuously, too, had been stuck a weed of evil odor and ugly aspect, which . . . destroyed the effect of all the rest," it is Zenobia who has placed the weed there, and Zenobia, too, who has decked Priscilla out with cherry blossoms and maple twigs. Similarly, it is Zenobia who dresses Priscilla in white in the city. Consciously or unconsciously, Hawthorne has so veiled Priscilla's actual nature that it is nearly impossible to determine between illusion and reality. But ambiguity does not equal complexity in this case. It makes little difference whether or not Priscilla was actually a prostitute; "the poor girl was enthralled in an intolerable bondage, from which she must either free herself or perish." If Priscilla's association with prostitution is deliberate on Hawthorne's part, then, probably it is intended as a symbol for her prostituted soul. (She may also stand for his own prostituted soul, for as I have shown in the section on Hester Prynne, the part of Hawthorne that sought societal approval by engaging in the "manly" pursuit of Uncle Sam's gold was at variance with his artistic nature.)

All that one can finally say about Priscilla is that she is a shadowy creature, a girl who exists only in relation to other people, and that other people use her. Everyone in the book uses her: Hollingsworth would use her first for her money, and later as a spiritual crutch; Zenobia and Westervelt use her as the Veiled Lady; Coverdale uses her as material for his ballad. As for any qualities of her own, she does not even exist "but for the fancy-work" with which she is decked out, and her shadowy substance makes her little more than "a figure in a dream." In Coverdale's dream of her, Zenobia and Hollingsworth stand on either side of his bed, bending across it to exchange a kiss of passion, but Priscilla, beholding this through the chamber-window "had melted gradually away, and left only the sadness of her expression in my heart. There it lingered, after I awoke; one of those unreasonable sadnesses that you know not how to deal with, because it involves nothing for common sense to clutch." With no identity of her own, then, Priscilla is, as Zenobia observes, "the type of womanhood, such as man has spent centuries in making"—a depressing and devastating portrait of woman in the nineteenth century.

Hilda

Hilda, in *The Marble Faun*, is less ambiguous, but more self-reliant than Priscilla. Robed always in spotless white, Hilda is associated with the shrine of the Virgin, whose lamp she keeps trimmed, and also—like Priscilla and like James's Milly Theale—with doves. Her hair is neither so bright blonde as Lucy's nor so dark as Isabel Archer's; she is "a slender, brown-haired New England girl" with "certain little house-wifely ways of accuracy and order." Kenyon (another cold Hawthornian artist) can safely marry her if he can just get her to come down from her tower.

Hilda is just as ethereal as, but certainly less compassionate than Lucy. Unlike Priscilla, she is never shown romping about in country pastures. Residing in her tower far above the profane world, the nearest Hilda gets to nature is her doves. "Only the domes of churches ascend into this airy region" where Hilda lives in her "dovecote." "You breathe sweet air, above all the evil scents of Rome," Miriam tells her; "in your maiden elevation, you dwell above our vanities and passions, our moral dust and mud, with the doves and the angels for your nearest neighbors." The doves recognize her as a sister, keeping a vigil outside her window, and the resident artists call Hilda "Dove." As for the angels, they are the subject of Hilda's art: "the Virgin's celestial sorrow, for example, or a hovering angel, imbued with immortal light, or a saint with the glow of heaven in his dying face." Hilda herself is "like an inhabitant of picture land, a partly ideal creature, not to be handled, nor even approached too closely." One representation of Hilda in art is the portrait entitled "Innocence, Dying of a Bloodstain," which depicts a maiden gazing "with sad and secret horror at a blood spot which she seemed . . . to have discovered on her white robe." Another is Kenyon's sculpture of her hand—"small, slender, so perfectly symmetrical," but cold, like the marble in which it is cast. Kenyon has little hope of winning the original, he tells Miriam: "Hilda does not dwell in our mortal atmosphere; and gentle and soft as she appears, it will be as difficult to win her heart as to entice down a white bird from its sunny freedom in the sky. It is strange, with all her delicacy and fragility, the impression she makes of being utterly sufficient to herself. No, I shall never win her. She is abundantly capable of sympathy, and delights to receive it, but she has no need of love."

Hilda is both angelic and self-sufficient only so long as she is not threatened by real life. She is not a real woman, but "the image of divine Womanhood." When her friend Miriam really needs her, Hilda withdraws her friendship with this pronouncement:

> If I were one of God's angels, with a nature incapable of stain, and garments that never could be spotted, I would keep ever at your side, and try to lead you upward. But I am a poor, lonely girl, whom God has set here in an evil world, and given her only a white robe, and bid her wear it back to Him, as white as when she put it on. Your powerful magnetism would be too much for me. The pure, white atmosphere, in which I try to discern what things are good and true, would be discolored. And therefore, Miriam, before it is too late, I mean to put faith in this awful heartquake, which warns me henceforth to avoid you.

Deeply saddened, Miriam responds, "As an angel, you are not amiss; but as a human creature, and a woman among earthly men and women, you need a sin to soften you." Hilda's lack of womanliness is further demonstrated by her feeling about Kenyon: "He cannot be my friend, . . . because—because—I have fancied that he sought to be something more." "What a discovery is here!" Kenyon later exclaims in almost contrapuntal comedy to Hilda's remark: "I seek for Hilda and find a marble woman! Is the omen good or ill?" But Hilda's coldness is not comic for Miriam, who, had she been given the choice between infamy in the eyes of the whole world, or in Hilda's eyes, "would unhesitatingly have accepted the former, on condition of remaining spotless in the estimation of her white-souled friend." Miriam later tells Kenyon, "She was all womanhood to me; and when she cast me off, I had no longer any terms to keep with the reserves of my sex."

Miriam's attraction to Hilda and her despair in response to Hilda's severity may seem implausible, but one must keep in mind Hilda's identification of herself as "a daughter of the Puritans" and the terrible force of Puritan repressiveness on Young Goodman Brown and on the Lord and Lady of the Maypole at Merry Mount. Hilda is like those Puritans who condemned Anne Hutchinson, the Salem witches, the Quakers and Hester Prynne. Her conception of herself as Elect allows for no flexibility; she can neither forgive nor accept forgiveness. As she tells the priest from whom she has sought relief, but refused absolution: "God forbid that I should ask absolution from mortal man!" God forbid Hilda should ever need forgiveness from her friends! But Hilda safeguards her elect status with "an elastic faculty of throwing off such recollections as would be too painful for endurance"—by closing her eyes, in other words, to human sinfulness. Although a great deal is made of Hilda's self-sufficiency, this quality is nothing more than a refusal to have anything to do with life. "Ah, Hilda," Kenyon tells her, "You do not know, for you could never learn it from your own heart, which is all purity and rectitude, what a mixture of good there may be in all things evil." *

* Kenyon's statement places Hawthorne (for whom I think he is a spokesman) much more nearly within the Transcendental camp than Melville, who saw the doctrine of "correspondence" as incestuous in *Pierre*, and with whom Hawthorne is usually linked in his rejection of Transcendental optimism.

Hilda's art, like her conception of herself, lacks "the reality which comes only from a close acquaintance with life." She seemed "to be looking at humanity with angels' eyes." This angelic vision gives her insight into the intentions of the great masters, however, and Hilda becomes a copyist. Like many another New England girl,[7] she opts for "generous self-surrender, and . . . brave, humble magnanimity in choosing to be the handmaid of those old magicians, instead of a minor enchantress within a circle of her own." Her work as a copyist is more valuable, Hawthorne thinks, than her originals would have been—most likely "pretty fancies of snow and moonlight." Whereas Hilda substitutes reason for feeling in her relationships with other people, in her copies she substitutes intuition for intellectual understanding. "She saw—no, not saw, but felt—through and through a picture; she bestowed upon it all the warmth and richness of a woman's sympathy; not by any intellectual effort, but by this strength of heart, and this guiding light of sympathy, she went straight to the central point, in which the master had conceived his work." She not only has given up any attempt at originality; she views the works of the masters with their own eyes, not with her own. "Reverencing these wonderful men so deeply, she was too grateful for all they bestowed upon her, too loyal, too humble in their awful presence, to think of enrolling herself in their society." So much for Hilda's self-reliance! Her complete submission to the spirit of the masters is almost mesmeric, like Priscilla's: "If Guido had not wrought through me," she exclaims at one point, "my pains would have been thrown away." There is no chance of her becoming one of those women like Miriam, "distinguished in art, literature, and science . . . who lead high, lonely lives, and are conscious of no sacrifice so far as . . . [the male sex] is concerned." As an American girl and as an "artist" Hilda has a certain amount of freedom granted her, as it were, only so long as she keeps herself "without a suspicion or a shadow upon the snowy whiteness of her fame." This is not likely to be a problem for Hilda—even when she finally comes down from her tower "to be herself enshrined and worshipped as a household saint, in the light of her husband's fireside."

DAISY MILLER

Where Hilda, one of the first American heroines to go to Europe, had kept her innocence by impersonating an angel, Daisy Miller goes to Europe to demonstrate that Hilda's kind of innocence is a myth. With *Daisy Miller* the American Princess comes to life. Still innocent, her innocence is not of the angelic sort, but of the naive and reckless very human sort. She shocks not only the American expatriates in the novel, who snub her, and her American observer, who is attracted to her, but her American reading public as well. The Philadelphia editor to whom James first sent the story in 1878 rejected it as "an outrage on American girlhood," [8] and even Howells, who himself managed to please the (mostly female) American reading public all his life with his own characterizations of the American girl, felt it necessary to apologize for Daisy: "The American woman would none of Daisy Miller . . . because the American woman . . . was too jealous of her own perfection to allow that innocence might be reckless, and angels in their ignorance of evil might not behave as discreetly as worse people." [9] Nevertheless, *Daisy Miller* became James's most popular book—perhaps because, as James says in his Preface, his "supposedly typical little figure" was "pure poetry," [10] perhaps because Daisy is punished for her audacity, or perhaps simply because *Daisy Miller* is so direct and accessible compared to James's later books.

I suspect that what Americans like about the book is Daisy's self-reliance, and that what they don't like is the idea that self-reliance is the chief characteristic of a *woman*. The women who condemned Daisy Miller would have liked to *be* Daisy Miller, but they were afraid to descend from their pedestals; the men needed to keep them there. This is why Win-

terbourne is so shocked at the end of the book when Giovanelli says at Daisy's funeral, "She was the most beautiful
young lady I ever saw, and the most amiable; . . . and she
was the most innocent." "The most innocent?" Winterbourne asks, feeling sore and angry.[11] The only way Winterbourne has been able to understand Daisy is finally to have
come to the conclusion that "she was a young lady whom a
gentleman need no longer be at pains to respect." This revelation comes to him when he sees her with Giovanelli at midnight in the Colosseum. He feels relief, because as a sort of
Coverdale who needs to *know*, not sympathize, he at last understands: "It was as if a sudden illumination had been
flashed upon the ambiguity of Daisy's behavior, and the riddle had become easy to read." Having classified Daisy as
"bad," no wonder Winterbourne's hearing from her supposed lover that she is "innocent" makes him angry; how
can a woman be self-reliant *and* innocent? Winterbourne has
obviously not read his Emerson, or if he has, he must have
thought that "Self-Reliance" applies only to men:

> What I must do is all that concerns me, not what the people
> think. . . . you will always find those who think they know
> what is your duty better than you know it. It is easy in the
> world to live after the world's opinion; it is easy in solitude to
> live after our own; but the great man is he who in the midst of
> the crowd keeps with perfect sweetness the independence of
> solitude.[12]

The reader can, if Winterbourne cannot, take the measure
of Daisy's innocent self-reliance from the moment of her first
appearance in the garden at Vevey. She is dressed all in
white, but her glance is "perfectly direct and unshrinking";
her eyes are "singularly honest *and* fresh" (emphasis added).
Winterbourne simply reflects, "What conditions could be
better than these?—a pretty American girl coming and standing in front of you in a garden." Although he is pleased with
Daisy's appearance, he cannot quite make her out. She *looks*
extremely innocent to him, and he tries to remember what he

has heard about American girls. Some people have told him that they are innocent, and others have told him that they are not. (Ironically, the Europeans will judge Daisy as innocent; it is the Americans living in Europe who will not—like Winterbourne, the coldness of whose name is reinforced by his fondness for Geneva, "the little metropolis of Calvinism," where both he and Mrs. Walker, Daisy's severest critic, have resided too long.)

Winterbourne decides that Daisy is "a flirt—a pretty American flirt," although he has never "had any relations with young ladies of this category." In Europe he has known "two or three women—perhaps older than Miss Daisy Miller, and provided, for respectability's sake, with husbands —who were great coquettes—dangerous, terrible women, with whom one's relations were liable to take a serious turn. But this young girl was not a coquette in that sense; she was very unsophisticated; she was only a pretty American flirt." The directness of Daisy's later observation, that "It seems to me much more proper in young unmarried women [to flirt] than in old married ones," makes clear that it is not so much her innocence that is in question—her honesty is more "innocent" than the hypocrisy of her critics—but rather her disregard for Old World customs.[13]

What bothers Daisy is that those who live in the Old World are concerned only with appearance; what bothers her critics is that Daisy is not concerned with appearance. This is the basis for Mrs. Costello's judgment that Daisy is "common" and Mrs. Walker's judgment that she is "naturally indelicate," and for their refusal to have anything to do with her. It is also the basis for Winterbourne's judgment of her as "an extraordinary mixture of innocence and crudity." All of them are not only disturbed by, but resentful of the fact that Daisy acts as if she were the first lady of an uncorrupted world, existing outside of time and custom. Thus Mrs. Costello observes, "She goes on from day to day, from hour to hour, as they did in the Golden Age. I can imagine nothing more vulgar." Daisy is "vulgar" because her disregard for custom is a rejection of the very values by which these people measure their lives. This aspect of Daisy makes her a deviant according to Old World standards, but James is very careful to insist upon her typical American-ness, to contrast the two communities rather than to set Daisy outside the boundaries of a single community. He is very careful, too, to insist on her innocence in the comments others make about her, and also by comparing her to Velasquez's portrait of Innocent X beneath which the pretty American girl sits.

Critics who believe that Daisy dies of a broken heart really miss the point of her self-reliance *and* innocence. They interpret her final message to Winterbourne to mean that she has really loved him all along. Daisy's message says that she was never engaged to Giovanelli and asks if Winterbourne remembers their visit to the Castle at Vevey. She has remained, in other words, *self*-reliant, not dependent on any man for her sense of identity; and her visit to the Colosseum with Giovanelli was as innocent as her visit to the castle with Winterbourne. Winterbourne doesn't understand this message at the time, but he realizes later that he has made a mistake in judging her. He has lived too long in foreign parts, as he tells his aunt, to realize that Daisy's association with servants and foreigners of dubious class, while flirtatious, has been as innocent as her relationship with himself. It is her American democratic spirit, rather than depravity, that has prevented Daisy from seeing the class lines that dictate to the more sophisticated Old World resident the kinds of people with whom it is proper to associate. She dies, literally and symbolically, not of any innate disease, not of a broken heart, but of the Roman fever. It is the Old World with its customs and judges that has killed her.

Daisy Miller is a special kind of American. One cannot say that she is "typical" in the sense that the ineffectual Mrs. Millers who are baffled by her, the proper Mrs. Walkers who criticize her, the cautious Winterbournes who try—without coming too close—to figure her out are typical. As Winterbourne observes, Daisy "had the tournure of a princess."

Princesses can be audacious, as Daisy Miller is, because they are special. It is Daisy's audacity that makes her a new and important type in American fiction.* Where innocence had been associated in Hawthorne with goodness and boldness with badness, James gives us here a type of American girl who is both bold and good. In *The Wings of the Dove* James will return to the Hawthorne formula and separate his innocent and bold heroine into good and bad, pale maiden and dark lady; and this American Princess, too, will die—clearly of a broken heart. It will not be until *The Golden Bowl* that the American Princess will live happily ever after, but that will happen only after she has learned to compromise with the imperfect Old World.

MILLY THEALE

Milly Theale is many things: she is James's eulogy to his cousin Minny Temple, she is the "good heroine" of Hawthorne and Melville and, like his own Jean Martle in *The Other House* paired for the struggle with the dark lady, she is the "dove," and she is the American Princess.[14] Yet Milly is not the richly complex heroine James hoped she might be. If one comes away from the novel with a feeling that she is vague and multiple, rather than singular and strong, it is because James deliberately presents her, as he tells us in his Preface, through the perceptions of others. He finds everywhere, he says (and finds "striking, charming and curious") "the indirect presentation" of his main image:

> I note how, again and again, I go but a little way with the direct—that is with the straight exhibition of Milly; it resorts for relief, this process, whenever it can, to some kinder, some merciful indirection: all as if to approach her circuitously, deal with

---

* She can be seen, for example, as the direct ancestor of Fitzgerald's Daisy Fay Buchanan, whose audacity is apparent whenever she speaks: her voice has the sound of the jingle of money.

her at second hand, as an unspotted princess is ever dealt with; the pressure all round her kept easy for her, the sounds, the movements regulated, the forms and ambiguities made charming. All of which proceeds, obviously, from her painter's tenderness of imagination about her, which reduces him to watching her, as it were, through the successive windows of other people's interest in her. So, if we talk of princesses, do the balconies opposite the palace gates, do the coigns of vantage and respect enjoyed for a fee, rake from afar the mystic figure in the gilded coach as it comes forth into the great *place*. [15]

The coigns of vantage through which Milly is perceived are those of Susan Shepherd Stringham, Kate Croy, Merton Densher, primarily, as well as Maud Manningham Lowder, Lord Mark and Sir Luke Strett. The perspectives of these characters are revealed through their names. Susan is both shepherd and one of those lady journalists with three names, her married name suggesting our current term "stringer." Kate Croy's name suggests coy, in the sense of devious, and crow, the French for which is *merle*, linking her to that earlier exploitative woman in *The Portrait of a Lady*. She is also related to Kate Theory and Georgina Roy in "Georgina's Reasons" and to Kate the shrew. Merton Densher is dense for a long time both to the evil of Kate's plan and to Milly's actual worth; he sees her throughout most of the book as simply an American girl. Aunt Maud's names suggest mannishness, loudness, aggressiveness, control—and that she will use whomever she can to gain her own ends. Both Mark and Luke have biblical connotations (as does Milly's prototype, Minny, whose real name was Mary Temple), but while Luke may refer to the evangelist who was also a physician, Mark, given the Wagnerian clues in the novel, may be meant to suggest King Mark in *Tristan and Isolde*. [16]

Susan Stringham finds herself, in relation to Milly, in the presence of "a muffled and intangible form." But dedicated to Milly as she is, she is confident that the form will take on sharpness and will become "the light in which Milly was to be read." This, James writes, is the way Milly affects people: "She worked—and seemingly quite without design—upon the sympathy, the curiosity, the fancy of her associates, and we shall really ourselves scarce otherwise come closer to her than by feeling their impression and sharing, if need be, their confusion." This indirection, this vagueness enshrouding Milly makes it difficult to fathom her as a *person;* [17] but this method is appropriate because it is fitting for Milly as sufferer to be acted upon rather than to act, and because indirection is the only way to approach a princess, as James makes clear in the Preface. This is the light in which Susan Stringham, the princess's confidante, will perceive her: "That a princess could only be a princess was a truth with which essentially, a confidant [sic.], however responsive, had to live."

Milly is a princess for Susan first because of her fabulous wealth: "it was in the fine folds of the helplessly expensive little black frock that she drew over the grass . . . it was in the curious and splendid coils of hair, 'done' with no eye whatever to the *mode du jour*. . . . She couldn't dress it away, nor walk it away, nor think it away; she could neither smile it away in any dreamy absence nor blow it away in any softened sight. She couldn't have lost it if she had tried—that was what it was to be really rich. It had to be *the* thing you were." Another regal quality is Milly's aloofness, through which she gives Mrs. Stringham the feeling of what it is to live with the great. Milly simply closes herself to the question of practical difficulty, and not by merely passing it on to others; "She kept it completely at a distance: it never entered the circle." Although this goes back, as Susan realizes, to the question of money, it goes back also to a quality of Milly's that is just as important as her money: her essential aloneness. Physically Milly is alone—she has recently experienced the "multitudinous . . . loss of parents, brothers, sisters, almost every human appendage, all on a scale and with a sweep that had required the greater stage"—and spiritually she is alone. Milly's is like a "legend of affecting, . . . romantic isolation," but her isolation is more than romantic; it is spiritually crippling. "She was alone, she was stricken, she was rich, and in particular, she was strange"—these are the qualities which sum up Milly for Mrs. Stringham. The aloneness, the strickenness, the richness are all explained by Milly's recent bereavement, but the strangeness for Susan is Milly's innocence. Susan believes she has found her own "note"—the art of "showing New England without showing it wholly in the kitchen"—in her "literary mission," but she is aware of her own limitations. She knows she is not the "real thing"—the "real thing" is Milly; and why Milly, "the potential heiress of all the ages" should admire Susan Stringham, "a mere typical subscriber, after all, to the 'Transcript,' " amazes Susan. It gives her "the key of knowledge"—that is, to Milly's innocence; it makes her ask herself "whom poor Mildred *had* then seen" and leads her to conclude that her friend is "starved for culture"—represented, of course, by herself. "Mrs. Stringham was a woman of the world," James, with irony, has that provincial woman reflect, "but Milly Theale was a princess."

Although James gently ridicules Susan and lets the reader know that Susan's "mission"—her dedication to Milly—is tied to Milly's wealth so that she, too, in her own way uses Milly, he mocks neither her final dedication to Milly nor her perception of Milly as princess. There is, for example, the scene when Milly goes off for a walk by herself and Susan follows. She finds Milly seated on the dizzy edge of a precipice: "Milly, with the promise of it from just above, had gone straight down to it, not stopping till it was all before her," like Milton's Eve. Mrs. Stringham retreats without revealing her presence because she realizes that "if the girl was deeply and recklessly meditating there, she was not meditating a jump; she was on the contrary, as she sat, much more in a state of uplifted and unlimited possession that had nothing to gain from violence. She was looking down on the kingdoms of the earth, and . . . [not with] a view of renouncing them. Was she choosing among them, or did she want them all?"

Princesses are often perched atop promontories: there is Hilda in her dovecote, Rapunzel imprisoned in the witch's tower, Sleeping Beauty slumbering in the castle turret where she climbed to prick her finger on the fatal spinning wheel. Each of them waits for her prince to rescue her. But only the American princess looks down on the kingdoms of the earth, spread before her for her choosing. Princesses in fairy tales seem to be of two sorts: either they are unattainable until the right young man overcomes an overwhelming number of obstacles and wins his prize, or they are unrecognized and rescued by the prince, often with the help of a fairy godmother or a wise old man. Milly Theale fits the archetype, but with a twist; she is doomed as the innocent Eve is doomed, as the self-reliant and innocent American girl, Daisy Miller, is doomed. Milly, as Susan has observed, is lonely, stricken, rich and strange. "Such was essentially the point: It was rich, romantic, abysmal, to have, as was evident, thousands and thousands a year, to have youth and intelligence and if not beauty, at least, in equal measure, a high, dim, charming, ambiguous oddity, which was even better, and then on top of all to enjoy boundless freedom, the freedom of the wind in the desert—it was unspeakably touching to be so equipped and yet to have been reduced by fortune to little humble-minded mistakes." This *American* princess is unique—she is "odd" rather than beautiful, and she is "stricken" (how stricken Susan does not at this point know); her freedom is that of the wind in the *desert*. The American princess seems not one who will live happily ever after, but a dying princess. This image will be emphasized later at Matcham when Lord Mark shows her the Bronzini portrait which she is said to resemble. Milly sees in the portrait a face "handsome in sadness . . . a very great personage—only unaccompanied by a joy." To Milly the significant thing about the lady in the portrait, and the thing that brings tears to her own eyes is that "she was dead, dead, dead."

While Susan Stringham's perception of Milly is as princess,

Kate Croy sees her as a dove. One must keep in mind the significance of Kate's relationship to her father; the fact that she is seen in the beginning and at the end of the book in terms of this relationship—that their relationship frames the action of the book—indicates that she can be as sordid, shady and selfish as Lionel Croy. James emphasized this in his Preface when he wrote, "The image of her so compromised and compromising father was all effectively to have pervaded her life, was in a certain particular way to have tampered with her spring." Thus it comes as no surprise when Kate, after posing for months as Milly's devoted friend, tells Merton, "I shouldn't care for her if she hadn't so much." Since Kate tends to manipulate people to her own advantage, "dove" can only mean mild, gentle and innocent—vulnerable, in other words, someone whom she can use. But Kate, being Kate, is also aware of Milly's wings—her freedom. She is, when she thinks about it, jealous of her companion's "liberty," which means for Kate not only Milly's immense wealth, but her not being "hideously relative to tiers and tiers of others." What Kate is expressing is envy of the self-reliant American girl: "You're an outsider, independent and standing by yourself." Yet Kate also feels "a latent impression that Mildred Theale was not, after all, a person to change places, to change even chances with."

This complete independence and freedom would be a plus for Kate, but for Milly it is part of her strickenness. Milly feels *inferior* to Kate. Remembering Kate's having said that she was at her best late at night makes Milly "wonder when *she* was at her best and how happy people must be who had such a fixed time. She had no time at all; she was never at her best—unless indeed it were exactly, as now, in listening, watching, admiring, collapsing." This is why when Kate, to her credit, warns Milly that "the English crowd" will use her, Milly fails to heed the warning and grasps instead at the role of "dove" which Kate offers her as a means of being a part of their group. "My honest advice to you would be . . . to drop us while you can," she tells Milly. "It would be funny if you didn't soon see how awfully better you can do. We've not really done for you the least thing worth speaking of nothing you mightn't easily have had in some other way. Therefore you're under no obligation. You won't want us next year; we shall only continue to want *you*. But that's no reason for you and you mustn't pay too dreadfully for poor Mrs. Stringham's having let you in. She has the best conscience in the world; she's enchanted with what she has done; but you shouldn't take your people from *her*. It has been quite awful to see you do it." Kate herself is so tied "to tiers and tiers of others" that she doesn't realize the extent of Milly's aloneness: Milly has nowhere else to go. She has seen Kate as her friend; she has no suspicion of "a rift within the lute," and so she asks her, "Why do you say such things to me?" Kate, who has earlier remarked to Milly, "You're impossibly without sin," now tells her, "Because you're a dove." When Kate delicately embraces Milly, it is "ceremonially and in the manner of an *accolade*; partly as if, though a dove who could perch on a finger, one were also a princess with whom forms were to be observed." The complexity of the image is just how Kate does perceive Milly: small, innocent, childlike, but at the same time one whose wealth gives her a certain power and distance which causes others to respond to her with ceremony. Milly accepts Kate's description of her with relief: it explains her to herself; it tells her what she must do to have Kate's friendship and a social identity. "It was . . . like an inspiration: she found herself accepting as the right one, while she caught her breath with relief, the name so given her. She met it on the instant as she would have met the revealed truth; it lighted up the strange dusk in which she lately had walked. *That* was what was the matter with her. She was a dove."

There is little that is innocent in Milly's doveness, however. From this moment on, now that her part has been named to her, she will play that part. Her first act as a dove is to lie to Aunt Maud, who has asked her to find out from Kate whether Merton Densher has returned to England. Milly feels her conversation with Aunt Maud as "that of dove cooing to dove," and understands "in a rush all the reasons that would make her answer the most dovelike." She tells Aunt Maud "I don't *think*, dear lady, he's here," but she believes the opposite. This lie gives her "straightway the measure of the success she could have as a dove." Aunt Maud's response, "Oh, you exquisite thing!" causes Milly, when she is left alone with Susan Stringham, to "study again the dovelike"—in this case by averting Susan's questions and getting Susan to indulge in her own "rich reporting." Milly's next dovelike act is to deceive Sir Luke Street when he comes by appointment to visit her. "He's to be told, please, deceptively, that I'm at home, and you, as my representative, when he comes up, are to see him instead," she instructs Susan. Kate has underestimated Milly: if by "dove" she meant innocence, Milly takes it to mean trying her wings.

"Dove," of course, brings to mind Hawthorne's Hilda, and James surely intends this association to be felt. When Milly's first two dovelike acts of deviousness lead her to the National Gallery, the lady-copyists engage her sympathy "to an absurd extent," for they seem to show her the right way to live. In fact, James writes, "she should have been a lady-copyist—it so met the case. The case was the case of escape, of living under water, of being at once impersonal and firm." Hilda and Milly are much alike: both are "impossibly without sin"; both are ready to give themselves up, for all their self-reliance, to the masculine mind (Hilda to the "masters," Milly to her "prince"); both experience alienation to a great degree, although Hilda seems to prefer hers while Milly's causes her despair; both seek absolution through "the wisdom of the serpent"—as Milly tells Kate after her visit to Sir Luke, "I feel—I can't otherwise describe it—as if I had been, on my knees, to the priest. I've confessed and I've been absolved. It has been lifted off." But for Hilda the word "dove" is one she accepts and one which expresses her purity; for Milly, although the Christ-like implications of her sacrifice are certainly there, the word "dove" is one applied to her by someone who will use her, by someone who uses the word to express Milly's gullibility. And while Milly accepts the term, she does not like Hilda accept it as descriptive, but rather as *pre*scriptive: it prescribes a role for her. Hilda, in other words, has known all along who she is: "I am a daughter of the Puritans." But Milly is aware, especially when she visits Sir Luke, "aware as she had never been, of really not having had from the beginning anything firm." As she tells him, she knows what it is "when one *is*—really alone."

It is Milly's "learning that she was in some way doomed," more than her being a "dove," that will tell her who and what she is. Here is where she goes beyond Hilda in richness and complexity. Hilda is not only not doomed; she is so "spotless," it will be remembered, that one artist portrays her as "Innocence Dying of a Bloodstain." The exact nature of Milly's fatal illness is never revealed. Kate tells Densher that it's "not lungs," but one has learned not to trust Kate, and Minny Temple did die of consumption. But the name of her disease doesn't really matter; in fact, its mysteriousness makes Milly more ethereal and emphasizes that her death is spiritual as well as physical. The point is that Milly is physically doomed by her illness, spiritually doomed by her alienation and doomed, too, through her entanglement with Kate Croy and Aunt Maud, who will use her, Merton Densher, who will idealize her only after she is dead, and even Susan Stringham, who introduces her to all of these predators.

It is not simply because Milly is a princess, nor because she is a dove, but because she is doomed *and* rich that everyone treats her with considerate ceremony. Her visits to Sir Luke are like visits to a confessional (priest or psychiatrist), but they are also like ceremonial visits of royalty. Sir Luke, always referred to as "distinguished," is the wise counselor, the wise old man of the fairy tale, who tells Milly, "My dear young lady, . . . isn't to 'live' exactly what I'm trying to persuade you to take the trouble to do?" And on another occasion the wise old man of another mythic paradigm, he tells her, "The world's before you." [18] It is because Milly is doomed and rich that Kate can risk her odious plan of using her own lover to toy with Milly: "I shouldn't trouble about her if there were one thing she did have," she tells Merton. That one thing, of course, is life. It is only because Milly is doomed and rich that Kate "want[s] to make things pleasant for her." As she tells Merton, "I use, for the purpose, what I have. You're what I have of most precious, and you're there-fore what I use most."

"Do it," Kate tells Densher, because "she's a dove"—a bejewelled dove, on that occasion when Milly for once sheds her mourning and appears dressed all in white with a long, priceless chain of pearls, heavy and pure, wound twice about her neck and hanging down the front of her breast. And all the while "the vision was actually in Kate's face" of how she herself would look in those pearls. "Do it," says Susan Stringham, because "she's, you know, my princess, and to one's princess"—"One makes the whole sacrifice?" Densher finishes for her. "Do it," says Aunt Maud, because I trust you as a man of the world. Perceiving that Kate, Susan and Aunt Maud all want the same thing, he wonders if he mightn't as well consent "to *be* the ass the whole thing in-volved," but he is glad there are no male witnesses: "it was a circle of petticoats; he shouldn't have liked a man to see him." Remembering the "incisive" London surgeon, Den-sher's reaction to Milly and the plan involving her is to feel castrated.* Densher walks all round the others' interpreta-tions of Milly—to use a Jamesian metaphor—but he sees Milly in his own way. He has seen her first in America, and to him she is just an American girl. "I quite understand," he tells Susan Shepherd, that she's your princess, "only, you see, she's not mine." And his perception of Milly as dove is very different from Kate's: "Milly was indeed a dove," he

---

* James's hero, like Hawthorne's, is caught between the spiritual woman whom he idealizes but cannot love in a physical way, and the sexual but dangerous woman. Milly makes him feel sexually impotent, and he can only idealize her; he needs to prove his sexual potency with Kate, but he will never marry her.

reflects on that evening when he sees just how much Kate is impressed by Milly's great wealth, but "dove-like only so far as one remembers that doves have wings and wondrous flights, have them as well as tender tints and soft sounds. It even came to Densher dimly that such wings could in a given case—had, in fact in the case in which he was concerned—spread themselves for protection. Hadn't they, for that matter, lately taken an inordinate reach, and weren't Kate and Mrs. Lowder, weren't Susan Shepherd and he . . . nestling under them to a great increase of immediate ease?"

It is ironic that Milly shelters them all: Susan the shepherd; Kate, who has transformed Milly into a dove for her own malicious purposes; Maud Manningham, the wicked stepmother; and Densher, the castrated prince who cannot say the magic words that will break the evil spell. When she learns (from Lord Mark) that Densher has all along been engaged to Kate, Milly turns her face to the wall. With her knowledge of the horror that surrounds her, she cannot live as Sir Luke has bid her do. For Milly, Sir Luke is the priest of a failed religion: as a princess she dies, but as a dove she escapes. The meaning of the title, then, is the meaning of the psalm from which it is taken:

> My heart doth writhe within me:
>   And the terrors of death are fallen upon me.
> Fearfulness and trembling are come upon me,
>   And horror hath overwhelmed me.
> And I said, "O that I had the wings like a dove!"
>   For then I would fly away and be at rest.

Milly has become a dove especially for Densher, a dove whose wings cover, protect and nestle him. In refusing, finally, to "use" her, he does not realize the same kind of moral rise as Silas Lapham; rather, as Kate understands, he has transformed her memory into an idealized image to which he can be faithful. This is Henry James's own idealization of his cousin Minny as expressed in his letter to his brother William after her death: "I slowly crawling from weakness and inaction and suffering into strength and health and hope: she sinking out of brightness and youth into decline and death. . . . It's almost as if she had passed away—as far as I am concerned—from having served her purpose, that of standing well within the world, inviting me onward by all the bright intensity of her example." [19]

MAGGIE VERVER

The Golden Bowl picks up where *The Wings of the Dove* leaves off—with the marriage of the princess. Maggie Verver is not, like Milly Theale, lonely, stricken, rich and strange; she is mainly rich. And she has her father, literally a New World Adam, who is a sort of reincarnation of Christopher Newman: representative of New World industrialism and finance capitalism, he has come to Europe to buy its treasures for his American City and to buy his daughter a prince. So where Maggie is physically a whole person, as a part of this father-daughter team she is an incomplete person, still a child attached to her father when she marries. *The Golden Bowl* is the story of her initiation.

The theme of initiation is one of the oldest of archetypal motifs. As Joseph Campbell writes: "All moments of separation and new birth produce anxiety. Whether it be the king's child about to be taken from the felicity of her established dual-unity with King-Daddy, or God's daughter Eve, now ripe to depart from the idyl of the Garden, or again, the supremely concentrated Future Buddha breaking past the last horizons of the created world, the same archetypal images are activated, symbolizing danger, reassurance, trial, passage, and the strange holiness of the mysteries of birth." [20] One is reminded, since James again uses the princess/fairy-tale theme deliberately, of the story of "Beauty and the Beast." In that tale Beauty's purity and her devotion to her father are symbolized by her asking only for a white rose, but the only way for the king to satisfy her request is to steal the rose from the garden of the Beast. When the king is caught, the Beast agrees to let him go in exchange for Beauty. Although it is difficult for the king to let Beauty go, she insists upon honoring his promise, and so goes to live with the Beast, remaining aloof from him, however, and longing for her father. The compassionate Beast allows her, after a time, to visit her father, warning her that she must not stay for more than a week. Beauty overstays her visit, but when she dreams that the Beast is dying, she rushes back to him, finds him indeed dying, and tells him that she loves him. Her words transform the Beast into a Prince. And they live happily ever after.[21]

Like Beauty, like Eve before the Fall, like Daisy Miller and Milly Theale, Maggie Verver isn't "born to know evil. She must never know it,"[22] Fanny Assingham decides early in the book. And Maggie herself says to her father in their garden, "Do you realise, father, that I've never had the least blow?" But by the end of the novel Maggie will have had her blow and survived it; unlike Daisy and Milly, she will not die in the process of discovering the world of experience. Innocence in this book is not a positive quality in mature persons; it is a stage from which one must grow to maturity, and one in which Maggie lingers too long. Take away her wealth, take away her daddy, and Maggie would have only her innocence; she would not be self-reliant. To gain what might be called self-reliance—or more precisely self-awareness, because it involves the interdependency of human relationships—Maggie must give up her innocence, give up her dependence on the King-Daddy and participate in acts of deviousness (like Milly's learning to play the role of "dove") in order to win the love of her husband.

Before her marriage Maggie is the only woman in her father's life. To hear her describe "the way we've sat together late, ever so late, in foreign restaurants, which he used to like; the way that, in every city in Europe, we've stayed on and on, with our elbows on the table and most of the lights put out, to talk over things" is to understand how she longs for "the *real* old days." In the early days of her marriage she has changed little; the relationship between Maggie and Adam is much like that of Beauty and the King: "She had only been his child—which she was indeed as much as ever; but there were sides on which she had protected him as if she were more than a daughter. She had done for him more than he knew—much and blissfully, as he always *had* known. If she did at present more than ever, through having what she called the change in his life to make up to him for, his situation still, all the same, kept pace with her activity—his situation being simply that there was more than ever to be done." Even the arrival of the Principino—for Maggie's is not a sterile marriage—does not forge a link between husband and wife. Instead, "Maggie and her father had, with every ingenuity, converted the precious creature into a link between a mamma and a grandpapa." The time that mamma, grandpapa and Principino spend each day in the garden of Fawns is a ritual; the Prince's connection with his son and his wife is "auxilliary." What is "clear at all events for the father and the daughter" is "their simply knowing they wanted, for the time, to be together—at any cost, as it were." Even after Adam's marriage to Charlotte, Maggie keeps her own room at her father's house, much of her clothing there, and a second nursery for her child. Maggie is so "at home" there, according to Fanny, that "if Charlotte, in her own house, so to speak, should wish a friend or two to stay with her, she really would be scarce able to put them up . . . Maggie and the child spread so." Charlotte herself tells Fanny, "I've simply to see the truth of the matter—see that Maggie thinks more on the whole of fathers than of husbands." The result for Adam and Maggie of Maggie's arranging their separate households as it suits her is "more contact and more intimacy. She likes him best alone. And it's the way . . . in which he best likes *her*. It's what I mean therefore by being 'placed.' And the great thing is . . . to 'know' one's place. Doesn't it all strike you . . . as rather placing the Prince too?"

As for the Prince (appropriately named Amerigo because he discovers Americans), he scarcely matters to Maggie and her father. As the naive Maggie has rather crassly told him on the eve of their marriage, "You're . . . a part of his collection . . . —one of the things that can only be got over here. You're a rarity, an object of beauty, an object of price. You're not perhaps absolutely unique, but you're so curious and eminent that there are very few others like you—you belong to a class about which everything is known. You're what they call a *morceau de musée*." This valuable museum piece, then, which Maggie and her father have chosen and paid for, is not to interfere with their relationship; their "clearance" comes "from the one prime fact that the Prince, by good fortune, hadn't proved angular." "You're round, my boy," Adam tells him—"you're *all*, you're variously and inexhaustibly round, when you might, by all the chances, have been abominably square." Angularity is "lovely in a building, but so damnable, for rubbing against, in a man, and especially in a near relation. . . . One would . . . [be] more or less reduced to a hash. As it is, for living with, you're a pure and perfect crystal." Clearly, Adam Verver can no more tell the real thing than can Christopher Newman. A pure and perfect crystal is what the Prince is not; like the golden bowl itself, he has a flaw which has been gilded over—by Fanny Assingham.

Prince Amerigo's flaw, specifically, is his relationship with Charlotte Stant prior to his marriage; he has loved Charlotte, and very likely still does, but he has married Maggie for her money. In a general way, however, he is simply an imperfect human being. "Personally," he considers, taking stock of himself, "he hadn't the vices in question—and that was so much to the good. His race, on the other hand, had had them handsomely enough, and he was somehow full of his race." But he never pretends to be what he is not. "There are two parts of me," he tells Maggie during their engagement. "One is made up of the history, the doings, the marriages, the crimes, the follies, the boundless *bêtises* of other people. . . .

Those things . . . are as public as they're abominable. . . .
But there's another part . . . which . . . represents my single
self, the unknown, unimportant—unimportant save to you—
personal quality. About this you've found out nothing." And
he asks, "You do believe I'm not a hypocrite? You recognize
that I don't lie nor dissemble nor deceive? Is *that* water-
tight?" In light of his and Charlotte's later deception of
Maggie and Adam, his question seems at least ironic; but it
is to be read not in that light, for when he asks it he has
given up Charlotte—she is away in America searching for a
marriage of her own—and he is offering himself to Maggie
for what he is. He is not prepared for the seriousness with
which she takes his question and realizes that Americans
have something which his race does not possess: the moral
sense.[23] Fanny Assingham—expatriated, but still American—
can teach him the moral sense, he decides. "I've of course
something that in our poor dear backward old Rome sufficiently passes for it," he tells her. "But it's no more like
yours than the tortuous stone staircase—half-ruined into the
bargain!—in some castle of our *quattro-cento* is like the 'lightning elevator' in one of Mr. Verver's fifteen-storey buildings.
Your moral sense works by steam—it sends you up like a
rocket. Ours is slow and steep and unlighted, with so many
of the steps missing that—well, it's as short in almost any
case to turn round and come down again." The Prince may
have no "moral sense" from an "American" point of view,
but he is amoral, not immoral, as is demonstrated, for example, by the way he looks at Charlotte Stant—which is not
so unlike the way Adam Verver considers *him*, different, of
course, in its frank sexual appreciation, but similar in the use
of the metaphor of money:

> . . . it was, strangely, as a cluster of possessions of his own
> that . . . Charlotte Stant now affected him; items in a full list,
> items recognized, each of them, as if, for the long interval, they
> had been "stored"—wrapped up, numbered, put away in a
> cabinet. . . . He saw again that her thick hair was, vulgarly
> speaking, brown, but that there was a shade of tawny autumn

leaf in it for "appreciation"—a colour indescribable, . . . something that gave her at moments the sylvan head of a huntress.
. . . He saw the sleeves of her jacket drawn to her wrists, but
he again made out the free arms within them to be of the completely rounded, the polished slimness that Florentine sculptors
in the great time had loved and of which the apparent firmness
is expressed in their old silver and old bronze. He knew her
narrow hands, he knew her long fingers and the shape and
colour of her finger-nails, he knew her special beauty of movement and line when she turned her back, and the perfect working of all her main attachments, that of some wonderful finished instrument, something intently made for exhibition, for a
prize. He knew above all the extraordinary fineness of her flexible waist, the stem of an expanded flower, which gave her like-
ness also to some long loose silk purse, well filled with gold-
pieces, but having been passed empty through a finger-ring
that held it together. It was as if, before she turned to him, he
had weighed the whole thing in his open palm and even heard
a little the chink of the metal.

Significantly, this is not the way the Prince looks at
Maggie—not through any disposition of his own, for his habitual response to women is "more or less to make love to
them"—but because Maggie, as the American Princess, totally lacks the sensuality of Charlotte Stant. One cannot sense
her body through her clothes. Maggie's innocence and her
wealth suggest that she would wear expensive, but stiff and
fluffy frocks; one would expect her to be elaborately or-
namented, to be clothed in gowns of tulle and net with full
skirts and puffy sleeves. She dresses, one learns, not for her
husband, but for her father—in other words, like a little girl.
On the occasion when she does dress deliberately for her
husband she puts on "her newest frock, worn for the first
time, sticking out, all round her, quite stiff and grand; even
perhaps a little too stiff and too grand for a familiar and
domestic frock." She "rustles" when she walks; she seems
"beautifully bedecked."

The Prince feels "placed," all right. He senses that it would
be "ridiculous," "absurd" and "grotesque" if, "being thrust,

systematically, with another woman, and a woman one happened, by the same token, exceedingly to like . . . to 'go about' . . . with such a person as Mrs. Verver in a state of childlike innocence, the state of our primitive parents before the Fall." James makes it abundantly clear, both in the text and in his notebooks (where he states that his intention is to describe adultery) that they do not "go about" in Edenic innocence. Critics who insist that there is no adultery between Charlotte and the Prince after their marriages, that Maggie is a neurotic witch who acts on trumped-up charges, cannot have read closely such passages as this, which is as close to a complete description of sexual passion as the squeamish James was ever to write: "And so for a minute they stood together as strongly held and as closely confronted as any hour of their easier past even had seen them. They were silent at first, on facing and faced, only grasping and grasped, only meeting and met. 'It's sacred,' he said at last. 'It's sacred,' she breathed back to him. They vowed it, gave it out and took it in, drawn, by their intensity, more closely together. Then of a sudden, through this tightened circle, as at the issue of a narrow strait into the sea beyond, everything broke up, broke down, gave way, melted and mingled. Their lips sought their lips, their pressure their response and their response their pressure; with a violence that had sighed itself the next moment to the longest and deepest of stillnesses they passionately sealed their pledge." Ironically, it is Maggie who has made the situation—made it, first of all, because she feels guilty in her own marriage of forsaking her father. "You'll always know that I know it's my fault," she tells him, and decides that perhaps it will help his loneliness if he marries. "It was as if you couldn't be in the market when you were married to *me*," she reasons. "Or rather as if I kept people off, innocently, by being married to you. Now that I'm married to some one else you're, as in consequence, married to nobody. . . . what you've lost . . . [is] the happiness of being just as you were—because I was just as *I* was— that's what you miss." Her father sees what she is driving at:

"So that you think . . . that I had better get married just in order to be as I was before?" And Maggie has made the situation even more what it is after her father's marriage to her old school-friend and her husband's former mistress, because the resumption of the adulterous-in-fact relationship between the Prince and Charlotte is no worse than the incestuous-in-spirit relationship that has been going on all along between Maggie and Adam.

I have not meant to infer that Maggie is to blame for the irregular conditions of these marriages; that would be to give her more responsibility than she deserves for the characters of Adam, the Prince and Charlotte—not to mention Fanny Assingham. (If there is a villain in the piece it is probably she, who with her machinations has engineered the whole quartette.) I see Maggie neither as Witch nor Saint [24] but as a human being with a flaw—not even a tragic flaw, for she has not enough nobility in her character to be a tragic heroine. She has grown up imperfectly, or not at all; she has remained—one might almost say she has chosen to remain—in the state of childhood innocence long past the point when it was time for her to grow up. To say that it is time for Maggie to grow up, time for the Princess to leave the King-Daddy or Eve to leave the Father in the Garden, is not new from either a critical or mythical perspective. What is striking is that the way in which Maggie will have to grow is the way of Fanny Assingham; the way of worldliness is the way of deviousness. Maggie, in order to win the love of her very imperfect husband, will have to do it on his terms, learning to practice the same kind of deceit which he and Charlotte have practiced. Maggie's growing up is really very sad; in growing up she becomes a more mature person, but not necessarily a better person. Or, metaphorically, for America to give up its "innocence" and become part of the world, it has to become more like the Old World—richer, more complex, but decadent and corrupt, too. It is appropriate, therefore, that Fanny Assingham is the one to declare that it is time for Maggie to grow up.

James seems to have an ambivalent attitude toward Fanny Assingham. Three words in her name suggest that she is an ass. Certainly, she is meddlesome, even to the point of villainy. Physically she seems a grotesque combination of Madame Merle and Ida Farange: "Type was there, at the worst, in Mrs. Assingham's dark neat head, on which the crisp black hair made waves so fine and so numerous that she looked even more in the fashion of the hour than she desired. . . . Her richness of hue, her generous nose, her eyebrows marked like those of an actress—these things, with an added amplitude of person on which middle age had set its seal, seemed to present her insistently as a daughter of the South, or still more of the East, a creature formed by hammocks and divans, fed upon sherbets and waited upon by slaves. . . . She wore yellow and purple because she thought it better, as she said, . . . to look like the Queen of Sheba than like a *revendeuse;* she put pearls in her hair and crimson and gold in her tea-gown for the same reason: it was her theory that nature itself had overdressed her and that her only course was to drown, as it was hopeless to try to chasten, the overdressing. . . . With her false indolence, in short, her false leisure, her false pearls and palms and courts and fountains, she was a person for whom life was multitudinous detail, detail that left her, as it at any moment found her, unappalled and unwearied." Given the "moral sense" of the resident Europeans in *Daisy Miller,* who thought it appropriate for married, but not unmarried women to have affairs with men other than their husbands, it is understandable that the Prince would go to Fanny for his lessons in the "moral sense." It is also understandable that Maggie would see in Fanny the worldly knowledge that she herself does not possess, and that Charlotte in her penniless state would use Fanny for her connections. But that James himself would use her for some of the "moral" pronouncements of the book would seem to indicate that he sees her both as the wicked old crone and as the wise old woman of the fairly tale—unless, of course, he views Maggie's "rise" not as the height of his achievement in his international novels, but as her decay. Fanny has said so many things in her time, she admits, "that they make a chance for my having once or twice spoken the truth. I never spoke it more, at all events, than when I declared, on that occasion, that Maggie was the creature in the world to whom a wrong thing could least be communicated. It was as if her imagination had been closed to it, her sense altogether sealed. That . . . is what will now *have* to happen. Her sense will have to open . . . To what's called Evil—with a very big E: for the first time in her life. To the discovery of it, to the knowledge of it, to the crude experience of it."

Maggie has begun to experience at least the imagination of the wider world when Fanny makes her pronouncement. While she waits for the return of the Prince from Matcham, where he and Charlotte have presumably consummated their reunion, Maggie suddenly feels imprisoned within her garden; it is as if she has literally eaten from the tree of knowledge, and she will offer the Prince not only her knowledge, but her new willingness to share his life. Maggie is not conscious of any inward voice that has spoken to her in a new tone, but her reflections

were the fruit, positively, of recognitions and perceptions already active; of the sense above all . . . [of] a difference in the situation so long present to her as practically unattackable. This situation had been occupying for months and months the very centre of *the garden of her life,* but it had reared itself there like some strange tall tower of ivory, or perhaps rather some wonderful, beautiful but outlandish pagoda, a structure plated with hard bright porcelain, coloured and figured and adorned at the overhanging eaves with silver bells that tinkled ever so charmingly when stirred by chance airs. She had walked round and round it—that was what she felt; she had carried on her existence in the space left her for circulation, a space that sometimes seemed ample and sometimes narrow: looking up all the while at the fair structure that spread itself so amply and rose so high, but never quite making out as yet where she might have entered had she wished. She hadn't wished till now—such was the odd case; and what was doubtless equally odd besides was that though her raised eyes seemed to distinguish places that must serve from within, and especially far aloft, as apertures and outlooks, no door appeared to give access *from her convenient garden level* [emphasis added].

I have quoted this long passage because *this* is the beginning of Maggie's initiation. It is not a tree which she sees for the first time in her garden, but a pagoda—not a natural (New World) image, but an artistic, and highly erotic Old World image. What she is feeling for the first time is sexual desire for her husband. She suddenly realizes that "she had been able to marry without breaking . . . with her past. She had surrendered herself to her husband without the shadow of a reserve or a condition and yet hadn't all the while given up her father by the least little inch." Now Maggie dresses for her husband for the first time. When he arrives, after her long wait, she is in the act of "plucking . . . in the garden of thought, . . . some full-blown flower that she could present to him. . . . It was the flower of participation." Although she is unable to tell him her thoughts—"I'm as much in love with you now as the first hour; except that there are some hours—which I know when they come, because they almost frighten me—that show me I'm even more so,"—she is able to show him "that she adored and missed and desired him." But Maggie knows, too, that she is "moving for the first time in her life as in the darkening shadow of a false position," that in order to get what she knows she wants she will have to play a game of art and artifice.

Maggie's first posture is to watch and wait: "She had but one rule of art—to keep within bounds and not lose her head; certainly she might see for a week how far that would take her. She said to herself in her excitement that it was perfectly simple: to bring about a difference, touch by touch, without letting either of the three, and least of all her father, so much as suspect her hand." Maggie's recognition of her situation as a game—"There was a card she could play, but there was only one, and to play it would be to end the game"—foreshadows the climactic scene of the book, when the Prince and Charlotte play as partners in a card game opposite Adam and Fanny Assignham while Maggie watches them from the terrace.

As Maggie watches through the window in that extraordinary scene, the sight of the card players "*told* her why, told her how, named to her, as with hard lips, named straight at her, so that she must take it full in the face. . . . It was extraordinary; they positively brought home to her that to feel about them in any of the immediate, inevitable, assuaging ways, the ways usually open to innocence outraged and generosity betrayed, would have been to give them up." That is why—to keep everything and give none of them up—Maggie lies to Charlotte when that lady follows Maggie to question her. "Have you any ground of complaint of me?" Charlotte demands. "Is there any wrong you consider I've done you? I feel at last that I've a right to ask you." Maggie's denial is not Charlotte's triumph, as it would seem, but the triumph of Maggie's learning to play the game. Even as she lies to Charlotte, she realizes that she has hit upon "the right . . . form of humbugging" that will help her to win in the end. "You must take it from me that your anxiety rests quite on a misconception. You must take it from me that I've never at any moment fancied I could suffer by you," she tells Charlotte. "You must take it from me that I've never thought of you but as beautiful, wonderful and good." Ironically, she is aware of "a chill that completed the coldness of their conscious perjury" between them at the exact moment that Charlotte publicly embraces Maggie for the benefit of the others who arrive at the doorway. The embrace is a demonstration not of their affection, but of their partnership in perjury; it is a signal of the depths of Maggie's growth—or the extent of her fall.

Maggie has learned this kind of game from Fanny Assingham. She has gone to Fanny for lessons, as it were, in gamesmanship, and when Maggie can tell her just how much "I make them do what I like," Fanny is surprised at how far

Maggie has come. She not only finds Maggie "amazing," but "terrible," and Maggie tells her that this is a measure of how much she can bear "for love."

> Fanny hesitated. "Of your father?"
> "For love," Maggie repeated.
> It kept her friend watching. "Of your husband?"
> "For love," Maggie said again.

It is fitting, then, that the Golden Bowl, symbol of this love that Maggie has grown to desire, to protect, and to insist upon as her right, should be revealed for what it is by Fanny.

In one sense the Golden Bowl is the Prince. It will be recalled that Adam Verver had seen his son-in-law as "a pure and perfect crystal." But the Prince knows, and Fanny knows as well, that the Prince has a flaw, and Fanny has gilded it over in introducing him to the Ververs. If Fanny has discovered the Prince for the Ververs, Charlotte has discovered the Golden Bowl itself. It was found in an old curiosity shop during what was ostensibly a search for a wedding gift for Maggie, but really a last opportunity for Charlotte to spend an hour alone with the Prince before his marriage. Both the Golden Bowl and the Prince, for whom she wants to buy it, are beyond her means. But the Prince will not accept it at any price because it has a flaw—which he perceives immediately, though she does not. "Per Dio I'm superstitious! A crack's a crack—and an omen's an omen," he tells her.

> "You'd be afraid—?"
> "Per Bacco!"
> "For your happiness?"
> "For my happiness."
> "For your safety?"
> "For my safety.
> . . . "For your marriage?"
> "For my marriage. For everything."

The rhythm of their speech is similar to the rhythm of the conversation between Fanny and Maggie, when Maggie declares how much she can bear for love—with the difference that during the time that has elapsed Maggie *will* be able to accept and to give a flawed bowl.

In another sense, the Golden Bowl is Maggie's marriage to the Prince. By a series of remarkable coincidences, Maggie picks out the same Golden Bowl in the same shop years later as a gift for her father. She thinks it is perfect when she buys it, but the dealer—the very one who had waited on Charlotte and the Prince—comes to Maggie, conscience-stricken that he has overcharged her for an imperfect piece. In her drawing room he recognizes the family portraits and tells what he knows. The flawed bowl is now an imperfect gift for her father (like their once-perfect love); what it has become is a symbol of Maggie's marriage. Fanny Assingham, present as usual at important moments, seizes the bowl and dashes it to the floor, proclaiming: "Whatever you meant by it—and I don't want to know *now*—has ceased to exist." At that moment, as if by a magic signal in a fairy tale, the Prince appears. The spell has been broken. There, before his eyes, Maggie picks up the shining fragments of the bowl—it has split neatly in half along its crack and become detached from its foot—and offers them to him. As a symbol of their marriage, it is significant that Maggie is able to carry only two of the three pieces of the bowl at a time. It is herself that she offers Amerigo in this flawed and womblike bowl.

The Golden Bowl becomes finally, for Maggie, the "golden fruit—the moment . . . that had shone from afar"; and with Charlotte and her father finally off to America and her husband coming to her, Maggie has a brief moment of terror wondering what is the price she has paid for this fruit. Perhaps Maggie's most important lesson in maturity occurs at the end of the novel: she learns compassion. Even before Amerigo speaks, Maggie knows she has "begun to be paid in full. With that consciousness in fact an extraordinary thing occurred; the assurance of her safety so making her terror drop that already . . . it had been changed to concern for his own anxiety." That extraordinary thing is Maggie's most redeeming quality. She has shown it before in her pity at Charlotte's animal-like wail, as she shows the treasures in Adam's house. And now that she knows that she has won and can exact a confession from Amerigo, she says instead of Charlotte, "Isn't she too splendid?" It is this redeeming quality in Maggie that makes her transformation a rise as well as a fall, and makes believable the fairy tale ending: "See?" the Prince asks her. "I see nothing but you."

ISABEL ARCHER

In 1883 one of Henry James's closest female friends, Constance Fenimore Woolson, wrote to him to ask why he did not create a real woman. She cited Claire de Bellegarde, Daisy Miller and Isabel Archer as examples of incomplete women, asking, "How did you ever dare to write a portrait of a lady?" How did he dare, indeed. What more logical way for an artist, alienated by the commercial "masculine" values of his society, to probe his own identity? But Woolson continued, "Why not give us a woman for whom we can feel a real love? There are surely such in the world. . . . I do not plead that she should be happy; or even fortunate; but let her be distinctly loveable; perhaps, let some one love her very much; but at any rate let *her* love very much, and let us see some that she does; let us care for her, and even greatly. If you will only care for her yourself, as you describe her, the thing is done." [25] Fenimore, as James called her, may well have been pleading for herself. Leon Edel suggests throughout his five-volume biography of James that she was more than a little in love with the novelist, but that although the two writers spent a good deal of time together in Venice, especially during 1880 while James was writing *The Portrait of a Lady*, he never found Fenimore "distinctly loveable." Still, her literary criticism is sound: James does not create "real women," for reasons more personal than artistic. I think he did care very much for Isabel Archer, however. In fact, I believe her to be, to borrow James's criticism of Hawthorne, his nearest approach to the creation of a *person*.

James knew what was wrong with fictional women: they were nearly always seen as "satellites" of men. Aware that to Dickens and Scott and even to Shakespeare women "are typical . . . of a class difficult, in the individual case, to make a centre of interest," James decided in *The Portrait of a Lady* to brave the difficulty, seeing it as "the beautiful incentive." He would not play the easy trick of presenting his heroine through the relation of others to her; instead, he said to himself: "Place the centre of the subject in the young woman's own consciousness." He warned himself, "To depend upon her and her little concerns wholly to see you through will necessitate, remember, your really 'doing' her." It would be "naturally of the essence that the young woman should be herself complex; that was rudimentary." [26]

James faced many of the same problems with Isabel that Hawthorne faced in creating Hester Prynne. James, too, centered tale after tale in the artist who struggled with the problem of listening only to his inner voice, of choosing between or somehow reconciling the needs of his artistic self with membership in a society which demanded that its (male) members do something "useful." It is not surprising, then, that James, like Hawthorne, would probe the concept of self-reliance most profoundly through a heroine. This was a difficult task for both novelists. Hawthorne could only deal with the self-reliant *woman* by making her deviant, and therefore punishable, in her community. James, on the other hand, set out to give Isabel Archer the context which Hester Prynne lacked: he would make her self-reliant by endowing her with a fortune * and by removing her from the sterile confines of

* It is ironic that James came to the same conclusion as the utopian socialists regarding the independence of women: the only way to make them self-reliant is to remove their economic dependence on men. But James, the elitist, makes Isabel Archer, like Milly Theale, independently wealthy, where the utopian writers either do away with money altogether or have the state give each man, woman and child a living wage. Of course James himself constantly worried about money and was pressed, like his Ralph Limpert in "The Next Time," with the need to sell what he wrote without prostituting his artistic self.

puritanical America. He failed, however, to give her *absolute* free choice: she has health, wealth and beauty; but because she is a woman, her choice is limited, finally, to which of her possible suitors she will marry—which one will interfere least with her freedom. Henry James was no more of a feminist than Hawthorne—as his vitriolic attack on lady reformers in *The Bostonians* makes clear. But like Hawthorne, his nearest approach to the complete creation of a person (and James to the contrary, I think Hester Prynne surpasses Zenobia in human richness and complexity), was his closest approximation of an androgynous character. Originally as innocent as Eve before the Fall and as self-reliant as the most idealistic of the Transcendentalists, Isabel Archer grows to become a deeply suffering and richly developed human being. She is "complex," but not because James "place[d] the centre" in her "own consciousness." Or, to put it another way, he defined that consciousness as her relation to others, and perhaps this is what troubled Fenimore.

The core of the novel is Isabel's initial assertion that she is her own person, not shaped by "circumstances," and Madame Merle's counter-pronouncement that "every human being has his shell," cited at the beginning of this chapter. Elsewhere James has offered a kind of resolution between these two points of view: "Experience, as I see it, is our apprehension and our measure of what happens to us as social creatures." [27] In only one place do we get a portrait of Isabel though her "own consciousness"—in the famous chapter 42 where Isabel sits musing through the night before the fire—and by that time she will have so changed as to have become very much Madame Merle's creature of circumstances. Isabel's "own consciousness," then, is her *measure* and *apprehension* of her experience; her measure and apprehension of her American background, her education, the places she visits and in which she will reside, and the people with whom she interacts will shape her—an initially innocent and self-reliant young woman—as a social being.

The circumstances are present for Isabel even before the

reader encounters her: the scene is richly set at Gardencourt, where she is discussed by Ralph Touchett and Lord Warburton as interesting and independent, qualities surmised from Mrs. Touchett's telegrams announcing the impending arrival of herself and her niece from America. But then James begins at the beginning, taking us back to Albany, New York, where Mrs. Touchett found Isabel "seated alone with a book"—a history of German thought—in the "large, square . . . house" beyond which slopes "a long garden," like the garden of James's grandmother's house in Albany evoked in his autobiographies, "containing peach-trees of barely credible familiarity." The house, the garden, the solitude, the Transcendental reading matter are at this point the circumstances which shape Isabel's consciousness. These are her "little concerns." This is the artist's "dream of some Paradise," to which James refers in the Preface, "the fruit of a tree he may not pretend to have shaken, . . . a golden apple for the writer's lap, straight from the wind-stirred tree." This is the key to the "square and spacious house" in which his heroine stands "in perfect isolation."

Her mother long dead, the most important person in Isabel's life seems to have been her father. Despite some frightening memories—such as the time her father left her in Europe with a governess who in turn abandoned her for a lover—and despite what his relatives characterize as his frivolity, the father and daughter seem to have had a close relationship, and in his recent death "the pain of separation from his clever, superior, his remarkable girl" has been great. Since her father's death, Isabel has lived alone; her two older sisters—Edith, the "pretty" one, and Lilian, the "sensible" one—are married. Isabel, the "intellectual" one, is thought to be "different" from other girls; she spends most of her time reading. Physically she is attractive, but in an unusual way. No "daughter of the Puritans," she is "undeniably spare, and ponderably light, and proveably tall," with hair "dark even to blackness," and light grey eyes. Nineteen men out of twenty, those whose norm is the blonde-haired, blue-eyed maiden, would not find her "pretty," but the twentieth finds her exquisite. A romantic heroine, she has had "kindness, admiration, bonbons, bouquets, . . . abundant opportunity for dancing, plenty of new dresses"—and "the latest publications." Young men are a bit afraid of her, perhaps because of her propensity to please herself, perhaps because of "her reputation of reading a good deal which hung about her like the cloudy envelope of a goddess in an epic." [28] She is also rather rigid, like the Puritan daughters she disowns, and she is brazen, like Daisy Miller. Her first words to Mrs. Touchett, for example, who has come to "do something" for her are, "Ah, . . . you must be our crazy Aunt Lydia." Although she has in the depths of her nature an even more unquenchable desire to please than does Edith, "the depths of her nature are a very out-of-the-way place," and in fact what others see in Isabel is "an unquenchable desire to think well of herself." She goes to Europe, then, both innocent and well developed—intellectually and physically, as her brother-in-law jokes—both virginal and attractive to every man she meets, but most of all with "a desire to leave the past behind her and . . . to begin afresh."

Isabel's educational background is similar to that of the younger members of the James family: she and her sisters have had no regular education and no permanent home; they have had a variety of governesses or been sent to superficial schools; their father has transported them three times across the Atlantic before Isabel's fourteenth year, whetting her curiosity for Europe without satisfying it. Like Margaret Fuller, too, Isabel's education has begun under her father's guidance and continued under her own. Her solitude does "not press upon her; for her love of knowledge had a fertilising quality and her imagination was strong." She is thoroughly grounded both in the classics (she is reported to have read them "in translation") and in Romanticism—"the music of Gounod, the poetry of Browning, the prose of George Eliot." The one thing missing from her education seems to be a knowledge of the unpleasant, which her father has kept from her, even though she has gathered from literature "that it was often a source of interest and even of instruction." Although she reads much of the time, Isabel's "great desire for knowledge" is not limited to books. A Transcendentalist at heart, "she really preferred almost any source of information to the printed page; she had an immense curiosity about life and was constantly staring and wondering." Mrs. Touchett arrives just at the right time: she will both supply a knowledge of the unpleasant and satisfy Isabel's curiosity about life by taking her to Europe to complete her education.

As important as one's psychological and intellectual background in the development of consciousness is one's physical "place." [29] The house at Albany, as the first of a number of places important to Isabel's development, is not only the home of her childhood, but contains her books and her garden, and becomes a metaphor for Isabel herself. There are two entrances to the Albany house: one is "condemned, . . . secured by bolts which a particularly slender little girl found . . . impossible to slide." It is on the other side of this door that Isabel sits reading, shutting out the world. "She knew that this silent, motionless portal opened into the street; if the side-lights had not been filled with green paper she might have looked out upon the little brown stoop and well-worn brick pavement." But like the novelist at work, "she had no wish to look out, for this would have interfered with her theory that there was a strange, unseen place on the other side—a place which became to the child's imagination, according to its different moods, a region of delight or of terror."

Isabel herself is a mixture of garden-like innocence and a desire for worldly knowledge: "Her nature had . . . a certain garden-like quality, a suggestion of perfume and murmuring boughs, of bowers and lengthening vistas, which made her feel that introspection was, after all, an exercise in the open air, and that a visit to the recesses of one's spirit was harmless when one returned from it with a lapful of roses. But she was often reminded that there were other gardens in the world than that of her remarkable soul, and that there were moreover a great many places which were not gardens at all."

Gardencourt, the Touchett estate in England, is a gentle mediating place between nature and civilization, between America and Europe, as its name suggests. It is a place where "the deep greenness outside . . . seemed always peeping in, . . . a place where sounds were felicitously accidental, where the tread was muffled by the earth itself and in the thick mild air all friction dropped out of contact and all shrillness out of talk." But as American innocents are always doomed to learn about nature, it is Gardencourt where first the elder Mr. Touchett and then Ralph Touchett die, where Isabel receives the £70,000 bequest and where she first meets Madame Merle. It is to Gardencourt that Isabel, a self-reliant innocent, comes in search of knowledge. It is to Gardencourt that she will return, full of the knowledge of evil, to see the ghost of human suffering. It is from Gardencourt that she must make her journey into the world.

Lockleigh is important, briefly, in Isabel's life because it is the home of the first of her European suitors, Lord Warburton. Like Gardencourt, its name is significant: it has the traditional romantic connotations appropriate to "a wilderness of faded chintz" (it could be the name of an estate in a Scott novel); but more important, it suggests again the "locks" which are a clue to Isabel's personality. Warburton shows Lockleigh to Isabel from the gardens, where it appears as "a stout grey pile," affecting her "as a castle in a legend." It must also affect her as a sort of nunnery, given Warburton's sisters who live there, the Misses Molyneux, with their eyes like "balanced basins," round, quiet and contented, and their "encased" figures, and his brother the Vicar who comes to call. The idea of living there fills Isabel with coldness and fear.

If Lockleigh suggests a convent, the houses of Italy, with their decaying gardens, suggest prisons to varying degrees. They are often full of ruins and statuary, like the shadowy

Rome of Hawthorne's *Marble Faun*. Osmond's villa in Florence has an "antique, weather-worn, yet imposing front" with "a somewhat incommunicative character"—like Osmond, himself. "It was the mask, not the face of the house. It had heavy lids, but no eyes; the house in reality looked another way—looked off behind." The massively cross-barred windows seemed "less to offer communication with the world than to defy the world to look in." There is a garden (really a terrace), narrow and full of "tangles of wild roses," but it seems to be used chiefly by Pansy, who has herself been imprisoned in a convent to be educated as the perfect *jeune fille*, a blank page. For Osmond the villa houses his prize possessions—hangings, carvings, chests and cabinets, pictorial art and other "perverse-looking relics." All of this—the façade, the possessions and especially the barred windows—should, but does not, suggest to Isabel both how much Osmond values appearance and what the chances are for the survival of a free spirit in such an environment. That it does not reveals the blindness of her own innocence.

Mrs. Touchett's Palazzo Crescentini suggests Mrs. Touchett herself. In her rooms, "the pompous frescoes of the sixteenth century looked down on the familiar commodities of the age of advertisement." To live in such a place is for Isabel "to hold to her ear all day a shell of the sea of the past." There is a bright garden "where nature itself looked as archaic as the architecture of the palace." It is here that Ralph tries to warn Isabel about Osmond: "You were the last person I expected to see caught," he tells her, but "you're going to be put into a cage."

Isabel, however, professes to like her cage, and accepts Osmond's proposal in a hotel in Rome which is "ugly to distress; the false colours, the sham splendour were like vulgar, bragging, lying talk"—like the union of Osmond and Isabel. Ironically, when Osmond proposes to her, she feels "the sharpness of the pang that suggested to her somehow the slipping of a fine bolt—backward, forward, she couldn't have said which"—ironic, for Isabel with her complete independence cannot tell whether the door is closing on her prison or opening to set her free.

Isabel's own house in Rome answers, too late, her question. Ned Rosier finds it to be a dungeon: "a kind of domestic fortress . . . which smelt of historic deeds, of crime and craft and violence." It has no garden, but only a damp court with frescoes by Caravaggio and "a row of mutilated statues and dusty urns." The "good things" in her rooms are of "a taste of Osmond's own—not at all of hers," although purchased with her money. By the time Isabel has "taken the measure of her dwelling," it is with "incredulous terror." She has followed Osmond, and "he had led her into the mansion of his own habitation, then, *then* she had seen where she really was. . . . It was the house of darkness, the house of dumbness, the house of suffocation."

Place, as I have said, is James's metaphor for person, and it is the people with whom one interacts who form the most important part of one's experience. Mrs. Touchett, a kind of fairy godmother who transforms Işabel from American girl to Princess, and Madame Merle, who uses Isabel for her own selfish ends, are crucial to her experience; but their influence—either destructive or instructive, depending on one's point of view—is discussed in the next chapter.

Henrietta Stackpole is Isabel's oldest friend. James treats this self-made lady journalist more as a vehicle for humor than as a model for what a truly liberated woman ought to be. Ralph's estimate of her, and probably James's, is that she "smells so of the Future—it almost knocks one down!" She figures for Isabel as a sort of American conscience, treasured, but ignored. She tells Isabel, for example, "The peril for you is that you live too much in the world of your own dreams. You're not enough in contact with reality—with the toiling, striving, suffering, I may even say sinning world that surrounds you. You're too fastidious; you've too many graceful illusions." This is not only a pronouncement about Isabel Archer; it is a description of Henry James as well.

Ralph Touchett's judgment of Isabel is much like Henrietta's. When she tells him, "I don't wish to touch the cup of experience. It's a poisoned drink! I only want to see for myself," he answers, "You want to see, but not to feel." Although Ralph is right in this case, he is not always right about Isabel; his "measure" of experience is often no more valid than her own. His disease is symbolic as well as literal; it perverts his vision. It is Ralph who thought that the £70,000 would set Isabel free, that her contact with Madame Merle "probably" would not harm her, that she would not marry Gilbert Osmond if one "did nothing." (Isabel's perceptions are equally skewed: she sees the money as something that must be shared, Madame Merle—initially—as the most charming of women, and Gilbert Osmond as a perfectly cultivated gentleman.) Ralph, of course, is also one of Isabel's lovers, but he loves her, as he tells her, without hope. "It was not exactly true that Ralph Touchett had had a key put into his hand," James says of the man who always keeps his hands in his pockets. "He surveyed the edifice [of his cousin] from the outside and admired it greatly; he looked in at the windows and received an impression of proportions equally fair. But he felt that he saw it only by glimpses and that he had not yet stood under the roof. The door was fastened, and though he had keys in his pocket he had a conviction that none of them would fit." Because of his limitations, Ralph, like many a Jamesian character, will live vicariously through Isabel. He decides to launch her, like a balloon, with £70,000 so that he can see what she will do with complete freedom. He is to declare later, sadly, "You seemed to me to be soaring far up in the blue—to be sailing in the bright light, over the heads of men. Suddenly some one tosses up a faded rosebud—a missile that should never have reached you—and straight you drop to the ground. It hurts me, . . . hurts me as if I had fallen myself." He is, then, the author of all her woe—for her money is finally a burden and the cause of her falling prey to the evil machinations of Osmond and Madame Merle—and the source of her salvation. His love for Isabel, like Milly Theale's for Merton Densher, is spiritual. He literally dies that Isabel might live, for his death is what draws Isabel from the morass of evil which Osmond and Madame Merle represent, and in which she has been ensnared. Ralph's real legacy to Isabel, like Milly's, is his love.

The men in Isabel's life all seem to love her except the one she marries—a comment both on how one "measures" one's experience and on the tragedy (or comedy or at least irony) of absolute free choice. Lord Warburton is almost too kindly, too good. Isabel's coldness toward him is based on "a certain fear." His proposal makes her imagine "she knew not what strange gardens," and makes her feel as if she were "some wild, caught creature in a vast cage." This fear is partly sexual fear, but Isabel really rejects Warburton because, "liberal" as he is, he represents a social system, a whole tradition of conventions and proprieties which she senses would stifle her.

If Lord Warburton presents a gentle threat, a threat of being socially immured, Caspar Goodwood, with his "hard manhood," presents a threat more dangerous and more directly personal. Isabel's first reaction to Henrietta's information that Goodwood will present himself at Gardencourt is alarm. What she fears is "that he seemed to deprive her of the sense of freedom. There was a disagreeably strong push, a kind of hardness in his presence, in his way of rising before her. . . . more than any man she had ever known . . . Caspar Goodwood expressed for her an energy—and she had already felt it as a power—that was of his very nature. . . . She might like it or not, but he insisted, ever, with his whole weight and force: even in one's usual contact with him one had to reckon with that. The idea of a diminished liberty was particularly disagreeable to her." Thus, although Caspar tells her that he supposes her with wings and the need of beautiful free movement, that the force in her, the independence is what appeals to him, that "It's to make you independent that I want to marry you," she calls this "a beautiful sophism" on his part. And she is right; his answer betrays his conventional male view of woman's independence: "An unmarried woman—a girl of your age—isn't independent. There are all sorts of things she can't do. She's hampered at every step." In addition to her strong sense of personal freedom which intuitively impels her to reject Caspar as overpowering, Isabel fears his sexuality as well. "I'm after all very much afraid of you," she tells him when he presses her to marry him, and after he leaves her she drops on her knees before the bed and hides her face in her arms: "She was not praying; she was trembling—trembling all over. . . . she found herself now humming like a smitten harp. She only asked, however, to put on the cover, to case herself again in brown holland, but she wished to resist her excitement. . . . it was a thing to be ashamed of—it was profane and out of place." The two are tied together: this sense of passion is irresistible, beyond her control; giving in to it means giving up herself, literally submitting to Goodwood.

Isabel chooses the one man who makes the least demands upon her—or so at least her misperceptions of him tell her before their marriage. As a matter of fact, Isabel chooses Osmond because with him she feels that *she* is in control. "That he was poor and lonely and yet that somehow he was noble—that was what had interested her and seemed to give her her opportunity," she reflects later. The sense that he is "helpless and ineffectual" had made her feel tenderness, made her decide, somewhat like Ralph, that "She would launch his boat for him; she would be his providence; it would be a good thing to love him." She had given herself to him "a good deal for what she found in him" (or didn't find in him), "but a good deal also for what she brought him and which might enrich the gift." In other words, "The finest—in the sense of being the subtlest—manly organism she had ever known had become her property." Gilbert Osmond, then, has a need which Isabel can fill. To help him will be a "noble" act; it will even have a "maternal strain" to it. Then, too, Osmond is the least passionate of Isabel's wooers, and for a variety of reasons—early childhood experiences which have made her wary of deep emotional commitments, the fear that a man to whom she gives herself will abandon her as her father did, the need to protect her own freedom and independence—passion terrifies her. "What made her dread great was precisely the force which, as it would seem ought to have banished all dread—the sense of something within herself, deep down, that she supposed to be inspired and trustful passion. It was there like a large sum stored in a bank—which there was a terror in having to begin to spend. If she touched it, it would all come out." That there is so little of the physical about Osmond, then, is a plus. He has "dense, delicate hair," "overdrawn, retouched features," a clear complexion and "that light, smooth slenderness of structure which made the movement of a single one of his fingers produce the effect of an expressive gesture." These are precise words, for what Osmond does primarily is to *produce effects* rather than to make actual gestures. He is fastidious, critical and governed—probably too much—by his sensibilities; but to Isabel's early apprehension these signs speak of "quality, of intensity, somehow as promises of interest."

Isabel's friends, except for Madame Merle, who has a great deal to gain from the match, recognize Osmond for what he is. Mrs. Touchett sees the alliance as having an air of "morbid perversity," while Henrietta, Ralph and Caspar all beg Isabel not to marry him. Even the Countess Gemini feels compelled to warn Isabel about her brother and compares him to Machiavelli. The self-reliant American innocent makes her own decision, however: believing she is giving up the least amount of freedom, she casts herself into a "dungeon." She chooses to repress rather than to experience passion—not, in other words, to become initiated; but ironically, she is initiated into things that are "hideously unclean." She believes Osmond to be cultured, clever, amiable, good-natured, knowledgeable, but underneath this façade "his egotism lay hidden like a serpent in a bank of flowers," and everything he touches, including Isabel herself, will wither.

This is the moment of Isabel's fall. It is after her marriage that James paraphrases the last lines of *Paradise Lost:* "The world lay before her—she could do whatever she chose." But Isabel's free-spirited traveling is over; she is confined to Osmond's cluttered drawing rooms, herself his chief "possession." Their marriage is as sterile as the one dead child Isabel and Osmond produce and the dungeonlike house without a garden in which they live. Isabel is indeed fallen. "She had taken all the first steps in the purest confidence, and then she had suddenly found the infinite vista of a multiplied life to be a dark, narrow alley with a dead wall at the end," she realizes later. "Instead of leading to the high places of happiness, from which the world would seem to lie below one, so that one could look down with a sense of exaltation and advantage, and judge and choose and pity, it led rather downward and earthward, into realms of restriction and depression where the sound of other lives, easier and freer, was heard as from above, and where it served to deepen the feeling of failure."

The most telling sign of Isabel's changed condition is that she ceases to be natural—a quality which once chiefly distinguished her. "Covert observation" becomes "a habit with her; an instinct of which it is not an exaggeration to say that it was allied to that of self-defence." Defensiveness describes very well her stance toward her husband, and no wonder, for the sentiment he most clearly manifests toward her after their marriage is disapproval. She is sure that he regards her sentiments as "worthy of a radical newspaper or a Unitarian preacher." The real offense is in "her having a mind of her own at all." Her mind was to be his—"attached to his own like a small garden-plot to a deer-park." He does not wish her to be stupid; far from desiring that her mind be a blank page, he had wished it to be richly receptive. "He had expected his wife to feel with him and for him, to enter into his opinions, his ambitions, his preferences." Not only does Isabel have a mind of her own, but as far as Osmond's goes, "there were certain things she could never take in." Such "hideously unclean" things have to do somehow with Madame Merle, but even when Isabel begins to perceive the relationship of these two persons to each other and to herself, she does nothing to change her situation. If Osmond is devoted to appearances, telling people at their receptions, "We're as united . . . as the candlestick and the snuffers," belying the fact that they haven't spoken to one another for weeks, Isabel, by playing beautifully the role of hostess at these receptions, does nothing to contradict him. She seems to have become a more beautiful and richly developed mature woman, but one who is as fastidious, defensive, unnatural and devoted to appearances as is Osmond himself.

It takes the revelation that Madame Merle has used her, and Ralph's death to shake Isabel out of her stupor. But because *she* is now a different person, her return to Gardencourt cannot be a rebirth. Gardencourt had been her starting point, but her return now to its "muffled chambers" is only a temporary solution: "She had gone forth in her strength; she would come back in her weakness, and if the place had been a rest to her before, it would be a sanctuary now." Her journey from Rome shows just how changed she is. Although the countries through which she passes are decked out "in the richest freshness of spring," Isabel's thoughts take her through other countries—"strange-looking, dimly-lighted, pathless lands, in which there was no change of seasons, but . . . a perpetual dreariness of winter." She who was once so richly endowed with life, now feels "as good as . . . dead." She envies Ralph his dying, "the most perfect rest," as she sits in a corner motionless, passive, detached. A flash of her old self-confidence wells up: "Deep in her soul—deeper than any appetite for renunciation—was the sense that life would be her business for a long time to come. And at moments there was something inspiring, almost enlivening, in the conviction. It was a proof of strength—it was a proof she should some day be happy again. It couldn't be she was to live only to suffer; she was still young, after all, and a great many things might happen to her yet. To live only to suffer—

only to feel the injury of life repeated and enlarged—it seemed to her she was too valuable, too capable, for that." But the flash is momentary. Quickly her confidence dies away as she realizes that all history "is full of the destruction of precious things." Drearily, "as the grey curtain of her indifference closed her in," she perceives that "she should never escape; she should last to the end."

Caspar Goodwood comes, finally, like a knight in shining armor, to rescue her. If this were a fairy tale, Isabel, like Beauty and like Maggie Verver, would wake up to her essential femininity and be saved in the strong arms of Caspar Goodwood. He even echoes the words of *Paradise Lost* to convince her of the garden of earthly delights that awaits her as his wife: "The world's all before us—and the world's very big." "Here I stand; I'm as firm as a rock," he tells her, but while she realizes that "the world, in truth, had never seemed so large; it seemed to open out, all round her," at the same time she is "like a creature in pain; it was as if he were pressing something that hurt her." Being passionately loved isn't rescue for Isabel Archer: "this was the hot wind of the desert, at the approach of which the others dropped dead, like the mere sweet airs of the garden. . . . the very taste of it, as of something potent, acrid and strange, forced open her set teeth." Caspar's kiss arouses her passion once again. It is like "white lightning, a flash that spread, and spread again, and stayed"; but "while she took it, she felt each thing in his hard manhood that had least pleased her, each aggressive fact of his face, his figure, his presence, justified of its intense identity and made one with this act of possession. So had she heard of those wrecked and under water following a train of images before they sink." When darkness returns, when the flash of white lightning is over, she is *free*. "She never looked about her; she only darted from the spot. . . . She had not known where to turn; but she knew now. There was a very straight path."

The path for Isabel is clearly away from Goodwood. The path out of the garden is into the world of maturity. Yet one does not really know where that straight path leads Isabel—to Italy to escape the passion which still seems the greatest threat to her freedom, to keep her promise to Pansy, to buy her freedom from Osmond, or to make the best of her self-made prison. Perhaps, as Leon Edel suggests, there can be no resolution because Henry James, in trying here to marry the opposite sides of his own personality, would necessarily fail until he was able to resolve the problem of human passion and maturity in his later years. Edel sees the writer of *The Portrait* as "a man of large sympathies and powerful passions, which are in some degree inhibited, and which are struggling to be set free, indeed which are using all kinds of indirection to find some liberating channel." [30]

It is because of the indirection, because James has presented Isabel in terms of her experience rather than through her "own consciousness," that the liberating channel is so hard to find. One thing, however, is clear: James's conclusion about the consequences of American innocence and self-reliance. Strangely enough, this statement of Emerson's in "The Transcendentalist" matches his own: "A picture, a book, a favorite spot in the hills or the woods . . . can give . . . often forms so vivid that these for the time shall seem real, and society the illusion. . . . But the good and wise must learn to act, and carry salvation to the combatants and demagogues in the dusty arena below." *This* must be the straight path. It *may* suggest redemption for Isabel. It *may* suggest a fortunate fall. Isabel Archer is what she is at the end of the novel—which is very different from what she was at its beginning—because of the way in which she has measured and apprehended her experience. This means, of course, that she might have become a different social creature had she measured differently; but it also means that if her experience has taught her new ways of apprehension, the possibility of further change might still be open to her. Perhaps one's view ultimately depends upon one's own measure and apprehension of experience. Such is the complexity, finally, of James's most fully developed American Princess.

Poster for the Gertrude Stein, Virgil Thompson opera, *The Mother of Us All,* by Robert Indiana, 1967. Courtesy, Robert Indiana.

~ IV ~
The Great Mother

The Great Mother, in her function of fixation and
not releasing what aspires toward independence and
freedom is dangerous. . . . To this context belongs a symbol that plays an important role in
myth and fairy tale, namely captivity. . . . Moreover, the function of ensnaring implies an aggressive tendency, which . . . belongs to the witch
character of the negative mother.

—Erich Neumann, *The Great Mother* [1]

THE ARCHETYPE: OLIVE CHANCELLOR

It is fascinating how the same myths are repeated in
the tales and rituals of all cultures, how the same figures
haunt the imaginations of all peoples. This deliberate retelling of Grimm's fairy tale, for example, is an unwitting retelling of Henry James's *The Bostonians*. Verena Tarrant is
Rapunzel, Basil Ransom is the Prince and Olive Chancellor is
Mother Gothel, the Great Mother.

Rapunzel

A woman
who loves a woman
is forever young.
The mentor
and the student
feed off each other.
Many a girl
had an old aunt
who locked her in the study
to keep the boys away.

They would play rummy
or lie on the couch
and touch and touch.
Old breast against young breast . . .

They play mother-me-do
all day.
A woman
who loves a woman
is forever young.

Once there was a witch's garden
more beautiful than Eve's
with carrots growing like little fish,
with many tomatoes rich as frogs,
onions as ingrown as hearts,
the squash singing like a dolphin
and one patch given over wholly to magic—
rampion, a kind of salad root,
a kind of harebell more potent than penicillin,
growing leaf by leaf, skin by skin,
as rapt and as fluid as Isadora Duncan.
However the witch's garden was kept locked
and each day a woman who was with child
looked upon the rampion wildly,
fancying that she would die
if she could not have it.
Her husband feared for her welfare

144

The Great Mother

And thus climbed into the garden
to fetch the life-giving tubers.

Ah ha, cried the witch,
whose proper name was Mother Gothel,
you are a thief and now you will die.

However they made a trade,
typical enough in those times.
He promised his child to Mother Gothel
so of course when it was born
she took the child away with her.
She gave the child the name Rapunzel,
another name for life-giving rampion.
Because Rapunzel was a beautiful girl
Mother Gothel treasured her beyond all things.
As she grew older Mother Gothel thought:
None but I will ever see her or touch her.
She locked her in a tower without a door
or a staircase. It had only a high window.
When the witch wanted to enter she cried:
Rapunzel, Rapunzel, let down your hair.
Rapunzel's hair fell to the ground like a rainbow.
It was yellow as a dandelion
and as strong as a dog leash.
Hand over hand she shinnied up
the hair like a sailor
and there in the stone-cold room,
as cold as a museum,
Mother Gothel cried:
Hold me, my young dear, hold me,
and thus they played mother-me-do.

Years later a prince came by
and heard Rapunzel singing in her loneliness.
That song pierced his heart like a valentine
but he could find no way to get to her.
Like a chameleon he hid himself among the trees
and watched the witch ascend the swinging hair.
The next day he himself called out:
Rapunzel, Rapunzel, let down your hair,

145

and thus they met and he declared his love.
What is this beast, she thought,
with muscles on his arms
like a bag of snakes?
What is this moss on his legs?
What prickly plant grows on his cheeks?
What is this voice as deep as a dog?
Yet he dazzled her with his answers.
Yet he dazzled her with his dancing stick.
They lay together upon the yellowy threads,
swimming through them
like minnows through kelp
and they sang out benedictions like the Pope.

Each day he brought her a skein of silk
to fashion a ladder so they could both escape.
But Mother Gothel discovered the plot
and cut off Rapunzel's hair to her ears
and took her to the forest to repent.
When the prince came the witch fastened
the hair to a hook and let it down.
When he saw that Rapunzel had been banished
he flung himself out of the tower, a side of beef.
He was blinded by thorns that pricked him like tacks.
As blind as Oedipus he wandered for years
until he heard a song that pierced his heart
like that long-ago valentine.
As he kissed Rapunzel her tears fell on his eyes
and in the manner of such cure-alls
his sight was suddenly restored.

They lived happily as you might expect
proving that mother-me-do
can be outgrown,
just as the fish on Friday,
just as a tricycle.
The world, some say,
is made up of couples.
A rose must have a stem.

As for Mother Gothel,
her heart shrank to the size of a pin,

never again to say: Hold me, my young dear,
hold me,
and only as she dreamt of the yellow hair
did moonlight sift into her mouth.

—Anne Sexton, from *Transformations*

There it amazingly is. Right down to Olive's smile: "It might have been likened to a thin ray of moonlight resting upon the wall of a prison." Like "Rapunzel," another name for life-giving rampion, the name "Verena" suggests the vernal qualities of spring, and Rapunzel and Verena are traded by their fathers to the witch-mother. Like Mother Gothel, Olive hides Verena from the Prince—Basil has "a longish pedigree [which] . . . had flowered at one time with English royalists and cavaliers." But wandering "blind as Oedipus," both princes find their princesses because "the world, some say,/ is made up of couples." And as for Verena, those tears she sheds as she enters "the union, so far from brilliant" at the close of the book "were not the last she was destined to shed."

Women were important to Henry James. As he recorded in his notebook on April 8, 1883, when the plot of the as yet unnamed *Bostonians* was forming itself in his mind, "I wished to write a very American tale, a tale very characteristic of our social conditions, and I asked myself what was the most salient and peculiar point in our social life. The answer was: the situation of women, the decline of the sentiment of sex, the agitation on their behalf." It is logical that James should have been preoccupied with American life at this time and that he would see "the situation of women" as its most salient point. In 1881 he paid his first visit to his native land since his decision several years earlier to make England his permanent home. The visit was a traumatic one: in January of 1882 he received a telegram announcing his mother's illness; by the time he reached Cambridge, she was dead.

Mary James was a figure of overwhelming importance to

her novelist son. "She was our life, she was the house, she was the keystone of the arch," he wrote just after her death.[2] The eulogy which follows is pure fantasy, as Leon Edel points out. The younger brothers and sister were in fact crushed by the irrationalities and contradictions of the familial environment over which Mary James presided, and the novelist, while he surmounted them, was to re-create in his fiction these very contradictions. "On a deeper level of feeling, which he inevitably concealed from himself," Edel writes, "James must have seen his mother as she was, not as he imagined and wanted her to be. She is incarnated in all his fiction, not as the fragile self-effacing and self-denying woman he pictured in his filial piety. . . . The mothers of Henry James, for all their maternal sweetness, are strong, determined, demanding, grasping women." [3] *The Bostonians*, then, was the novel in which James "wrote out the hidden emotional anguish of the collapse of his old American ties," and in particular the disappearance from his life of the "keystone of the arch," which must have evoked on a subconscious level some "dim passage of his childhood" in which he was involved in a struggle with his powerful mother.[4]

No wonder James's hero in *The Bostonians* rants about the decline of the sentiment of sex. "I want to save my sex," he tells Verena, "from the most damnable feminization! . . . The whole generation is womanized; the masculine tone is passing out of the world; it's a feminine, a nervous, hysterical, chattering, canting age, an age of hollow phrases and false delicacy and exaggerated solicitudes and coddled sensibilities, which if we don't soon look out, will usher in the reign of mediocrity, of the feeblest and the most pretentious that has ever been." Ransom's speech is hysterical, nearly as hysterical as some of Olive Chancellor's. This is not an example of James's irony or humor, but rather the thinly veiled point of view of a man and writer deeply concerned with preserving the "masculine" character—preserving it from all the mothers he created in his fiction: the governesses and the housekeepers—the surrogate mothers, the mother-neglecters and the witch mothers. James perceived "an abyss of inequality" in America, "the like of which has never before been seen under the sun." This inequality lay in "the growing divorce between the American woman (with her comparative leisure, culture, grace, social instincts, artistic ambitions) and the male American immersed in the ferocity of business, with no time for any but the most sordid interests, purely commercial, professional, democratic and political." [5] Women in James's America have all the power, and in his fiction they are often strong and terrifying women—especially in their ability to manipulate others.

Possession is the key to the mother-figure in James's fiction, and in *The Bostonians* the struggle for the possession of Verena between Olive Chancellor and Basil Ransom is the central issue. Olive's "glance," the first time Verena comes to visit her, is "the beginning; it was with this quick survey, omitting nothing, that Olive *took possession* of her" (emphasis added). And "before the girl had been five minutes in the room she jumped to her point—inquired of her, interrupting herself, interrupting everything: 'Will you be my friend, my friend of friends, beyond every one, everything, forever and forever?' " Such excessive expression from a woman who is repeatedly described as cold, and whose behavior with others is reserved in the extreme is a clue to the *com*pulsive as well as *im*pulsive nature of Olive's relationship with Verena. It indicates a real human need on Olive's part that makes her pitiful as well as frightening. This compulsive possessiveness is to characterize their relationship from this point forward. Thus when Olive returns Verena's visit she attempts to extract from the young girl a promise not to marry, exclaiming passionately, "I am so afraid I shall lose you. Verena, don't fail me—don't fail me." One can ridicule this passage, as does Matthias Pardon, the newspaper reporter, who observes them and remarks wryly, "You ladies had better look out, or you'll freeze together!" but Pardon is himself treated with some irony by James. The point is rather the terrible emptiness of Olive's own life, which her compulsive need for Verena's exclusive fidelity to herself makes clear. Making the sexual overtones of the scene ridiculous is one way for James to avoid coming too close to the issue of sexuality (like Freud's "tendency-wit," which masks in a safe way the hostility or anxiety of the witmaker)—he cannot let the reader pity Olive *too* much—and to keep the focus on the main point: the possession of one human being by another.

As Olive's life becomes "a matter for whispered communications," so does her passion for Verena deepen and her fear of losing Verena increase. With Verena she is whole; but without Verena she is nothing. "How can I help the dread of losing you," Olive wonders on one occasion, lifting Verena's hand to her lips and holding it there, "when you are so divinely docile?" Clearly, the relationship has homosexual overtones, but whether or not this is the case is not so important as the attempt at *possession* itself. Drawing Verena to her bosom, stroking her hair, extracting promises of loyalty are maternal actions on Olive's part as well; such endearing words as "You're so simple—so much like a child" are as indicative of a mother-child relationship as of a lesbian relationship. In fact, Olive as powerful mother figure is the more terrifying way to see her.

One of the things that makes the Jamesian mother so strong is her belief in the righteousness of her cause with what amounts to a religious zeal. For Olive feminism is such a cause, and losing Verena is more than losing control over the one person she cares about; it is losing a consecrated maiden to the devil. The passion Olive feels for Verena is therefore often described in religious terms. When Verena has satisfied Olive that she has renounced men for "the cause," for example, Olive "came to her slowly, took her in her arms and held her long—giving her a silent kiss." The kiss is a benediction for a "quivering, spotless, consecrated maiden." On another occasion the two women are described as nuns, "pacing quietly side by side, in their winter robes, like women consecrated to some holy office." The holiness with which the women view their "office" is emphasized in Verena's later speech which compares the world of sexual equality with the new Eden. "Good gentlemen all," she says, "if I could make you believe how much brighter and fairer and sweeter the garden of life would be for you if you would only let us help you keep it in order! You would like so much better to walk there, and you would find grass and trees and flowers that would make you think you were in Eden." Like the utopian visionaries evoked by her speech, some of whom saw marriage as bondage, Verena must remain single because "sacredly, brightly single . . . her only espousals would be at the altar of a great cause." In fact, Olive perceives how *fatally* "without Verena's tender notes, her crusade would lack . . . what the Catholics call unction." Together they serve a religious cause: Olive with her money, Verena with her "gift."

Religious dedication usually implies martyrdom, and Olive is no exception. It is because she is a martyr that she forces herself to use the abhorrent public streetcar rather than a comfortable private conveyance. Her great guilt about her money makes her wish to befriend some poor shopgirl, but her attempts in this direction founder when the shopgirls inevitably fail to understand what it is that Olive wants from them and become "odiously mixed up with Charlie." Like Henry James, she envies Basil Ransom because he has served in the Civil War, as she envies her two brothers who had died martyrs' deaths in the War. In fact Olive envies anyone who has had the opportunity to offer his life for a cause: "The most secret, the most sacred hope of her nature was that she might be a martyr and die for something."

Olive does die a sort of symbolic death at the end of the novel. *If* Basil, who now has possession of Verena, had observed her, James writes, "It *might* have seemed to him that she hoped to find the fierce expiation she sought for in exposure to the thousands she had disappointed and deceived, in offering herself to be trampled to death and torn to pieces. She *might* have suggested to him some feminine firebrand of Paris revolutions, erect on a barricade, or even the sacrificial figure of Hypatia, whirled through the furious mob of Alexandria" (emphasis added). Olive, of course, will not be trampled to death and torn to pieces; James makes clear that this is fantasy, that she is neither a firebrand nor a beautiful and wise woman of Alexandria. But a fantasy, no matter how ridiculous it might be to others, still exerts power over its holder—in Olive's case, in Basil's and in Henry James's as well. He has succeeded in rendering the great mother impotent. Probably, like Mother Gothel, her heart shrank to the size of a pin, and never again will moonlight sift into her mouth. As for Verena, she only escapes with the lesser of two evils (and she is nearly the only child or child-woman who does escape at all). *The Bostonians* is about the struggle for the possession of Verena between two opposing forces—not between good and evil, for possession in itself destroys—but between two forces each determined to control, manipulate, possess.

Like Mother Gothel, Olive Chancellor is not a "real" mother: she is "unmarried by every implication of her being." But like Mother Gothel she is the archetype. Her characteristics—a desperate determination to possess and control coupled with an equally desperate fear of a loss of control, a strength born of a belief in the rightness of her cause which amounts to a religious zeal, martyrdom—are those of the mother surrogates who haunt, or dominate, James's novels. The Governess, Mrs. Grose, Mrs. Bread, Mrs. Wix are all "mother surrogates" who possess such qualities in varying degrees. The "neglecters," on the other hand, are those actual mothers who are devoid of any maternal feelings: Mrs. Farange, Mrs. Moreen and Mrs. Touchett. And finally there are the real witch-bitches: Rose Armiger, Madame de Bellegarde and Madame Merle, who deliberately set out to destroy their victims.

THE MOTHER-SURROGATES

The Governess

The governess could just as well have served as the archetype of the Jamesian Great Mother as Olive Chancellor were she not such a controversial figure to literary critics. Not all readers are willing to see the governess as a corrupter, let alone as a character worthy of study in herself: some choose to see her as a "saviour," [6] while others see her as merely an observer—Pelham Edgar insists, for example, that "save for courage and devotion she has no discussable characteristics." [7] Most of the criticism of *The Turn of the Screw* has centered on the ghosts; a voluminous controversy has attempted to settle whether they are "real" or hallucinations of the deranged or sexually repressed governess's mind. Eminent Freudians and anti-Freudians notwithstanding, I would maintain that whether or not the ghosts are "real" is not important; they do not function as characters in the novel—real or imagined. What is important is the governess. Her words, whether recollection or fiction, are all one has to evaluate. The story is about *her*. Furthermore, the evil done to the children—Flora is driven mad and Miles is literally frightened to death—is done by the governess and far outweighs any potential evil effected through the machinations of any ghosts, real or imagined. The governess destroys the children by attempting to *possess* them.

Are there any "facts" about the governess with which to begin? There is Douglas's statement in the Prologue that "She was the most agreeable woman I've ever known in her position: she would have been worthy of any whatever." But Douglas also reveals that "she was in love. That is, she had been." [8] And since the possibility exists that it is Douglas with whom she had been in love, his estimation of the governess counts only as so much "moonlight in a familiar room" in the Hawthornian sense, necessary to set the scene for this tale which is both supernatural and as real and horrifying as a nightmare. The youngest of several daughters of a poor and "eccentric" country parson (whose family, one later learns, write "disturbing" letters to her at Bly), this young woman of twenty has secured her first job as governess for the orphaned niece and nephew of a handsome bachelor. The children have been established at a remote country estate by their uncle, who, wishing to be relieved of all responsibility for their care, has insisted as his "main condition" of employment that the person in charge never bother him. The governess, according to Douglas, sees all of this in the nature of a mission: the handsome bachelor had put the thing to her as "a kind of favour, an obligation he should gratefully incur," and when he held her hand, thanking her for the *sacrifice*, she felt rewarded. Before the governess begins her story, then, the reader knows that she is young and inexperienced, that she has probably had a strict or at least meager upbringing, that she has become infatuated with her employer (Douglas mentions the fact that she only saw him twice as "the beauty of her passion"), and that she tends to regard herself as a martyr.

The governess's own first words are about a "succession of flights and drops"—which, along with her ensuing insomnia, the Freudians see as symptoms of a neurotic or even manic-depressive personality, but which could well be seen as the trepidations of a sensitive and inexperienced person about to assume a large responsibility in a secluded place. But this is to focus on the psychological and ignore the literary aspects of the novel; these "flights and drops" offer a clue to the governess's perceptions of things. She will tend, throughout the novel, to see everything in terms of white and black, or good and evil. Her original perception of Bly, for example, is as a veritable Eden with its wide lawns, bright flowers, clustered treetops and golden sky. But when she first sees Quint, just a few weeks later, the garden seems "stricken with death," foreshadowing her later vision of Bly: "The summer had turned, the summer had gone; the autumn had dropped upon Bly and had blown out half our lights. The place, with its grey sky and withered garlands, its bared spaces and scattered dead leaves, was like a theatre after the performance—all strewn with crumpled playbills." Similarly, the governess sees the children in terms of good and evil. Flora's "radiant image" is described as "beatific"; she is a little girl of "angelic beauty," with "the deep, sweet serenity indeed of one of Raphael's holy infants." Miles is immediately perceived to have "without and within, in the great glow of freshness, the same positive fragrance of purity, in which I had, from the first moment, seen his little sister"; he is "incredibly beautiful," "something divine," and has an "indescribable little air of knowing nothing in the world but love." But later Flora, like Bly, withers: "her incomparable childish beauty had suddenly failed, had quite vanished. . . . she was literally, she was hideously, hard; she had turned common and almost ugly." And Miles is revealed to her as conniving and wise beyond his years; he is extraordinary not in his innocence and beauty, but in his deception, for she knows that "the imagination of all evil *had* been opened up to him."

One learns two more things about the governess from her opening words: she *expects* something to happen—"I suppose I had expected, or had dreaded, something so melancholy that what greeted me was a good surprise"—and she is suspicious—"I wondered even then a little why she [Mrs. Grose] should wish not to show it, and that, with reflection, with suspicion, might of course have made me uneasy." These clues ought to suggest that what happens at Bly is a self-fulfilling prophecy on the part of the governess, for she sees herself as the heroine of the play to which she has referred. This suggestion is further strengthened by her remarks, still in the opening chapter, that she was "carried away [by the bachelor uncle] in London" and by her fancy "of our being almost as lost as a handful of passengers in a great drifting ship. Well, I was, strangely, at the helm!" The word "drifting" is important here, but so is the fact that the governess is at the helm: she has imagined a role for herself in which she will provide the direction for the lost passengers, thus earning for herself the admiration of the master in Harley Street. One final important observation about the first chapter: the governess immediately takes verbal possession of the children by referring to them as *my* children; physically, she moves Flora's bed into her own room.

Here one has not only all of the elements of *The Turn of the Screw*, but of the Jamesian mother figure as well: great strength derived from an almost religious sense of mission, martyrdom and determined possession. *I* would almost be willing to rest my case on this initial chapter—*before* the ghosts are even mentioned, but I must quote the following important paragraph upon which John Lydenberg bases his case, because it so clearly sums up these qualities.[9] The paragraph occurs exactly between the identification of the first "ghost" as Peter Quint and the initial visit of "Miss Jessel" to the governess and Flora.

> I scarce know how to put my story into words that shall be a credible picture of my state of mind; but I was in these days literally able to find a joy in the extraordinary flight of heroism the occasion demanded of me. I now saw that I had been asked for a service admirable and difficult; and there would be a greatness in letting it be seen—oh, in the right quarter!—that I could succeed where many another girl might have failed. It was an immense help to me—I confess I rather applaud myself as I look back!—that I saw my service so strongly and so simply. I was there to protect and defend the little creatures in the world the most bereaved and loveable, the appeal of whose helplessness had suddenly become only too explicit, a deep, constant ache of one's own committed heart. We were cut off, really, together; we were united in our danger. They had nothing but me, and I—well, I had *them*. It was in short a magnificent chance. This chance presented itself to me in an image richly material. I was a screen—I was to stand before them. The more I saw, the less they would. I began to watch them in a stifled suspense, a disguised excitement that might well, had it continued too long, have turned to something like madness. What saved me, as I now see, was that it turned to something

else altogether. It didn't last as suspense—it was superseded by horrible proofs. Proofs, I say, yes—from the moment I really took hold.

Flights and drops, mission and martyrdom, the governess at the helm of a drifting ship and that horrible sentence—"I had *them*." Is it not clear that what so horribly happens to the children is not the ghosts, but the governess? She stands before them as a screen and they are to see nothing but what they see *through* her—nothing but what she wants them to see, in other words. Her watching them with stifled suspense is literally that—stifling; she never lets them out of her sight for a moment, scrutinizing their every word, their every move. Yes, from the moment the governess "really took hold"—of the children, that is—their "Edenic innocence" began to turn to something like madness.

That Edenic innocence is itself, like everything else in the tale, the governess's perception of the situation. As has been mentioned, she sees things only in terms of black and white; thus the children are beautiful and innocent at the beginning of the tale and ugly and evil at its conclusion. They are never just children—a mixture of good *and* bad, mischievous and angelic, serious and frivolous—as children often are. She decides, for example, that Miles has an "indescribable little air of knowing nothing in the world but love." Certainly we must doubt this kind of perception, for Miles is an orphan, has had a variety of "caretakers" and has been abandoned by his nearest relative, his uncle, who used to visit him frequently. Later she describes the children as "quite unpunishable," as "cherubs of the anecdote, who had—morally, at any rate—nothing to whack!" One wonders why, then, Miles was dismissed from school. Again, she says of Miles: "He had never for a second suffered. I took this as a direct disproof of his having really been chastised. If he had been wicked he would have 'caught' it, and I should have caught it by the rebound—I should have found the trace. I found nothing at all, and he was therefore an angel." Such logic is suspect: the governess's finding nothing at all proves only her own inability to find things. The point is that these children are not necessarily absolutely good or absolutely evil; they are children who have suffered (through their orphanage), who have been exposed to a variety of caretakers—two of whom presumably engaged in sexual activity in front of them so that they may be said to be "experienced" rather than naive, one child at least has been "bad" enough to have been expelled from school. Even this information comes through the governess. Standing as a screen between these children—abnormally perfect or abnormally corrupt—and the world, and between these children and the reader as well, she sees *herself* as a martyr-saviour. All knowledge, including the "knowledge of all evil," is filtered through the governess: in that way she not only has *them;* she has *us* as well.

The Turn of the Screw is, as I have said, about the struggle—real enough for the governess—for the possession of the children. In her capacity as "screen" she prevents one's seeing at first just how completely she attempts to control them. It soon becomes evident that these prodigious children are not only clever; they are "too clever"—too clever, that is, "for a bad governess, for a parson's daughter, to spoil." That is why she can allude to her "unnatural composure" on the subject of another school for Miles. All the same, she is aware of a strange and bright thread in her "pensive embroidery" which she does not dare to work out: the impression that Miles was "under some influence operating in his small intellectual life as a tremendous incitement." This influence is not Peter Quint's, as she tries to convey, but her own. Her influence is often overt as well as covert: when Flora gets up in the night to look out the window, the governess "gripped *my* little girl with a spasm that, wonderfully, she submitted to without a cry or a sign of fright" (emphasis added). It turns out that Flora has been looking down at Miles, who has gone out on the lawn so that the governess would think him, for a change, bad. When the governess goes out to lead Miles into the house, she feels a

"curious thrill of triumph." She is anxious to discuss the evening's events with Mrs. Grose, but it is difficult to find a time
to do so because of "the rigour with which I kept my pupils
in sight." She even goes so far as to intercept the children's
letters to their uncle: "They were too beautiful to be posted; I
kept them myself." After all, any indication that all was not
well at Bly might cause a breakdown of "the fine machinery I
had set in motion to attract his attention to my slighted
charms." Miles finally lets the governess know that he resents his captivity and makes her aware, in his request to return to school, that she has "all but pinned the boy to my
shawl and that, in the way our companions were marshalled
before me, I might have appeared to provide against some
danger of rebellion. I was like a gaoler with an eye to possible surprises and escapes."

Miles's indication to the governess that he is becoming a
man ("I'm a fellow, don't you see? that's—well, getting on")
is a sign that underlying the governess's overprotection of
the boy is the threat of possession in a sexual sense. James
provides several kinds of clues. There is an immediate association of this kind of love with death, foreshadowing just
what possession will mean for Miles, when their conversation and walk bring them to the graveyard. The governess, in
fact, sinks down on a stone slab when Miles first inquires
whether his uncle knows what is going on at Bly and then
rebelliously marches into the church, leaving the governess
alone on her tomb. Her love for the boy is associated with
sickness; as her watchfulness becomes "my endless obses-
sion," she even begins to listen outside his closed bed-
room door. When he catches her there and refers to "this
queer business of ours," she sees him as "some wistful patient in a children's hospital," "like a convalescent slightly
fatigued" who needs mothering. Miles, however, feels that
she smothers him and tells her, "I want to get away." But the
governess is aware that "I should never be able to bear that
and it made me let myself go. I threw myself upon him and
in the tenderness of my pity I embraced him. 'Dear little

Miles, dear little Miles—!'·'' Her kiss is not the "mother-kiss" savored by Henry Roth's David Schearl or James Joyce's Stephen Dedalus, but one that makes Miles look "as . . . sick children look," makes him face the wall and beg her to let him alone. For the governess to accede to his request, however, is "to abandon or, to put it more truly, to lose him." Seeing only what she wishes to see, she catches for the first time "a small faint quaver of consenting consciousness" which impels her to drop on her knees beside the bed "and seize one more chance of possessing him." It is at this point that the candle in Miles's room goes out.

Flora, meanwhile, has also grown older; in fact, she has become for the governess "an old, old woman," quite like the big, ugly spray of withered fern which the child picks up. Mrs. Grose, however, suggests that it is the governess who, in her insistence that the child see Miss Jessel, has made Flora old, and she may be right, for the governess is not consistent about what she sees and hears. When she sees Miss Jessel in the schoolroom, the latter appears "dishonoured and tragic . . . dark as midnight in her black dress, her haggard beauty and her unutterable woe" before "the awful image passed away," and the governess addresses her as "You terrible, miserable woman." That is all. But she tells Mrs. Grose that she has had a "talk with Miss Jessel":

> "Do you mean she spoke?"
> "It came to that."
> "And what did she say?"
> "That she suffers the torments of the lost. Of the damned.
> And that's why, to share them . . . she wants Flora."

But it is Mrs. Grose who wins possession of Flora, as she removes the raving child first to her own room once again, and then takes her to London, away from the horrors of Bly, but especially away from the governess.

This leaves the governess alone with Miles, and she imagines that they are like "some young couple . . . on their wedding-journey." Their relationship is now described repeatedly as having "the possibilities of a beautiful inter-course"—frightening to Miles, who strains to get away from the governess, but enticing to the governess who, perceiving this, springs up in "the mere blind movement of getting hold of him, drawing him close." Forcing from him the confession that he has taken her letter to his uncle, she relates, "with a moan of joy, I enfolded, I drew him close; and . . . held him to my breast." Indeed, the more tormented and white-faced Miles becomes, the more sure is she of her possession: "I almost shouted in my joy . . . I was infatuated—I was blind with victory." It is she who measures "the very distance of his fall in the world," and it is she who will catch him as she forces the surrender of the name "Peter Quint." "What does he matter now, my own?" she murmurs in satisfaction. "I have you." It takes but a moment for the governess to realize that her possession has destroyed the child:

> But he had already jerked straight round, stared, glared again, and seen but the quiet day. With the stroke of the loss I was so proud of he uttered the cry of a creature hurled over an abyss, and the grasp with which I recovered him might have been that of catching him in his fall. I caught him, yes, I held him—it may be imagined with what a passion; but at the end of a minute I began to feel what it truly was that I held. We were alone with the quiet day, and his little heart, dispossessed, had stopped.

One is reminded of Hawthorne, and beyond him of Poe: the governess loses the struggle for possession of the children (they *are* lost even if their souls are saved) because she attempts to know too much. In the Poe-Hawthorne-James tradition, knowledge is equated with evil, possession with destruction; to know, to possess is to destroy. One has only to think of "Rappaccini's Daughter," "The Birthmark," "Ethan Brand" or "Young Goodman Brown" to understand that superhuman knowledge or the quest for perfection leads only to destruction. Possession by intellectual knowledge (or in this case, supernatural knowledge) is opposed to the more subtle and intuitive knowledge of the heart. To possess one's lover by complete knowledge inevitably leads to the destruction of the loved one—in this case the destruction of the children by the passionate devouring of the governess.

Mrs. Grose

James himself was subject to a "bevy of educative ladies," as he recounts in *A Small Boy and Others*. He recalls the humiliation he felt that small boys should have for instructors *instructresses*, "a grave reflection," he felt, not unlike Miles, "both on our attainments and our spirit." Evidently, they left a lasting impression, for he goes on to recall in detail the names, the characteristics, the costumes of these "aggravational representative[s] of the compromising sex." [10] His creation of the destructive mother-figure of the governess in *The Turn of the Screw* is an implicit statement of his feeling about "the compromising sex," but there are explicit statements as well, for example the governess's amazement that Miles is so nice to his little sister, "that there was a little boy in the world who could have for the inferior age, sex and intelligence so fine a consideration." Again, the governess reflects that the master never writes to inquire about the children because "the way in which a man pays his highest tribute to a woman is apt to be but by the more festal celebration of one of the sacred laws of his comfort." These are not only the governess's words, but the words of Henry James. It behooves a reader, therefore, to look carefully at any Jamesian woman in whose care small children are placed, no matter how stout and homely she appears on the surface.

The first of these that merits consideration is Mrs. Grose. She is the only one who can definitely be said to have won any sort of possession: she goes off to London with Flora. C. Knight Aldrich, a psychiatrist, has written a fine essay in which he unmasks Mrs. Grose as the true villain of the piece. [11] He goes as far as to suggest that Mrs. Grose is the real mother of the children and their father the master in

Harley Street. My only quarrel with Dr. Aldrich is that he fails to account for the fact that it is the governess who tells the story, that Mrs. Grose is seen through *her* eyes. I would not go so far as he in seeing Mrs. Grose as *the* villain, but rather as another Jamesian mother-figure, potentially destructive in her capacity for possessiveness. It is to that end that I recount some of the evidence which shows us the "under side of the tapestry" of that plain, homely, good-natured woman.

One learns from Douglas's Prologue that Mrs. Grose, formerly the maid of the master's mother, is not only housekeeper, but has been acting as superintendent to the little girl, "of whom, without children of her own, she was, by good luck, extremely fond." At the head of this little establishment—"but below stairs only"—she might well feel resentment when the governess arrives to supersede her, visibly taking possession by removing Flora's bed from Mrs. Grose's room to her own. The governess, when she reaches Bly, perceives a "stout, plain, clean, wholesome woman" (but the governess's perceptions are not to be trusted) and wonders why Mrs. Grose is "positively on her guard" against showing too much pleasure at the governess's arrival. That might be a cause for suspicion, the governess reflects uneasily.

It does not seem odd that Mrs. Grose might not be too glad to see the new governess. She is probably jealous. For example, when the new governess remarks, "He seems to like us young and pretty," Mrs. Grose answers, "Oh, he *did* . . . it was the way he liked everyone!" Quickly catching herself up, she adds, "I mean that's *his* way—the master's." The first emphasis is on *did*—that is, the master liked them young and pretty in the past, too, perhaps when Mrs. Grose was his mother's maid and, presumably, less plain and stout. The second emphasis is on *his*, a hint of another man, which puzzles the governess, who asks, "But of whom did you speak first?" Mrs. Grose looks blank, but colors, responding, "Why, of *him*." "Of the master?" "Of who else?" This is important: it is Mrs. Grose who first suggests that there might be someone else, and later it is Mrs. Grose who identifies the mysterious visitor as Peter Quint, the former valet. It is she who suggests that the man the governess saw on the tower is a man who is dead. It is entirely possible that resentful of her demotion from supreme authority to "below stairs," she sets out to drive this governess away as she has possibly driven the others away. Once this suggestion is conceded as a possibility, then everything Mrs. Grose says and does should be regarded with suspicion. One must remember that everything the governess learns about Quint and Miss Jessel is learned from Mrs. Grose; the master never mentions them. Discussing the influence Quint had on the children, Mrs. Grose cries, "I couldn't [bear it]—and I can't now!" Does she mean that she can't bear to remember Quint or that she can't bear the governess? Mrs. Grose at every point supports the governess as to the credibility of her visions: "She went all the way with me as to its being beyond doubt that I had seen exactly what I had seen." Why? If Mrs Grose is all that plain and wholesome, would *she* be apt to believe in ghosts? Could it be to her advantage to support the governess, supplying and encouraging her fantasies until she drives the governess mad and gets rid of her?

The governess is only fleetingly suspicious of Mrs. Grose: "She had told me a great deal . . . but a small shifty spot on the wrong side of it all still sometimes brushed my brow like the wing of a bat." This wrong side of things comes up again when the governess and Mrs. Grose sit watching the children and discussing the ghosts. "I caught," the governess says, "the suppressed intellectual creak with which she conscientiously turned to take from me a view of the back of the tapestry. I had made her a receptacle of lurid things, but there was an odd recognition of my superiority—my accomplishments and my function—in her patience under my pain. She offered her mind to my disclosures as, had I wished to mix a witch's broth and proposed it with assurance, she would have held out a large clean saucepan." Who, then, weaves the tapestry? Who supplies the ingredients for the witch's broth?

Finally, there are two inconsistencies about Mrs. Grose which ought to be mentioned. One is her ability to read. The governess assumes that Mrs. Grose cannot read when the lady refuses to take the headmaster's letter (but all Mrs. Grose says is, "Such things are not for me, Miss" of a letter that was not addressed to her). Later Mrs. Grose says that she will write to the master, and then quickly covers up by saying that the bailiff will write the letter for her. This suggests that the governess may be overestimating Mrs. Grose's "simplicity." The other, more important inconsistency is Mrs. Grose's information about Quint and Miss Jessel. Originally she tells the governess that Quint was the master's personal valet and that the master put Quint in complete charge when Miss Jessel had to leave. Later she says, turning quite pale, "He didn't really in the least know them. The fault's mine." This is a puzzling admission on Mrs. Grose's part. It seems to reveal that she was content to ignore the "infamy" of Quint and Miss Jessel (presumably their open and intimate sexual relationship) so that she could have complete control of the children. Whether or not she is actually the children's mother, as Dr. Aldrich maintains (and this seems to be a likely possibility, although there is not enough evidence in the text to prove the case), she is clearly a mother-surrogate. One must not only regard her, like other Jamesian mothers, with suspicion, but take the clue from her to clear away the obscurity surrounding those other plain, clean, wholesome caretaker-mothers, Mrs. Bread, and Mrs. Wix, as well.

Mrs. Bread

If it can be argued that Mrs. Grose, more gross than homely, has a secret, it can be stated with even greater certainty that so has Mrs. Bread, her counterpart in *The American,* who presumably represents the wholesome qualities associated with the staff of life. While there is evidence to support Mrs.

Bread's account of the death of M. de Bellegarde, one must keep in mind that she was the only one present when the marquis accused his wife and that anything Valentin knows about his father's death he learned from Mrs. Bread, who, in fact, "taught him to speak." When Newman confronts Madame de Bellegarde with her husband's letter, the only defense she makes in her own behalf is that Mrs. Bread "was my husband's mistress." And somehow, bad as she is—and she comes across as one of the most evil, most destructive, most viciously possessive women in all of the James canon—she is believable at that point.

Mrs. Bread tells Newman when she first meets him that she has lived with the de Bellegardes for more than forty years; she came over with the Lady Emmeline as "my lady's own woman," much as Mrs. Grose had been maid to the mother of the master in Harley Street. And forty-some years ago when she was "much younger and very different looking to what I am now," with "a very high color . . . indeed . . . a very smart lass, the marquis, also young and high-spirited, was "fond of his pleasure," and "sometimes went rather below him to take it." This made the marquise, understandably, very jealous. One day, Mrs. Bread recounts to Newman, "I had a red ribbon in my cap, and my lady flew out at me and ordered me to take it off. She accused me of putting it on to make the marquis look at me. I don't know that I was impertinent, but I spoke up like an honest girl and didn't count my words. A red ribbon indeed! As if it was my ribbons the marquis looked at!" The jealousy was probably justified, for Mrs. Bread keeps the ribbon, faded now like Mrs. Bread herself, pinned to her undergarments.

Just how young she was when she attracted the master's attention is suggested when she tells Newman that she was never a nurse to the present marquis: "When he was a baby I was too young; they wouldn't trust me with him." When she came over with "the lady Emmeline," then, she was even younger. Was she old enough to have been married? Was there ever a Mr. Bread? It is interesting to remember at this point that in the note written by the old marquis on his deathbed, he refers to her only as "Mrs. B—."

Her relationship with Claire and Valentin has been quite different from that with Urbain de Bellegarde. She regards both Claire and Valentin as "my own children." Of Claire she says, "If she were my own child I couldn't love her more. . . . I received her in my arms when she came into the world and her first wedding day was the saddest of my life. She owes it to me to show me another and a brighter one." And of Valentin: "The poor count was my own boy, sir, for the first year of his life he was hardly out of my arms; I taught him to speak." Moreover, long before Newman meets Mrs. Bread he forms his own theory about the difference between Urbain, on the one hand, and Claire and Valentin, on the other—that Urbain "is the old woman at second hand," but that the other two take after their father. "The late marquis had been a very amiable foreigner," he decides, "with an inclination to take life easily and a sense that it was difficult for the husband of the stilted little lady . . . to do so. But if he had taken little comfort in his wife he had taken much in his two younger children, who were after his own heart, while Madame de Bellegarde had paired with her eldest-born." So unlike their brother and mother are Claire and Valentin that one wonders if they might be the children of Mrs. Bread. James provides two more pieces of evidence to support this theory. One is the old woman's name—and she names herself only once: "poor Catherine Bread." Urbain later tells Christopher Newman that his mother would rather that Claire become "Soeur Catherine" than Mrs. Newman. In fact, she becomes Sister Veronica, but why does Urbain assume that the name will be Catherine? The other piece of evidence is the mystery of Claire's refusal to Newman. James never makes clear what terrible pressure Madame de Bellegarde and Urbain have put upon Claire to make her change her mind, but Mrs. Bread offers a hint, and this hint, perhaps, supplies the answer to the mystery. "She was like a fair peach," Mrs. Bread says of Claire, "with just one little speck. She had one little sad spot. You pushed her into the sunshine, sir, and it almost disappeared. Then they pulled her back into the shade and in a moment it began to spread." Since Mrs. Bread has already sworn that Claire knew nothing of the circumstances of her father's death, what else could the speck be but her illegitimacy? Why else was Madame de Bellegarde so anxious to push her off onto the much older M. de Cintré when Claire was beautiful, rich and titled? What else could Madame de Bellegarde and Urbain have told her to make her withdraw from Newman and the world but the secret of her illegitimacy?

"Poor Catherine Bread" is not central to *The American;* but she is interesting evidence of James's propensity to leave clues to the mothering qualities of even the most obscure women he creates. Moreover, occurring in his first important novel, she is significant as a model, instructing the reader to look closely at his other innocuous old women—archetypal old crones all, most of them not so benign as Mrs. Bread.[12]

Mrs. Wix

The most malicious of these old crones is Mrs Wix, who like her predecessor Mrs. Grose, triumphs through winning possession of a child. James is never careless with names (sometimes he is blatantly didactic, as with the "urbanity" of Urbain who "guards" the "belle" Claire, or the "grossness" of Mrs. Grose). In naming Mrs. Wix he must have had in mind not the sense, but the sound of her name: Wix, wicked, witch; Mrs. Wix is the wicked witch of *What Maisie Knew.* And lest one's ears miss this hint of Mrs. Wix's character, James provides another—Mrs. Wix's "straighteners," her spectacles through which, with her own crooked vision, she views the world. These straighteners, she tells Maisie, are "put on for the sake of others, whom, as she believed, they helped to recognise the bearing, otherwise doubtful, of her regard." [13] The rest of her melancholy garb, James observes, could only have been put on for herself: "With the added suggestion of her goggles it reminded her pupil of the polished shell or corslet of a horrid beetle. At first she had looked cross and almost cruel; but this impression passed away with the child's increased perception of her being in the eyes of the world a figure mainly to laugh at." Jamesian children are preternaturally wise; their first impressions are to be trusted. Mrs. Wix *is* horrid and cruel, and she shows herself to be a person to be dealt with. Maisie perceives two more things during her first meeting with Mrs. Wix. One, as her mother pushes her towards the new governess with "Take her, Mrs. Wix," is that Mrs. Wix "would never let her go." The other is that Mrs. Wix had been "with passion and anguish a mother."

Indeed, a good part of Maisie's lessons, which are lessons only in Mrs. Wix's version of "the moral sense" since that lady is totally ignorant in "subjects," are devoted to "the little dead Clara Matilda"—Maisie's "little dead sister," as Mrs. Wix tells her. It is not too much to say that Maisie *becomes* poor little dead Clara Matilda, for Mrs. Wix, and to explain thus her determination to save the child from those without the moral sense, although, as shall be seen, there are other reasons. The rest of Maisie's education consists of stories related by Mrs. Wix from novels she has read. They are all about "love and beauty and countesses and wickedness," and somehow entangled beyond magic and monsters with Mrs. Wix's own "gushing fountains of homeliness," giving Maisie a vivid impression of "everyone who had ever, in her phrase, knocked against her." It must be remembered that the punishment for wickedness in fairy tales—that which is usually necessary to the triumph of the hero—is death. Add to this Mrs. Wix's instructing Maisie, when they discuss the child's relationships to her various parents and governesses, to "hold on like grim death," the visits to the grave of Clara Matilda, and the "rather remarkably absent" dead Mr. Wix, and it is not surprising that Maisie, at the end of the novel, comes up with a supreme proof of her "moral sense": if Mrs. Beale were unkind to Sir Claude, Maisie tells Mrs. Wix, "I'd *kill* her!"

Maisie has learned her lesson well, insofar as Mrs. Wix is concerned, for that lady "adores" Sir Claude. If Mrs. Wix is the old crone—and she is literally so named by Mr. Perriam, who tells her, ". . . you ain't a myth, . . . though you might be, to be sure!"—Sir Claude is the prince who will turn her into a fairy princess. Outrageous and downright funny as it seems for this ugly old woman who peers through her straighteners and alternately neighs like a horse or moans to be in love with the golden-haired Sir Claude, the evidence is there. Maisie cannot believe her eyes when she sees "the good lady, with whom she had associated no faintest shade of any act of provocation, actually after an upward grimace" give Sir Claude "a great giggling insinuating naughty slap." Mrs. Wix not only tells Maisie she is in love with him "over head and ears. I've *never*, since you ask me, been so far gone"; she tells Sir Claude himself: "Take me, take me. . . . Here I am, here I am!" spreading herself "into an exhibition that, combined with her intensity and her decorations, appeared to suggest her for strange offices and devotions, for ridiculous replacements and substitutions." But this causes Sir Claude to squirm and he realizes that "If Mrs. Wix clung it was all the more reason for shaking Mrs. Wix off." If Mrs. Wix, in spite of such evidence, is so often seen as the "good" governess who "saves" Maisie from the forces of evil, it is because James has succeeded in playing upon the reader's psychological defenses. The story of Mrs. Wix and Sir Claude calls to mind this tale with which Norman Holland opens his book, *The Dynamics of Literary Response*:

> The young executive had taken $100,000 from his company's safe, lost it playing the stock market, and now he was certain to be caught, and his career ruined. In despair, down to the river he went.
>
> He was just clambering over the bridge railing when a gnarled hand fell upon his arm. He turned and saw an ancient crone in a black cloak, with wrinkled face and stringy gray hair.

"Don't jump," she rasped. "I'm a witch, and I'll grant you three wishes for a slight consideration."

"I'm beyond help," he replied, but he told her his troubles anyway.

"Nothing to it," she said, cackling, and she passed her hand before his eyes, "You now have a personal bank account of $200,000!" She passed her hand again. "The money is back in the company vault!" She covered his eyes for the third time. "And you have just been elected first vice-president."

The young man, stunned speechless, was finally able to ask, "What—what is the consideration I owe you?"

"You must spend the night making love to me," she smiled toothlessly.

The thought of making love to the old crone revolted him, but it was certainly worth it, he thought, and together they retired to a nearby motel. In the morning, the distasteful ordeal over, he was dressing to go home when the old crone in the bed rolled over and asked, "Say, sonny, how old are you?"

"I'm forty-two years old," he said. "Why?"

"Ain't you a little old to believe in witches?" [14]

Mrs. Wix, like the "witch" in the story, is no purer in her motives for hanging on to Maisie than any of the others. She does not, like Ida or Beale, seek revenge, but like Mrs. Beale and Sir Claude, she regards Maisie as a ticket to the possession of the object of her sexual desire. Mrs. Wix's idea of "the moral sense," as she teaches it to Maisie, is a strange one. This code, like that of fairy tales where one *marries* and lives happily ever after, seems to be that sex in marriage is good, but sex outside of marriage is bad. Sir Claude and Mrs. Beale, therefore, are committing a crime "branded by the Bible." But Maisie cannot comprehend this, for to her marriage has been only a reason for hatred and revenge; the great thing is to be "free." No wonder Maisie cannot understand Mrs. Wix and loses her "moral sense" as soon as she has found it when Sir Claude offers her a refuge of warmth. Mrs. Wix's code can also embrace murder in its service—she presses Maisie's hand when Maisie swears she would kill

Mrs. Beale for mistreating Sir Claude—and would allow Mrs. Wix to live with Sir Claude where it will not allow for Mrs. Beale to do so.

Mrs. Wix's additional motive for possession of Maisie is also like that of others: Maisie promises material security; whoever takes care of Maisie will be supported by Ida's money. Maisie is aware that Mrs. Wix "quivered with insecurity," that she was "more scared on her own behalf than on that of her pupil. A governess who had only one frock was not likely to have either two fathers or two mothers: accordingly if even with these resources Maisie was to be in the streets, where in the name of all that was dreadful was poor Mrs. Wix to be?" Later Mrs. Wix throws herself on Maisie's neck crying, "They'll take you, they'll take you, and what in the world will then become of me?" No wonder, then, that Mrs. Wix is determined to hold on like grim death, that the dim straighteners are always fixed on Maisie as Mrs. Wix intently waits.

Mrs. Wix, like Olive Chancellor and the governess, is willing to play up her martyrdom—"I'll work my fingers to the bone in your service!"—and like her predecessors, it makes her possession of the child all the more terrible because it allows her self-righteously to justify her selfishness. The terrible quality of her possessiveness is rendered most forcefully when Maisie likens her separation from Mrs. Wix to the extraction of a rotten tooth (which would leave the old crone toothless!): "the 'arrangement,' as her periodical uprootings were called, played the part of the horrible forceps. Embedded in Mrs. Wix's nature as her tooth had been socketed in her gum, the operation of extracting her would really have been a case for chloroform." The hug of Maisie and Mrs. Wix on that occasion was one that "fortunately left nothing to say." Thus we are prepared for the final struggle when Mrs. Wix literally girds her loins for battle: " 'I don't leave the child—I don't, I don't!' she thundered from the threshold, advancing . . . girded—positively harnessed . . . and armed with a small fat rusty reticule which, almost in the manner of a battle-axe, she brandished in support of her words." She leaves triumphantly with Maisie, but the final words of the book remind us of the governess's final possession of Miles "alone with the quiet day"; Mrs. Wix and Maisie in mid-channel are "surrounded by the quiet sea."

THE NEGLECTERS

Ida Farange

What Maisie Knew also provides an opportunity to look at one of the "real" Jamesian mothers. These "neglecters," as I call them, differ completely from the mother-surrogates; they ignore their maternal responsibilities. If it is clear that Mrs. Wix, "with passion and anguish," has been a mother, the same is not clear with Ida Farange, Maisie's mother, whose conception of duty takes "at times the form of not seeing her child for days together." Maisie knows that "Mama doesn't care for me . . . not really." Yet in spite of this knowledge, or perhaps because of it, Ida holds tremendous power over Maisie. Realizing that nothing she can do will make her mother love her, Maisie tells Sir Claude that she is more afraid of her mother than of anything in the world—even more, as she thinks over all objects of dread, "than of a wild elephant!"

Ida's power, for Maisie, is a result of the distance which she maintains between herself and her daughter; Ida is more an idol to be worshipped than a human being. She gives off a nonfeeling of coldness and harshness instead of warmth and security. Her huge painted eyes are "like Japanese lanterns swung under festal arches," and "the intense marks in her face formed an *éclairage* as distinct and public as a lamp set in a window." The foreignness of Japanese lanterns and *éclairage* is deliberate, emphasizing Ida's foreignness to Maisie. Against her mother's breast, Maisie, "amid a wilderness of trinkets," feels "as if she had been suddenly thrust, with a smash of glass, into a jeweller's shop-front, but only to be as suddenly ejected with a push." Maisie very early learns of Ida that "the lower the bosom was cut the more it was to be gathered she was wanted elsewhere," and, of course, the less Maisie is wanted near her.

Neglecting Maisie is bad enough, but Ida does irreparable damage to Maisie by depriving her of a sense of self-worth. Her lack of self-esteem is reinforced by her father, who calls her a "dirty little donkey," and by Mrs. Wix, who tells her she has no moral sense. When she goes to galleries she sees only "ugly Madonnas and uglier babies." Ida continually tells Maisie she is "a dreadful dismal deplorable little thing," and builds herself up by contrast as a martyr:

> I *am* good—I'm crazily, I'm criminally good. But it won't do for *you* any more, and if I've ceased to contend with him, and with you too, who have made most of the trouble between us, it's for reasons that you'll understand one of these days but too well— one of these days when I hope you'll know what it is to have lost a mother. I'm awfully ill but you mustn't ask me anything about it. If I don't get off somewhere my doctor won't answer for the consequences. He's stupefied at what I've borne—he says it has been put on me because I was formed to suffer. I'm thinking of South Africa, but that's none of your business. You must take your choice—you can't ask me questions if you're so ready to give me up. No, I won't tell you; you can find out for yourself. . . . I've struck my last blow for you; I can follow you no longer from pillar to post. I must live for myself at last, while there's still a handful left of me. I'm very, very ill; I'm very, very tired; I'm very, very determined. There you have it. Make the most of it. Your frock's too filthy; but I came to sacrifice myself.

Of course from the beginning Ida is shown to have none of the qualities of a real mother: the judge of the divorce case, "in a manner worthy of the judgment-seat of Solomon," had divided Maisie in two and tossed the portions impartially to the disputants. A real mother, as we know from the Bible, is recognized by her willingness to give up her right of possession rather than see her child destroyed.

Mrs. Moreen

Morgan Moreen's mother in "The Pupil," on the other hand, gives up possession and her child *is* destroyed. Her relationship with her son is exactly like her relationship with the rest of the world—a sham. From the opening lines where Mrs. Moreen is described as drawing a pair of "soiled *gants de Suède* through a fat jewelled hand," to the closing scene of upheaval where the family is being forcibly ejected from their Parisian lodgings, the impression is one of the lady's *false* "expensive identity." [15] Everything about her is false: when the "storm" comes, as James calls the final humiliation of the Moreens, Mrs. Moreen worries only about protecting herself, hurrying into the "hatches" and pulling the covers closed after her, hoping that someone will "take" each of her children off her hands. But the final abandonment of Morgan—one of those sensitive and precocious Jamesian children—has been predictable from the initial glimpse of Mrs. Moreen addressing her son with mock tenderness as "you pompous little person" and telling him, "My darling, you're too quaint." She is exactly as tender as T. S. Eliot's lady typist, "putting out to caress him a practised but ineffectual hand."

Pemberton, whom Mrs. Moreen hires as Morgan's tutor but neglects to pay, sees right away that "her elegance was intermittent and her parts didn't always match." Her material shabbiness is indicative of her internal shabbiness. Just as the Moreens attempt to put on an appearance of opulence and disguise the reality of their meager means, "they contrived to reconcile the appearance, and indeed the essential fact, of adoring the child with their eagerness to wash their hands of him." And their physical neglect of Morgan betrays their real neglect of him—after all, he didn't "show"—that is, he didn't care for appearances. Pemberton can trace perfectly "the degrees by which, in proportion as her little son confined himself to his tutor for society, Mrs. Moreen shrewdly forbore to renew his garments. She did nothing that didn't show, neglected him because he escaped notice, and then, as he illustrated this clever policy, discouraged at home his public appearances."

Mrs. Moreen isn't malicious in her neglect of Morgan; she isn't an Ida Farange seeking revenge. She simply and selfishly neglects her son; but for a child as sensitive as Morgan, one who craves warmth and love, this is tantamount to destroying him. Even Pemberton, who has the most reason to despise Morgan's family, comes to see them not as malicious, but as "toadies and snobs": "The Moreens were adventurers not merely because they didn't pay their debts, because they lived on society, but because their whole view of life, dim and confused and instinctive, like that of clever colour-blind animals, was speculative and rapacious and mean. Oh they were 'respectable,' and that only made them more *immondes!*" Although "immondes" (unclean, impure) is Pemberton's judgment (and James may intend it as an ironic comment on the tutor's relationship with the boy—the homosexual overtones to their relationship and the final abandonment by Pemberton of Morgan), using people, as the Moreens do, is one of the most cruel and evil things one human being can do to another in the James canon of morality. And while Morgan may literally die of a broken heart, it is his family and his tutor, but *especially his mother* who has broken his heart. Pemberton, after all, is entitled to a life of his own, but Morgan is entitled to love from his mother. And so far is he from getting his due that Pemberton, when he first considers leaving the Moreens for a job that will pay, is unable to decide because he is afraid to leave Morgan with his mother. "You practise on one's fears—one's fears about the child if one should go away," he tells her. "And pray what would happen to him in that event?" Mrs. Moreen demands. "Why," Pemberton answers, "he'd be alone with *you.*" For Morgan to be alone with his mother is to be *alone.*

Even in the crisis scene, when it seems with all of James's usual vagueness that Morgan is having a heart attack, Mrs. Moreen touches her son "no more than if he had been a gilded idol." As for Morgan, he begs Pemberton to take him away, calling his parents "awful frauds" and saying that he can't take any more of such scenes. When the Moreens finally do give Morgan up in fact—as they had done long ago in deed—it is with the same protestations of sacrifice that Ida Farange utters to Maisie. And although the final blow to Morgan is Pemberton's lack of enthusiasm at this "sacrifice," it is the final blow to a long-overburdened heart, a long-neglected spirit. Mr. Moreen, who has been able to do no more than stroke his son with a "tentative paternal forefinger" and who "takes his bereavement as a man of the world," tells his wife: "I *told* you he didn't [want to be given up], my dear." But Mrs. Moreen disclaims all responsibility: "You walked him too far, you hurried him too fast!" she hurls over her shoulder at Pemberton as for the first time, now that he is dead, she takes her son in her arms.

Mrs. Touchett

Mrs. Touchett, in *The Portrait of a Lady*, in living only for herself seems to be the least harmful of the Jamesian mothers. Although she never goes out of her way to see her son, believing that when he wishes to see her "he was at liberty to remember that the Palazzo Crescentini contained a large apartment known as the quarter of the signorino," probably she is not responsible for his ill health; he is a young man tubercular, and she gives him up less than he remains with his father in damp London through his own choice—formed, of course, by the temperaments of his father and of his mother. The problem with all of the Touchetts is that they *touch* too little of life: Mrs. Touchett "embrace[s] her boy with gloved hands" after a separation of many months, and Ralph knows that "in her thoughts and her thoroughly arranged and servanted life his turn always came after the other nearest objects of her solicitude." Like Mrs. Moreen, she is only able to show feeling for her son when he is dead. James does not condemn "crazy Aunt Lydia" Touchett, as she is called by her nieces. He describes her as cold, hard, dry, and often he ridicules her, but most of all, I think, he feels sorry for her because the quality by which she is chiefly characterized—her taciturnity—prevents her from forming close relationships with other people. Mrs. Touchett knows that she has failed somehow, Isabel feels, "that she saw herself in the future as an old woman without memories." One understands immediately as much as will ever be known about her from her telegrams, her chief way of communicating with people:

> Tired America, hot weather awful, return England with niece, first decent steamer cabin.
>
> Changed hotel, very bad, impudent clerk, address here. Taken sister's girl, died last year, go to Europe, two sisters, quite independent.

Separated from her husband, separated from her son, separated from her country, Mrs. Touchett has become "a person of many oddities." She is not a bad person; in fact she does "a great deal of good, but she never pleased. This way of her own, of which she was so fond, was not intrinsically offensive—it was just unmistakeably distinguished from the ways of others. The edges of her conduct were so very clear-cut that for susceptible persons it sometimes had a knife-like effect." Interesting words here. Ralph may no longer be a susceptible person; he is grown and seems to have withdrawn into "private apartments," protected by his "ante-room." Both his disease and his habitual stance with his hands in his pockets symbolize his inaction. But the combination of "knife-like effect" and "hands in his pockets" gives one pause—a Jamesian mother, no matter how seemingly benign, is never very far away from being the castrating terrible witch-mother. The choice of words is not accidental; it is used again when Isabel reflects that Mrs. Touchett's "offered, her passive extent . . . was about that of a knife-edge." Perhaps it is for his own protection that Ralph sees his father as the more motherly, his mother as the more paternal.

The person who *is* more susceptible than Ralph is Isabel. Isabel has been described both as totally responsible for her own conduct and as used and betrayed by the poisonous pair, Gilbert Osmond and Madame Merle; but no one seems to have taken into account the influence upon her of her aunt. Mrs. Touchett comes upon her orphaned, self-reliant niece in America. She introduces her to knowledge by taking her to Europe; she introduces her to money by taking her to Ralph and Daniel Touchett; she introduces her to Madame Merle—the most evil character in the book. As she tells Ralph:

> I found her in an old house in Albany, sitting in a dreary room on a rainy day, reading a heavy book and boring herself to death. She didn't know she was bored, but when I left her no doubt of it—she seemed very grateful for the service. You may say I shouldn't have enlightened her—I should have let her alone. There's a good deal in that, but I acted conscientiously; I thought she was meant for something better. It occurred to me that it would be a kindness to take her about and introduce her to the world. She thinks she knows a great deal of it—like most American girls; but like most American girls she's ridiculously mistaken. If you want to know, I thought she would *do me credit*. I like to be well thought of, and for a woman of my age there's no greater *convenience*, in some ways, than an attractive niece [emphasis added].

Thus Mrs. Touchett, neglecter of her own son and husband, is not as insignificant a character as she first appears; she is once again a mother to beware. Even Madame Merle, that master of selfishness who ought to be able to judge it in others, reflects that Mrs. Touchett has never exhibited the smallest preference for anyone but herself, that she has never done anything for another. What she sees is that Mrs. Touchett, too, commits the great Jamesian sin of using someone; she wants to bring Isabel "out" from some obscure sense of duty, but this means using her by interfering with and attempting to shape her life: "She had taken up her niece—there was little doubt of that."

Other than her taciturnity, the main quality one notices about Mrs. Touchett is her eccentricity. Although Mrs. Touchett immediately tells Isabel that there is nothing "crazy" about her, Isabel sees that her aunt is just as eccentric as she had always supposed—but her definition of "eccentric" changes after she encounters her aunt. While it *had* meant offensive and alarming, even grotesque and sinister, Isabel comes to see it as "a matter of high but easy irony, or comedy," and wonders whether "the common tone, which was all she had ever known, had been half as interesting." I need hardly mention that Isabel's perceptions are changing as her eyes are opened to knowledge. She is at this point "held" by this "little thin-lipped, bright-eyed, foreign-looking woman, who retrieved an insignificant appearance by a distinguished manner and . . . talked with striking familiarity of the courts of Europe," but her aunt will never again appear so brilliant as on that first afternoon in Albany—never again, that is, after Isabel's own experience has begun. Mrs. Touchett, for her part, enjoys "the consciousness of making an impression on a susceptible mind."

Mrs. Touchett, except for her lack of beauty, has much in common with her niece, so much in fact, in her independence of spirit, that one wonders if she is not trying to relive her own life vicariously through Isabel. Mrs. Touchett has neither beauty nor vanity; "she was a plain-faced old woman, without graces and without any great elegance, but with an extreme respect for her own motives." She has married an expatriated American, as her niece will later do, and recognizes, as Isabel will recognize, that she and her husband "should never desire the same thing at the same moment." Isabel's unfortunate marriage, in fact, should come as no surprise once the reader has determined the extent of Mrs. Touchett's influence upon her niece, for that lady has tried to teach Isabel that one marries not for love, but to make use of

people. She is disappointed when Isabel rejects Lord Warburton, for one's dislike of the English "is all the greater
reason for making use of them"—especially if they are rich
and titled. Like her Aunt Lydia, I would venture to suggest
further, Isabel chooses the one among her suitors who
threatens her the least—that is, the one who seems likely to
demand the least from her sexually and personally. One child
comes from both sterile marriages, but Mrs. Touchett's is
only diseased, while Isabel's dies. Unlike Isabel, however,
Mrs. Touchett is prepared to "rescue disagreement from the
vulgar realm of accident," while Isabel, at least at the end of
the novel, prepares to go back to Rome. Mrs. Touchett's independence seems to be mixed with hardness, a shrewdness
that Isabel doesn't possess; not evil herself, Mrs. Touchett
has what Harold Frederic's Sister Soulsby calls the wisdom of
the serpent. But that is just why, in offering herself as a
model to Isabel, she is dangerous. Isabel's independence is
mixed with romantic idealism. Mrs. Touchett will be an old
woman without memories, while Isabel, because she feels
she has to live with the consequences of her mistakes, will be
an old woman with bitter memories. She, not Mrs. Touchett,
sees the ghost at Gardencourt.

Mrs. Touchett's great merit, from Isabel's point of view, is
her honesty, and one can accept that; Mrs. Touchett admits
from the beginning that she plans to make a convenience of
Isabel—she admits everything. Her honesty, aptly, is compared to something mechanical: a pair of compasses. "There
was a comfort in her stiffness and firmness," James says,
"you knew exactly where to find her and were never liable to
chance encounters and concussions." Isabel comes to have at
last "an undemonstrable pity for her; there seemed something so dreary in the condition of a person whose nature
had, as it were, so little surface—offered so limited a face to
the accretions of human contact. Nothing tender, nothing
sympathetic, had ever had a chance to fasten upon it—no
wind-sown blossom, no familiar softening moss." From
James's point of view, of course, one would rather be Isabel

than Mrs. Touchett. It is better to have experienced pain than to have experienced nothing; Isabel at least has experienced something of life, while Mrs. Touchett cannot be said to have lived at all. She needs, unlike Hawthorne's Hilda, more than a sin to soften her.

THE REAL WITCH-BITCHES

This final section of the analysis of the great-mother arche-type as seen in the fiction of Henry James is a study of the portraits of three ladies so evil that one wonders what terri-ble monsters lurked in the nightmares of their creator, so tor-menting him that he had to translate their horror to a con-scious level. Rose Armiger cold-bloodedly murders a little child. Madame de Bellegarde, if she has not committed mur-der, at least has willed someone to die; but this deed is insig-nificant beside her spiritual suffocation of her daughter. Ma-dame Merle not only chooses not to recognize her own daughter, but manipulates and spiritually destroys the most promising of all the James heroines, Isabel Archer. Serena Merle's crime is the most devastating because her victim is the most fully developed human being, the one whose suffer-ing is the greatest.

As studies of patriarchal myth demonstrate, the arche-typal mother comes from the male unconscious:

> The symbolism of the Terrible Mother draws its images pre-dominantly from the "inside"; that is to say, the negative ele-mentary character of the Feminine expresses itself in fantas-tic and chimerical images that do not originate in the outside world. The reason for this is that the Terrible Female is a sym-bol for the unconscious. And the dark side of the Terrible Mother takes the form of monsters, whether in Egypt or India, Mexico or Etruria, Bali or Rome. In the myths and tales of all peoples, ages and countries—and even in the nightmares of our own nights—witches and vampires, ghouls and specters as-sail us, all terrifyingly alike.[16]

These witches and vampires, ghouls and specters, haunted James from the beginning of his career as a writer. His earliest tale, "A Tragedy of Error" (1864), is about a woman who hires a boatman—a man malicious enough to steal a child's milk—to murder her husband. Like the despoiler of the first Garden, Madame Bernier stands in the middle of the garden when she learns that her assassin has mistakenly killed not her husband, but her lover. "De Grey," published four years later, is another vampire tale. A curse has hung over the house of De Grey, whereby all males who marry into the family are destroyed, until a woman reverses the curse. When Margaret marries Paul De Grey, she blooms while her husband languishes. Dying, he tells her, "You're enchanted, baleful, fatal." [17] In "Osborne's Revenge," published the same year, Osborne's friend Robert Graham dies because a young woman has charmed him and kept him at poisoned waters. Osborne is puzzled by the idea that "a young woman could unite so much loveliness with so much darkness. He was as certain of the bright surface of her nature as of its cold and dark reverse, and he was utterly unable to discover a link of connection between the two." [18] "Longstaff's Marriage," published in 1878, like the earlier "De Grey" and the later *Sacred Fount,* is a restatement of the love-death equation: love between a man and a woman is destructive; the strength of one increases only as the other languishes. In "The Author of Beltraffio" (1884), Beatrice Ambient draws her strength from her power over her husband. The pawn in that struggle is their son, Mark; his mother lets him die rather than grow up to read his father's books.

We seldom *see* the crimes committed by these witch-mothers. Rose Armiger, like Beatrice Ambient, murders a child offstage. Madame de Bellegarde, in James's first important novel, murders her husband before the book opens, and stifles her daughter in a way that Christopher Newman, the self-reliant hero pitted against that decadent symbol of Old World depravity, is never able to fathom. And Madam Merle's crime is hidden even from the reader; one *senses* her horror before understanding it. This is James's way of intensifying the horror. He says of his method, "To narrow the meaning was to be specific: to start naming the horrors was to limit the imagination. To use the word 'horrors' and leave it at that was to suggest *all* the horrors a reader wanted to imagine." [19] The horrors have to be pieced together by the reader like the fragments of a nightmare; but they are *there* as clearly in these three books as any reader could wish—or dread.

Rose Armiger

"Oh, blest *Other House,* which gives me thus at every step a precedent, a support, a divine little light to walk by," Henry James wrote in his notebook toward the end of his career. [20] And indeed it does provide a "divine little light"—for the reader as well as for the writer. That *The Other House* is not widely read, probably because James did not include it in the New York Edition of his collected works, does not diminish its significance. As Leon Edel points out in his introduction to *The Other House,* the novel was first conceived as a play, and James, forced to limit himself to twenty-three volumes (although he spilled over to a twenty-fourth), automatically excluded the dramas. [21]

The Other House is a book about mothers. A visit from Julia Bream's wicked stepmother shortly after the birth of Julia's child has seemingly contributed to the death of Julia in some mysterious way. Her hatred of this woman is such that before she dies, Julia extracts from her husband Tony a promise never to marry during the life of their child. Next door lives an officious meddlesome mother, Mrs. Beever, who represents "the public," according to James's *Notebook.* Throughout the novel, she is busily engaged in making a match for her son Paul and in running things at the other house. There is, finally and most importantly, a "Good Heroine" and a "Bad Heroine"—and James so named them in his *Notebook* [22]—both of whom wish to be mother to little Effie, or wife to Tony Bream. The Good Heroine is fair-haired Jean

Martle; the Bad Heroine is dark-haired Rose Armiger, the cold-blooded villain who deliberately murders the child and then compounds her crime by attempting to fix it on the Good Heroine.

The time of *The Other House* is important: in 1893 James was at work both on *Guy Domville* and on *The Other House*, then called *The Promise*. He was, in other words, in the midst of his attempts to establish himself as a playwright. He not only saw Rose Armiger as the center of his play, but assigned her role to Elizabeth Robins, the celebrated Ibsen actress whom James had seen play Hedda Gabler, Hilda Wangel (*The Master Builder*) and Rebecca West (*Romersholm*), and who had played Claire in James's dramatic version of *The American*. He referred at this time to being under an "Ibsen spell," writing:

> Her motives are just her passions. . . . She is infinitely perverse. . . . one isn't so sure she is wicked and by no means sure that she is disagreeable. She is various and sinuous . . . complicated and natural; she suffers, she struggles, she is human, and by that fact exposed to a dozen interpretations.[23]

The Good Heroine and the Bad Heroine were stock literary conventions in the nineteenth century, but rarely is there a Bad Heroine of such intensity as Rose Armiger. To trust the tale and not the teller, one is very sure that she is wicked and that her wickedness is motivated by her passion. That one finds her attractive as often as one finds her disagreeable makes her all the more dangerous. Like the other Jamesian mothers, her aim, her threat is possession—not, this time, of a child, but of the man she loves. Since the child stands in the way, however, she must be sacrificed.

Early in the novel James establishes Rose as a mother figure. She and Julia have shared a common aversion to Julia's stepmother, who is Rose's aunt. Close friends at school, Rose, the elder, has always been a kind of mother to Julia. "I'm the one thing of her own that dear Julia has ever had," Rose tells Mrs. Beever. And when that lady asks if Rose doesn't count Julia's husband, Rose answers, "I count Tony immensely; but in another way." The other way, of course, is as *hers;* that is why Rose is the only thing of her own Julia has ever had. Rose is also a "mother" to Tony. When Dennis, her fiancé, questions her closeness with Tony she tells him, "Oh, he comes to me . . . as he might come to talk of her with the mother that, poor darling, it's her misfortune never to have known." "He treats you, you mean," Dennis asks, "as his mother-in-law?" "Very much," she answers. She is a sort of mother figure even to Dennis, referring to him as "My dear child" and "My dear boy." For poor Effie, Rose is the incarnation of all of Julia's worst fears about stepmothers. Rose not only will have nothing to do with the child; she makes it very clear that she despises children. When Tony asks her to take care of Effie for a few minutes, her "ominous face" as she refuses causes him to exclaim, "Good God, how you stand off from the poor little thing!" And when Jean makes the same request, Rose curtly replies that she has a letter to write. Although Tony imagines that Rose is scrupulously avoiding contact with the child out of deference to her dead friend's memory, and even goes so far as to suggest, "It's . . . as if she couldn't trust herself," Rose's actual dislike for the child comes through clearly. The child's lack of response to Rose, in contrast to her cries of "Auntie Jean!" when Miss Martle appears, and the contrast of Rose's assumed affection for the child with Dennis's spontaneous affection, both point this up.

James carefully makes Rose various *and* sinuous. He dresses her in white on the day she murders Effie, for example, reminding one of the seeming purity of her motives on that day when Julia lay dying in the Breams' house. Yet hints of her duplicity are there from the initial pages. True, it is Rose who encourages Tony to please his wife by vowing never to marry if she should die, but it is also Rose who suggests to him that he promise never to marry *during the lifetime of their daughter.* Put this together with her counting Tony "in quite another way" and Dennis's uneasiness over

the relationship between Rose and Tony (Dennis's perceptions are to be trusted; if he seems impetuous in this first
part, later he is shown to be one of the most straightforward
and direct characters ever created by James), and one begins
to fear for Effie's safety even before her mother is dead.

The other characters in Part I present sharp contrasts to
Rose: Dennis in his straightforwardness, Jean in her freshness (James makes her a Diana), Tony in his easygoing natu-
ralness. "I've never known anyone like you for not having
two grains of observation," Rose tells Tony. "You've no sus-
picions and no fears and no doubts; you're natural and generous and easy." Since Rose herself is continually observing
others, this makes her the opposite of natural. In fact, Rose
typically puts on a face to meet the faces that she meets.
Sometimes she appears beautiful and sometimes she is ugly,
depending upon which face she shows—at least until the end
of the book, when her mask has become the snakelike mask
of Medusa. It is the omniscient Mrs. Beever who tells her
what she is: "clever." Mrs. Beever, however, recognizes
Rose because they share many of the same attributes: both
try to run the affairs of the other house; both try to make a
match for Mrs. Beever's son Paul for their own selfish reasons; both are unnatural, or even inhuman in their inability
to weep; both are diabolically clever. But where Rose is the
more attractive of the two, Mrs. Beever is the more clever: *she*
wouldn't have slipped up; she would have covered her
traces.

Their function, however, is somewhat different. Mrs.
Beever nourishes: seated in her garden, she is the priestess of
the tea ceremony. Rose, on the other hand, is sexually aggressive; more than once she is shown digging up the turf of
the garden with the point of her blood-red parasol. *She* is
"the priestess of a threatened altar."

Mrs. Beever's garden is the scene of the murder of little
Effie. The lushness of its creepers and clusters, the velvet of
the lawn, puts the other house "all out of countenance by the
mere breath of the garden." Mrs. Beever, James continues,

had everything: "She had space and time and the river." Jamesian gardens are rarely Edenic, however. Mrs. Beever's garden is the scene of deceit, manipulation, intrigue, fierce struggles for possession, and finally death. As Rose herself says, this "isn't peace, my dear Tony. You give me just the occasion to let you know formally that it's war." Both Rose and Mrs. Beever are there "at last gathering the fruit of the tree she so long ago so fondly and so carefully planted." For Rose the garden becomes "foolish greenness," then "vague," and finally closed to her; she is at the end literally locked out of the garden, with Dennis guarding the door and Paul guarding the window.

The struggle for possession is the great horror of *The Other House*; it is always the great horror of the mother archetype. Rose's struggle with Jean for possession of Effie, which is really her struggle for possession of Tony Bream, recalls both the struggle of the parents for Mark Ambient in "The Author of Beltraffio," written the same year, and the struggle of the Governess for possession of Miles and Flora in *The Turn of the Screw*. Rose seizes the child "almost with violence, and holding her as she had held her before, dropped again upon the bench and presented her as a yielding captive. This act of appropriation was confirmed by the flash of a fine glance—a single gleam, but direct." Victorious, Rose says to Jean: "*I* want her for another reason. . . . I adored her poor mother— and she's hers. That's *my* ground, that's *my* love, that's *my* faith." Dealing Effie "a kiss that was a long consecration," she tells her, "It's as your dear dead mother's, my own sweet, that—if it's time—I shall carry you to bed!" As she escapes with Effie, Jean watches Rose, "as if in triumph—a great open-air insolence—of possession, press her face to the little girl's." Where she carries her, of course, is to the river to drown her. When she returns, she will blame the death on Jean Martle. But one could almost believe in her martyrdom; like all the mother figures analyzed in this chapter, her determination to possess is motivated by an almost religious belief in the rightness of her cause. Rose's possession of Dennis echoes her possession of Effie: "You came to me through doubts—you spoke to me through fears. You're mine!" The final attempt at possession, the possession of Tony Bream, presents the horrible truth that possessive love is equal to death: "She loves me!"—Tony's face reflected the mere monstrous fact. "It has made what it has made—her awful act and my silence."

James, however, was not silent. He would go on to create other awful acts of other witch-mothers. How ironic his words seem: *The Other House* provides a "divine little light to walk by."

Madame de Bellegarde

Madame de Bellegarde, too, commits murder, but a great deal of what the reader learns about her crime comes through Mrs. Bread, whose veracity and objectivity are somewhat suspect. There is no doubt, however, about the depravity of Madame de Bellegarde. As the guard of the beautiful Claire and in her manipulation of Valentin, she is even more terrible than in the murder of a man unknown to the reader. She is the "terrible devouring mother," and her children might well be the "victims" * described in Erich Neumann's psychoanalytic study of that archetype:

> A psychic depression . . . is characterized by . . . a loss of libido in the consciousness, expressed in lack of enthusiasm and initiative, weakness of will, fatigue, incapacity for concentration and work, and in "negative contents," such as thoughts of death and failure, weariness of life, suicidal leanings and so on. Often . . . this psychic process also becomes visible; that is to say it appears in the familiar symbolism of the light, the sun, the moon, or the hero being swallowed up by darkness in the form of night, the abyss, hell, monsters. A deep . . . analysis then reveals the irruption of an archetype, e.g. the Terrible Devouring Mother, whose psychic attraction is so great because of its energetic charge that the charge of the ego complex, unable to withstand it, "sinks" and is "swallowed up." [24]

* I do not count Urbain as a victim; he is, as Christopher Newman remarks, "the old woman at second-hand."

The first lines describe what happened to M. de Bellegarde: his wife seems to have *willed* him to die. Even Mrs. Bread, the only witness of the crime, doubts that Madame de Bellegarde touched the marquis with her hands. "I believe it was this way," she tells Christopher Newman:

> He had a fit of his great pain, and he asked her for his medicine. Instead of giving it to him she went and poured it away before his eyes. Then he saw what she meant, and, weak and helpless as he was, he was frightened, he was terrified. "You want to kill me," he said. "Yes, M. de Marquis, I want to kill you," says my lady, and sits down and fixes her eyes upon him. You know my lady's eyes, I think, sir; it was with them she killed him; it was with the terrible strong will she put into them. It was like a frost on flowers.

Although this is Mrs. Bread's interpretation, Valentin's belief that his father did not die a natural death, Claire's feeling that there is a curse upon the house, the dissatisfaction of the doctor from Poitiers (which again is reported by Mrs. Bread, but which is corroborated by Urbain's worry about what Newman has learned from the doctors), and Urbain's asking Newman how much he wants for the accusatory deathbed letter of his father, all support the substance of Mrs. Bread's story as true.

Pursuing Neumann's description of the "victim" further, the "negative contents"—thoughts of death and failure, weariness of life, suicidal leanings and so on—are characteristic of Valentin. I am good for nothing, he tells Newman:

> When I was twenty, I looked around me and saw a world with everything ticketed "Hands off!" and the deuce of it was that the ticket seemed meant only for me. . . . I do nothing! I am supposed to amuse myself. One can, if one knows how. But you can't keep it up forever. I am good for another five years, perhaps, but I foresee that after that I shall lose my appetite.

He reminds Mrs. Tristram of the hero in Keats's "La Belle Dame sans Merci": "Oh, what can ail thee knight-at-arms,/ Alone and palely loitering?" There can be no doubt that "La

Belle Dame" is Madame de Bellegarde, his mother. Although he dies in a duel, Valentin's death seems suicidal. When Newman suggests to the dying young man that he might have prevented his death, Valentin tells him:

> You said some very good things; I have thought them over. But, my dear friend, I was right, all the same. This is the regular way. . . . I'm a very small boy, now, . . . I'm rather less than an infant. An infant is helpless, but it's generally voted promising. I'm not promising, eh? Society can't lose a less valuable member.

The symbol of the archetype, Neumann goes on to say, is light, the sun, the moon, or the hero's being swallowed up by darkness in the form of night or hell. Both symbols here describe the destructiveness of Madame de Bellegarde, whose face literally suggests the moon: it is white and intense, with "formal gaze" and "circumscribed smile." Her daughter-in-law sees fit to celebrate the engagement of Claire and Newman in an audacious gown of crimson crape bestrewn with huge silver moons. "If it [her dress] is strange, it matches the occasion," she tells Newman when he comments on the dissimilarity of the color to a midnight sky. "That," she says, "is my originality; any one could have chosen blue. . . . But I think crimson is much more amusing. And I give my idea, which is moonshine." "Moonshine and bloodshed," is Newman's comment, to which she laughingly replies, "A murder by moonlight." This refers, of course, not only to the murder of Newman's hopes of marriage to Claire, which the old marquise will effect, but also quite literally to Madame de Bellegarde's murder of her husband. Claire, finally, to complete the parallel, is literally swallowed up in darkness; she becomes a Carmelite nun interred for life in the Rue d'Infer—hell. When Newman goes to see the place for himself, he finds that there is nothing to see:

> . . . no light came through the crevices. . . . behind it there was darkness, with nothing stirring. . . . Suddenly there arose from the depths of the chapel . . . a sound of a strange, lugu-

brious chant. It began softly, but it became more of a wail and a dirge. . . . The chant kept on, mechanical and monotonous, with dismal repetitions and despairing cadences. It was hideous, it was horrible, . . . this confused, impersonal wail was all that . . . the world she had deserted should ever hear of the voice he had found so sweet.

Madame de Bellegarde, then, is infinitely worse than someone like Olive Chancellor, who is also involved in a struggle for possession. It isn't just because Olive loses while Madame de Bellegarde wins that we pity Olive and despise and fear Madame de Bellegarde; it isn't because Christopher Newman, with all his faults, is an appealing hero—one cannot help responding to his attractiveness, his good humor, his buoyancy and directness—while Basil Ransom is as repulsive in his way as Olive is in hers; it isn't because Verena, weak willed though she is, is condemned to a less-than-brilliant marriage and a life of tears through her own choice while Claire is swallowed up in darkness. Madame de Bellegarde is evil incarnate. She murders her husband. She destroys her children—Valentin by depriving him of the self-esteem that means for him the will to live, Claire by seeing her literally condemned to hell rather than see her own will thwarted. She uses people—the cardinal Jamesian sin. Willing to use Newman's money, when she finds she cannot use him in a deeper sense—when she cannot dominate him—she dishonorably reneges on her bargain. It is when Newman takes the initiative at the engagement party, when *he takes her* on a circuit of the room, that she tells him, "This is enough, sir," and moonshine turns to bloodshed.

The reader has already found reason to dislike and distrust Madame de Bellegarde, however. "She never laughs," Valentin had told Newman in his first description of his mother. Newman himself finds her to be "a woman of conventions and proprieties." Her intense, respectable, formal countenance suggests to him, perhaps because he is a businessman, "a document signed and sealed; a thing of parchment, ink and ruled lines." He says to himself as he looks at her: "Her world is the world of things immutably decreed. But how she is at home in it, and what a paradise she finds it! She walks about in it as if it were a blooming park, a Garden of Eden; and when she sees 'This is genteel,' or 'This is improper' written on a mile-stone she stops ecstatically." The image is apt. The scene of the murder of the marquis, of Valentin's burial, and Newman's final meeting with Claire is *Fleurières*, or flowers, referred to as an "old city on a hill." Like other Jamesian heroes and heroines, Newman has come from the New World with its innocence and sterility to the gardens of the Old, rich with experience, fertile with corruption. Madame de Bellegarde describes herself to Newman as "a very proud and meddlesome old woman," but his description of her to Mrs. Tristram is worse than that: "I shouldn't wonder if she had murdered some one," he says, "all from a sense of duty, of course." At this point Newman is speaking from intuition, not knowledge—and intuition is the way he usually knows things. Unable to tell an original painting from a copy, nevertheless Newman is usually intuitively right about people; while one may laugh at his crudities and his aesthetic headaches, one trusts him from the moment of his decision not to avenge himself upon a man who has swindled him out of a pile of money. One trusts him further when he forms a friendship with the heart-warming Valentin and disdains the urbane Urbain. One even *expects* his decision not to avenge himself on the de Bellegardes. Thus, when he *feels* "that he is in the presence of something evil," as, for example, when he enters the Hotel Bellegarde to learn that his engagement is broken off, the reader feels it too. In fact, it is precisely Newman's capacity to feel and Madame de Bellegarde's lack of feeling that distinguish his goodness from her badness. With her sense of conventions and proprieties, she *feels* nothing: "I feel no emotion that I was not perfectly prepared for," she tells Newman when he announces to her that Claire has accepted him.

Claire feels; she feels fear, telling Newman, for example, "I am afraid of my mother." Valentin feels; he feels dismay and a sense of his own inadequacy. Christopher Newman feels, in contrast, a great sense of his own worth, and he feels anger at being mistreated. And the young marquise is completely a person of feeling to the exclusion of other qualities. But Madame de Bellegarde only *knows,* and what she knows is a sense of her own power. When Newman demands that she tell him what has been done to Claire to make her change her mind, she responds "in a rich bell-like voice": "We have used authority. . . . My power . . . is in my children's obedience."

What Madame de Bellegarde does not know is how much the others know: she is suspicious of Mrs. Bread, but continues to employ her husband's former mistress in order to watch and control her; she is unsure of the doctor from Poitiers, but makes certain he is sent away; and most important, she does not know how much Valentin and Claire understand. It has already been suggested that she is afraid of losing control, and that it is this seeming threat from the strong Newman during their promenade that gives her the excuse for breaking off the engagement. She has probably an even greater fear of losing control over Valentin and Claire, as James suggests by referring to the brother and sister as Orestes and Electra, who in the Greek tragedy avenge the murder of their Father Menelaus by their mother Clytemnestra. She is, then, not unlike Olive Chancellor of *The Bostonians* in that her determination to *possess* is founded on a fear of losing control. She is further like Olive in seeing her role in a religious sense: the religion of the Bellegardes is the "religion simply of family laws," where their "implacable little mother was the high priestess."

Woman as "priestess" brings to mind James's concern with women as the "salient point" of American life in his notebook entry on *The Bostonians.* James's own attitude toward women is the salient point in his creation of witch-mothers like Madame de Bellegarde. But that attitude is expressed even by Christopher Newman, his benevolent hero, who responds to Valentin's description of Mlle. Nioche as "a very curious and ingenious piece of machinery" with: "Well, I have seen some very curious machines, too, . . . and once, in a needle factory, I saw a gentleman from the city, who had stepped too near one of them, picked up as neatly as if he had been prodded by a fork, swallowed down straight, and ground into small pieces."

Madame Merle

By 1881, in his portrayal in *The Portrait of a Lady* of the ultimate witch-mother, Serena Merle, James had grown more subtle. Madame Merle's complexity is skillfully introduced by the juxtaposition of her name—*Merle* or "blackbird"— with her physical lightness. She is described as "tall, fair, smooth"; everything in her person is "round and replete" and she has "thick, fair hair, arranged somehow 'classically' as if she were a Bust . . . —a Juno or a Niobe." But Juno, wife of Jupiter, is a pagan priestess, and Niobe is a mother of *dead* children.

Madame Merle's "repleteness" is her most important asset. It is because of the completeness of Madame Merle's knowledge that Mrs. Touchett wants Isabel to know her: "She knows absolutely everything on earth there is to know," Mrs. Touchett tells her niece. "I wish you to know her. I think it will be a good thing for you. Serena Merle hasn't a fault." If this seems like a lack of perception on the part of Mrs. Touchett, who becomes aware long before her niece of the reason for Madame Merle's interest in Isabel's marriage, one must remember Madame Merle's own awareness that for Mrs. Touchett, having no faults means never being late for dinner, answering a letter the day one gets it, and not bringing too much luggage when one comes to visit. Perhaps because of these virtues, Ralph sees Madame Merle as being "as universally 'liked' as some new volume of smooth twaddle." As for knowing everything there is to know, this indeed is what draws Isabel to Madame Merle—literally, on that first occasion when the girl hears Madame Merle play the piano.

Isabel learns later that Madame Merle practices all the arts and graces of society: she has innumerable acquaintances to whom she writes innumerable letters; she paints, making "no more of brushing in a sketch than of pulling off her gloves"; she reads "everything important"; and if not reading, writing, playing the piano or painting, she busies herself with "rich embroidery, cushions, curtains, decorations for the chimney-piece, an art in which her bold, free invention was as noted as the agility of her needle." If this dilettante has a fault for Isabel, it is that she is not natural: "her nature had been too much overlaid by custom and her angles too much rubbed away.* She had become too flexible, too useful, was too ripe and too final. She was in a word too perfectly the social animal. . . ." Unfortunately, this is the direction in which Isabel herself moves as her involvement with Madame Merle deepens. When Isabel first meets her she feels as if she wanders "as by the wrong side of the wall of a private garden, round the enclosed talents, accomplishments, aptitudes of Madame Merle." By the end of the novel, both Isabel and Madame Merle are on the wrong side of the garden; their confrontation in the convent takes place in a room with "a collection of wax flowers under glass," but "on the other side of the window lay the garden." It is tempting to say here that in the first image Isabel looks longingly *from* the garden to the forbidden knowledge that Madame Merle represents, that Isabel is on the right side of that garden wall. But it is importnat to remember that the Old World is full of Jamesian gardens—Garden-court, the tangles of wild roses in Osmond's garden, the garden of Mrs. Touchett's Palazzo Crescentini in Florence where Ralph warns Isabel about Osmond, the damp court that takes the place of a garden at the Palazzo Roccanera, Isabel and Osmond's home in Rome, with its rows of mutilated statues and dusty urns—and that the image is usually used ironically; European gardens are

* This is also what Adam Verver says of Prince Amerigo in *The Golden Bowl*, where it is a positive quality.

fallen and cultivated gardens, to a greater or lesser degree poisonous, like Rappaccini's garden. Madame Merle is the great mother of the fallen garden.

If Isabel's perception of Madame Merle's fault is that she is not natural, it is to be expected that that lady's influence on Isabel will be to acquaint her with the importance of the "things" of this world. In one of the most important speeches of the book (one, in fact, which provides a clue to the method of Henry James in his lingering descriptions of the houses in which his characters live), Madame Merle tells Isabel:

> . . . every human being has his shell and . . . you must take the shell into account. By the shell I mean the whole envelope of circumstances. There's no such thing as an isolated man or woman; we're each of us made up of some cluster of appurtenances. What shall we call our "self?" Where does it begin? Where does it end? It overflows into everything that belongs to us—and then it flows back again. I know a large part of myself is in the clothes I choose to wear. I've a great respect for *things!* One's self—for other people—is one's expression of one's self; and one's house, one's furniture, one's garments, the books one reads, the company one keeps—these things are all expressive.

Madame Merle's own house, interestingly, is a small apartment in an old Roman house; her diminutive drawing-room is crowded with "things": "The room was small and densely filled with furniture; it gave an impression of faded silk and little statuettes which might totter if one moved." "By Jove," Edward Rosier exclaims (unwittingly reinforcing the Juno reference), as he looks at her bric-a-brac through his eyeglass, "she's got some jolly good things!" Rosier, however, is a lightweight. Madame Merle's faded silk and little statuettes reveal not elegance, but the faded and spiritually small quality of Madame Merle herself. As a matter of fact, on first meeting Isabel she describes herself as "old and stale and faded." Although her pretensions are great—like her old Venetian lace—she came into the world in a Brooklyn navy yard and her husband was a horrid little Swiss merchant. Madame

Merle's shell, then, unlike that of the other characters in the book, is a disguise for what she really is. Her shell is more than this brief glimpse of her own house; it is the social fabric with which she surrounds herself—not just the arts and graces which she has cultivated, but also other people's houses in which she spends most of her time. She is like a chameleon, a certain kind of reptile which assumes the protective coloration of its surroundings.

The suggestion of Madame Merle's reptilian qualities brings to mind that her knowledge, like that of the Governess, is the knowledge of all evil; like Eve's, it is the wisdom of the serpent. "She knew how to think—an accomplishment rare in women," James remarks in one of his more venomous asides. And Madame Merle identifies herself as belonging "to the old, old world." Her final bit of evil is to give Isabel the knowledge that her beloved cousin Ralph is, at bottom, responsible for her inheritance. But there are physical hints as well. In one of her early conversations with Isabel she tells her that she likes to remain in the quiet, dusky cupboard, "But when I've to come out into a strong light—then, my dear, I'm a horror!" "A woman," she later says, "has no natural place anywhere; wherever she finds herself she has to remain on the surface and, more or less, to crawl." And when she finds out about Isabel's inheritance of 70,000 pounds, "her eyes, a little dilated, fixed themselves on those of her friend."

Madame Merle covets Isabel's money, of course. She has none of her own, and her abandoned daughter needs a dowry if she is to make a "successful" marriage. But had she managed merely to get Isabel's money for herself, her horror would not be so great. The horror—and like all Jamesian horrors it is felt rather than told—is that she covets Isabel herself.

Madame Merle is guilty of a great many "horrors." She is to be condemned as a mother for renouncing her own child. According to the Countess Gemini, Osmond's sister—and one has no reason to doubt her veracity; she is meddlesome, but she is goodhearted—Madame Merle gave up her interest in Pansy and in Pansy's father because of her own ambitions: "She hoped she might marry a great man; that has always been her idea. She has waited and watched and plotted and prayed; but she has never succeeded." Beyond this, she is guilty of that sin for which Jamesian characters are most severely judged: she uses people. As the Countess tells Isabel, "the only tangible result she has ever achieved—except of course, getting to know everyone and staying with them free of expense—has been her bringing you and Osmond together." That "except," using people for free room and board and social connections, is negligible compared to her use of Isabel in the hopes that Isabel's money and her fondness for Pansy would secure for her daughter a good match. That is her overt motive—not seen until the end by the idealistic Isabel, but seen clearly quite early by such close-minded persons as Mrs. Touchett and such scatterbrains as the Countess Gemini. One can only conjecture about what sort of payoff Madame Merle anticipates or receives from Osmond for finding him such a rich wife, or beyond that what satisfaction Madame Merle receives from the thrill of possession itself, from causing the fall of such a creature as Isabel. James alludes most specifically to this horror when Isabel kisses Madame Merle as proof of their friendship: "There are kisses and kisses, and this embrace was satisfactory to Madame Merle." The reader is reminded of the horror of Olive Chancellor's attempted possession of Verena, with the difference that one feels no pity for Serena Merle: she is too calculating and Isabel is too good. One suspects, in fact, that in her final scene with Isabel, Madame Merle only feigns humiliation as she has feigned everything else—how could she send forth her final poisonous barb about Ralph if she were truly feeling remorse? Her "I shall go to America," then, is said not in defeat, but in triumph: having felled Isabel, she is now ready to take on the New World itself.

From the beginning Madame Merle has had no scruples. As she tells Osmond, "I don't pretend to know what people are meant for, . . . I only know what I can do with them."

Her cold-bloodedness might well be a result of her own alienation. Although she identifies herself as being of the "old, old world," she is well aware of her lowly American birth, and in fact she has no country. Although she has her own diminutive drawing-room and takes her place in many people's houses, she is really at home nowhere. Although she has, as Isabel points out, "memories, graces, talents," she is well aware that "As for my graces and memories the less said about them the better." She has been involved in a lifelong process of creating illusions, but she is under no illusions about herself: "What have I got?" she asks Isabel. "Neither husband, nor child, nor fortune, nor position, nor the traces of a beauty that I never had." As for friends, "You'll be my friend," she prophesies, "until you find a better use for your friendship." This is a true speech—a true martyr's speech. But it is, from one who knows what to do with people, a calculated speech. "You must reward me," she tells Isabel of their friendship, "by believing in me." Isabel answers with that kiss "satisfactory to Madame Merle," but Madame Merle does not return the kiss until Isabel has inherited Daniel Touchett's 70,000 pounds. It is, for Isabel, the kiss of death.

For Mrs. Touchett, Madame Merle's crime consists in deceiving *her*. "She can do anything," Mrs. Touchett tells Isabel; "that's what I've always liked her for. I knew she could play any part; but I understood that she played them one by one. I didn't understand that she would play two at the same time." For the Countess Gemini, Madame Merle's badness is a result of her association with her brother Osmond. By herself her main fault is worship of propriety—a fault which the Countess Gemini seems not to share—but combined with Osmond, her cleverness amounts to evil: "You're capable of anything, you and Osmond. I don't mean Osmond by himself, and I don't mean you by yourself. But together you're dangerous—like some chemical combination." Madame Merle recognizes the truth of this when she later tells Osmond, "You've not only dried up my tears; you've dried up my soul." Her crime for Gilbert Osmond is that she has failed to deliver the goods: Isabel has not turned out to be what he wished, and for that he blames Madame Merle. In a tone that suggests he is sexually frustrated, he complains to Madame Merle: "If you didn't understand me before I married it was cruelly rash of you to put me into such a box. However, I took a fancy to the box myself; I thought it would be a comfortable fit. I asked very little; I only asked that she should like me. . . . That she should adore me, if you will. . . . My wife has declined—declined to do anything of the sort. . . . If you're determined to make a tragedy of that, the tragedy's hardly for her." Madame Merle's crime for Pansy is simply that she's odious; with the instinct of an unsophisticated child, Pansy intuitively knows that she does not like Madame Merle. But her crime for Isabel is the worst because Isabel was the best: she uses Isabel, who of all people believed herself to be free and self-reliant.

In that scene where she at last recognizes the full horror of Madame Merle and demands to know *what* she is, Isabel asks, "What have you to do with me?" "Everything!" Madame Merele answers. That is the final horror for Isabel, that this woman has controlled her, possessed her, as it were, deprived her of her own will. Isabel's knowledge, unfortunately, has to include knowledge of this fact—that this woman who cannot weep has practiced her unnaturalness upon Isabel herself. Although she has come to see Madame Merle as "armed" for the social battle at all points with "weapons [of] . . . polished steel" which she used with the skill of a veteran, it has taken, despite the warnings of Ralph and Henrietta, the use of those weapons on herself for Isabel really to see Madame Merle for what she is. She learns about Madame Merle in much the same way as the Countess has learned—by seeing Madame Merle and Osmond together. The scene makes an "image, like a sudden flicker of light," which is over in a moment, but which remains with her, conveying to her intuitively what the Countess is later to tell her. That Isabel can now *perceive* evil, however, means that she herself has changed. By the time she is ready to confront her husband, having recognized the evil that he and Madame

Merle together comprise, she is no longer natural. She watches Osmond, in that scene by the fire, with the "covert observation" which is "allied to self-defense" and has become habitual. This is what her association with Madame Merle has done to her; this once free, brave creature, now herself surrounded with fine "things," has need to be covert, suspicious, defensive. Like her confrontation with her husband, her confrontation with Madame Merle arouses defensiveness on Isabel's part when she perceives her visitor's critical attitude: "More clearly than ever before Isabel heard a cold, mocking voice proceed from she knew not where, in the dim void that surrounded her, and declare that this bright, strong, definite, worldly woman, this incarnation of the practical, the personal, the immediate, was a powerful agent in her destiny. . . . her nearness was not the charming accident she had so long supposed." At their final confrontation, when "all the bitterness of this knowledge [has] surged into her soul," her impulse is to "hiss like a lash," but she is silent. Possessed finally by Madame Merle's knowledge, she reduces Madame Merle, too, to silence: "What remained was the cleverest woman in the world standing there within a few feet of her and knowing as little what to think as the meanest." If Isabel was once aware that Madame Merle was "the product of a different moral or social clime from her own," her awareness that she has been brought down to Madame Merle's own plane is her tragedy. Lovers of the same man, mothers to the same daughter, possessors of the same knowledge, they are both finally on the other side of the window from the garden. What Isabel will do with her knowledge, however, is open to conjecture. Unlike Madame Merle, she does not return to America. Although she returns to Rome, she knows now where to turn; she sees a very straight path. One hopes that she is not to be interred like Pansy, like Claire de Bellegarde, in her own hell. One wants to believe that "the world, in truth, had never seemed so large; it seemed to open out, all round her." But one fears that for the changed Isabel, the new world is the world of Madame Merle.

V

The New Woman

"She is the freshest fruit of our great American
evolution . . . the self-made girl."
                                —Henry James, *Pandora*

THE NEW MYTH OF ATALANTA

"Once upon a time, not long ago, there lived a princess named Atalanta, who could run as fast as the wind. She was so bright, and so clever, and could build things and fix things so wonderfully, that many young men wished to marry her. . . .

"The king . . . told her, 'I have decided how to choose the young man you will marry. I will hold a great race, and the winner—the swiftest, fleetest young man of all—will win the right to marry you.'

"Now Atalanta was a clever girl as well as a swift runner. . . . 'Very well,' she said. 'But you must let me race along with the others. If I am not the winner, I will accept the wishes of the young man who is.' . . .

"As the day of the race grew nearer, young men began to crowd into the town. Each was sure he could win the prize, except for one; that was Young John, who lived in the town.

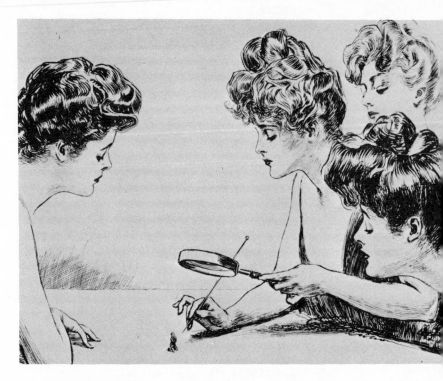

"The Weaker Sex," by Charles Dana Gibson, 1903. Courtesy, *The Saturday Evening Post*.

He saw Atalanta day by day as she bought nails and wood to make a pigeon house, or chose parts for her telescope, or laughed with her friends. Young John saw the princess only from a distance, but near enough to know how bright and clever she was. He wished very much to race with her, to win, and to earn the right to talk with her and become her friend. . . .

"At last the day of the race arrived. . . . The crowds cheered as the young men and Atalanta began to race across the field. . . . Atalanta soon pulled ahead, with three of the young men close after her. . . . Atalanta smiled as she ran out. I have almost won, she thought.

"But then another young man came near. This was Young John, running like the wind, as steadily and swiftly as Atalanta herself. Atalanta felt his closeness, and in a sudden burst she dashed ahead. Young John might have given up at this, but he never stopped running. Nothing at all, thought he, will keep me from winning the chance to speak with Atalanta. And on he ran, swift as the wind, until he ran as her equal, side by side with her, toward the golden ribbon that marked the race's end. Atalanta raced even faster to pull ahead, but Young John was a strong match for her. Smiling with the pleasure of the race, Atalanta and Young John reached the finish line together. . . .

" 'Very well, Young John,' said the king, as John and Atalanta stood before him, exhausted and jubilant from their efforts. 'You have not won the race, but you have come closer to winning than any man here. And so I give you the prize that was promised—the right to marry my daughter.' . . .

" 'Thank you, sir,' said John to the king, 'but I could not possibly marry your daughter unless she wished to marry me. I have run this race for the chance to talk with Atalanta, and, if she is willing, I am ready to claim my prize.'

"Atalanta laughed with pleasure. 'And I,' she said to John, 'could not possibly marry before I have seen the world. But I would like nothing better than to spend the afternoon with you.'

"Then the two of them sat and talked on the grassy field. . . . Atalanta told John about her telescopes and her pigeons, and John told Atalanta about his globes and his studies of geography. At the end of the day, they were friends.

"On the next day, John sailed off to discover new lands. And Atalanta set off to visit the great cities.

"By this time, each of them has had wonderful adventures, and seen marvelous sights. Perhaps some day they will be married, and perhaps they will not. In any case they are friends. And it is certain that they are both living happily ever after." [1]

—Betty Miles, from "Atalanta"

This is the new myth, the tale of the princess who is a person, not a doll or a dangerous temptress or a terrible mother. But there is nothing like it in classical mythology, in the fairy tales, or in the Judeo-Christian tradition; the myths of these traditions are masculine myths, drawn from a patriarchal culture. [2]

This is not a healthy state of affairs. According to Erich Neumann, "the peril of present-day mankind springs in large part from the one-sidedly patriarchal development of the male intellectual consciousness. . . . Western mankind must arrive at a synthesis that includes the feminine world—which is also one-sided in its isolation. Only then will the individual human being be able to develop the psychic wholeness that is urgently needed. . . . Only this wholeness of the individual can make possible a fertile and living community." [3]

To the novelists of the nineteenth century the "woman question" was the burning issue of the day. Yet within the half-century framed by the two important utopian attempts to develop a fertile and living community, those novelists who devoted themselves to this question and portrayed the "new woman" in their art created not women, but caricatures. Hawthorne's Zenobia, an early leader of the women's movement, commits suicide because of her unrequited love for an inferior man. Henry James's Olive Chancellor, a later feminist, is portrayed only in terms of her perverted sexuality and destructive possessiveness. The other "new women" in *The Bostonians,* Miss Birdseye, Mrs. Farrinder and Dr. Prance, are mere sketches; drawn with less maliciousness, they are for their author still "abnormal," characters to laugh at. Howells's Dr. Breen is a sympathetic figure, but as a lady doctor, she is first of all a lady, for Howells could not conceive of a woman (like Elizabeth Blackwell in real life, for example) being seriously dedicated to her work. And his Eveleth Strange is decidedly strange; she chooses to live in a fantasy world. All of these novelists are male. Only a woman, it seems, can write realistically about the awakening of a woman to her own identity. As Larzer Ziff observes in his study of the 1890s, "To be a serious female author in the '90s was to be a writer of stories about women and their demands. The woman novelist was trapped by her affiliations to her sex in precisely the same manner as was the twentieth-century Negro writer in the 1950s trapped by affiliation to his race. The condition of women inescapably had to be the material of her art." [4] When a woman finally did make the "woman question" the material of her art in 1899, Kate Chopin's *The Awakening* shocked reviewers, libraries refused to circulate it and the Fine Arts Club of St. Louis refused her membership because of it. Ziff calls it "the most important piece of fiction about the sexual life of a woman written to date in America, and the first fully to face the fact that marriage . . . was but an episode in her continuous growth. It did not reject the institution of the family, but it rejected the family as the automatic equivalent of feminine self-fulfillment." [5]

It is difficult today to see why *The Awakening* was viewed as "shocking" in 1899. The woman's movement had been launched in 1848 at the Seneca Falls convention. Margaret Fuller's *Woman in the Nineteenth Century* has been published five years before that. The Shakers, the free lovers at Oneida, the Mormon polygamists and the intellectuals at New Harmony, Brook Farm and Modern Times had attempted to undermine the traditional family structure a half-century earlier, and Edward Bellamy's *Looking Backward,* which would revolutionize both the social and economic structures, assuming as a matter of course equality between the sexes, had been met a decade earlier not with shock, but with acclaim. Victoria Woodhull had come upon the stage as a "live" new woman in the 1870s and published her own newspaper, run her own brokerage office, advocated free love as well as women's rights from public platforms across the country, appeared before Congress and had even twice run for President of the United States. Not only that, but Edna Pontellier, in *The Awakening,* does not find an answer; like Zenobia a half-century earlier, she commits suicide. Her suicide, however, is different from Zenobia's. And Hawthorne's portrayal of sexuality is different from Chopin's—not because the end of the century was a more propitious time to write about sexuality and experiment with nontraditional sexual relationships between men and women. Hawthorne portrays Zenobia as a deviant; she is very unlike the ideal maiden whom Coverdale finally confesses he loves. Edna Pontellier is a respected member of society who awakens to herself as a sexual being. She has a real sexual identity, and her awareness of that identity is not damning, as is Zenobia's or even Theron Ware's; it is an awakening. In this chapter, then, Edna Pontellier stands as a contrast to Zenobia, Olive Chancellor and the other Bostonians, Dr. Breen and Eveleth Strange; but she, too, chooses to die, asking, perhaps, the same question that Zenobia had asked: where is the place for the woman who swerves from the path laid down for her by tradition? Where is the new myth of Atalanta in American literature?

ZENOBIA: THE NEW WOMAN AS TRAGEDY-QUEEN

Henry James found *The Blithedale Romance* to be "the lightest, the brightest, the liveliest, of this company of unhumorous fictions" and Zenobia to be "the nearest approach that Hawthorne has made to the complete creation of a *person.*" [6] Zenobia is certainly a more believable woman than Miriam, but I am not convinced that she is more complete than Hester Prynne. Hester is not split into the dark and light lady; she is a whole person. Hester would never kill herself for love; she is too strong for that. But Zenobia may well have been more real for Hawthorne, so real that he had to kill her off.

Once having read *The Blithedale Romance,* one's conception of Zenobia is colored by her suicide; or to put it another way, the two poles of Zenobia's character around which one's attention focuses are her voluptuous, life-affirming vitality and her violent death. By saying that Hawthorne had to kill her off I do not mean that Zenobia's death is artistically inconsistent, that once having created such a full-blooded woman he did not know how to handle her, and so had to get rid of her abruptly. No, Zenobia's death is fitting within the context of the novel. She sees herself, and Hawthorne saw her, as a "tragedy queen." By definition, then, she has a flaw—several, in fact: her mysterious connection through Westervelt with evil and, therefore, with the manipulation of Priscilla; her radical stance on the position of women, which runs counter to the divine order of human relationships laid down by God and His spokesmen; or simply the classic sin of pride, "the pride and pomp which had a luxurious growth in Zenobia's character" indicated by the exotic flower in her hair. She is doomed; therefore, she must die.

If Zenobia were cast as "temptress," then her death would not be so bothersome—but she is not simply the temptress. Hollingsworth isn't much of a man for her to tempt, for one thing; he lacks the innocence and purity of a Dimmesdale or a Donatello. Purity in Hollingsworth becomes singleness of purpose: he is a monomaniac. Devoted solely to his scheme of the reformation of criminals, he will use anyone who will help him achieve his ends—first Zenobia, and then when he finds her wealth to be an illusion, Priscilla, the true owner of the purse. He is no Adam. He becomes his own first criminal, but Zenobia has not caused his fall. This powerfully built man ends his days in depression and melancholy, with "self-distrustful weakness, and a child-like or childish tendency to press close, and closer still, to the side of the slender woman whose arm was within his"—the shadowy Priscilla. The only man whom Zenobia does tempt is Coverdale/Hawthorne. But it is safer for narrator Coverdale, a thinly veiled disguise for the author, to see himself as a sort of Ethan Brand who would pry into the hearts of all of his fellow human beings but truly sympathize with none, than to acknowledge his sexual attraction to Zenobia. Hawthorne, after all, was engaged to be married to a pale maiden of his own when he joined the Brook Farm community. His own "dove," Sophia Peabody, would write to him about Margaret Fuller, Zenobia's probable prototype: "It seems to me that if she were married truly, she would no longer be puzzled about the rights of woman. . . . Home, I think, is the great arena for woman." [7] What choice had he, finally, but to kill off the dark lady and (ironically) confess his love for the pale maiden?

I challenge Zenobia's death, then, not in terms of artistic consistency; but I do challenge Hawthorne's conception of a spokeswoman for women's rights—someone whose philosophical position is that women can have rich and full lives apart from their "vocation" as wives—as a person with no real sense of personal independence, one who is so *dependent* on a man's love that if he does not return her love she must kill herself. I believe that Hawthorne makes Zenobia both a spokeswoman for women's rights and a "tragedy-queen" because one is a disguise for the other. The spokeswoman for women's rights whom Hawthorne knew, Margaret Fuller, was certainly no temptress. Zenobia, on the other hand, with the usual hair—"dark, glossy, and of singular abundance"— is "an admirable figure of a woman, just on the hither verge of her richest maturity . . . bloom, health, and vigor . . . she possessed in such overflow that a man might well have fallen in love with her for their sake only." Like Hester, she is identified with a single object; her exotic flower is as explicit a token of her sexuality as Hester's "A." Zenobia's physical beauty, her threatening sexuality, are emblematic of the threatening philosophy she espouses. Hawthorne, who has elsewhere written disparagingly of the "lady-scribblers," clearly feels threatened in his own sphere, for he has Zenobia prophesy: "when my sex shall achieve its rights, there will be ten eloquent women where there is now one eloquent man." But he is careful to have her add that "the pen is not for woman. Her power is too natural and immediate. It is with the living voice alone that she can compel the world to recognize the light of her intellect and the depth of her heart!" If an independent woman, a woman like Margaret Fuller, was a threat to his sense of masculinity, then artistically he would transform this trait into disturbing sexuality. This makes sense in terms of the romance as a whole, for its central device is the veil—from the Veiled Lady to the mysteries behind the figures of Priscilla, Old Moodie, Westervelt and Zenobia herself, to the "counterfeit Arcadia," the illusion of the happiness that the new community of Blithedale was to have created. The very name "Zenobia" is a veil, "a sort of mask in which she comes before the world, retaining all the privileges of privacy,—a contrivance, in short, like the white drapery of the Veiled Lady, only a little more transparent."

Whether or not Zenobia, beneath her mask, *is* Margaret Fuller is not important. As Henry James pointed out, it is an idle inquiry "to compare the image at all strictly with the model"; an author takes what he needs from a germ of life and supplies the rest from his imagination:

> If there is this amount of reason for referring the wayward heroine of Blithedale to Hawthorne's impression of the most distinguished woman of her day in Boston, that Margaret Fuller was the only literary lady of eminence whom there is any sign of his having known, that she was proud, passionate, and eloquent, that she was much connected with the little world of Transcendentalism out of which the experiment of Brook Farm

sprung, and that she had a miserable end and a watery grave—
if these are facts to be noted on one side, I say; on the other, the
beautiful and sumptuous Zenobia, with her rich and picturesque temperament and physical aspects, offers many points of
divergence from the plain and strenuous invalid who represented feminine culture in the suburbs of the New England metropolis. This picturesqueness of Zenobia is very happily indicated and maintained; she is a woman, in all the force of the
term, and there is something very vivid and powerful in her
large expression of womanly gifts and weaknesses.[8]

James is convincing that the *germ* of Zenobia came from
Margaret Fuller, and Margaret Fuller was a person who outraged, bothered and threatened Hawthorne. Why else would
he write such vindictive and ugly words about her after her
death as these?

> She had not the charm of womanhood. . . . she had a strong
> and coarse nature, which she had done the utmost to refine,
> with infinite pains; but of course it could only be superficially
> changed. . . . Margaret has not left in the hearts and minds of
> those who knew her any deep witness of her integrity and pu-
> rity. She was a great humbug. . . . she had stuck herself full of
> borrowed qualities, which she chose to provide herself with,
> but which had no root in her. . . . It was such an awful joke,
> that she should have resolved to make herself the greatest, wis-
> est, best woman of the age. And to that end she set to work on
> her strong, heavy, unpliable, and in many respects, defective
> and evil nature, and adorned it with a mosaic of admirable
> qualities such as she chose to possess.[9]

Coverdale, both attracted to and repelled by Zenobia, makes
similar pronouncements: "Her mind was full of weeds," he
says at one point (but he goes on to describe "the flesh-
warmth over her round arms, and what was visible of her full
bust,—in a word, her womanliness incarnated," which com-
pels him to close his eyes). And gazing at her grave he thinks
about "the tuft of ranker vegetation that grew out of Zenobia's heart."

Hawthorne, after all, needed to protect that part of himself that was engaged to be married to Sophia Peabody, to whom he wrote in 1841: "And what wilt thou do today, my persecuted little Dove, when thy abiding place will be a Babel of talkers? Would that Miss Margaret Fuller might lose her tongue!" [10] Margaret Fuller, meanwhile, was committing the ideas of her tongue to her pen, and it was probably from such notions that the economic dependence of woman upon man makes her "a child, or a ward only, not an equal partner," [11] that he wished to shield Sophia. Fuller's words sound much like Zenobia's when she writes: "The very fault of marriage, and of the present relation of the sexes, [is] that the woman does belong to the man instead of forming a whole with him. . . . Woman, self-centered, would never be absorbed by any relation; it would be only an experience to her as to men. It is a vulgar error that love, a love to woman is her whole existence; she is also born for Truth and Love in their universal energy." [12]

This is the inconsistency of Zenobia's death—that a woman who speaks out for the independence of woman should be totally absorbed by her relation to a man who discards her. Like Milton's Eve, Zenobia would correct "what wants in female sex"—a female identity separate from that of her husband. "Did you ever see a happy woman in your life?" she asks Coverdale. "How can she be happy, after discovering that fate has assigned her but one single event, which she must contrive to make the substance of her whole life?" "Thus far," she says later, "no woman in the world has ever once spoken out her whole heart and her whole mind. The mistrust and disapproval of the vast bulk of society throttles us, as with two gigantic hands at our throats!" Zenobia—at least that part of her which is modeled after Margaret Fuller—is an intellectual. Her knowledge, like Eve's, is dangerous: it gives her the ability to speak out against traditional attitudes; it gives her an awareness of her own identity, and the courage to refuse to stay in her prescribed place. She is dangerous not because she is intrinsically evil, but because she is willing to suspend the law of established convention and authority and operate according to her own moral law. *Her* sphere threatens to encroach upon that of the male because "The sphere of ordinary womanhood was felt to be narrower than her development required."

Attempting to transcend the limits of one's traditional role is the classical manifestation of the "flaw" which dooms the tragic hero or heroine. Thus in confusing (or choosing to ignore) traditional sexual roles, Zenobia is doomed from the beginning, for her knowledge and her attempt to take for herself traditionally "male" privileges are incompatible with her "feminine" passion for Hollingsworth. Zenobia's attempted subversion of traditional roles has also made her vulnerable to a devil like Westervelt, and Hawthorne emphasizes this point by having Westervelt be the only one to see her death as ironic. Coverdale, at Zenobia's funeral, rationalizes her death: "Everything had failed her;—prosperity in the world's sense, for her opulence was gone,—the heart's prosperity, in love. And there was a secret burthen on her. . . . Young as she was, she had tried life fully, had no more to hope, and something, perhaps, to fear." But Westervelt judges her death as "an idle thing—a foolish thing. . . . She was the last woman in the world to whom death could have been necessary. It was too absurd!" These are the words of the devil—that the life of woman should have meaning in itself, apart from her relationship to a man.

It is tragic and ironic that Zenobia loves Hollingsworth, this man who intended only to use her to gain his own selfish ends. His sentiments are those of patriarchal society beginning with Adam [13] when he says of woman: "She is the most admirable handiwork of God, *in her true place and character.* Her place is at man's side. . . . the echo of God's own voice, pronouncing, 'It is well done!' All the separate action of woman is, and ever has been and always shall be, false, foolish, vain, destructive of her own best and holiest qualities, void of every good effect, and productive of intolerable mischiefs! Man is a wretch without woman; but woman is a monster . . . without man as her acknowledged principal!

. . . The heart of true womanhood knows where its sphere is, and never seeks to stray beyond it!" (emphasis added). Yet Hollingsworth offers nothing in return for these demands. The reason women are dissatisfied with their conventional role, Zenobia says, is because men are not godlike—and she has good examples in the men she knows. Old Moodie, her shabby father, "had laid no real touch on any mortal's heart," while Westervelt, Hollingsworth and Coverdale would use her for their own purposes—Westervelt for something insidious and mysterious, Hollingsworth to fulfill his monomaniacal fantasy of reforming criminals and Coverdale "to turn the whole affair into a ballad." In her final words to Hollingsworth she blames the fallibility of woman *and* man ultimately on God:

> I am a woman, with every fault, it may be, that a woman ever had—weak, vain, unprincipled . . . passionate, too, and by pursuing my foolish and unattainable ends by indirect and cunning, through absurdly chosen means, as an hereditary bond-slave must; false, moreover, to the whole circle of good I saw before me,—but still a woman! A creature whom only a little change of earthly fortune, a little kinder smile of Him who sent me hither, and one true heart to encourage and direct me, might have made all that a woman can be!

Does Zenobia mean that "a little change of . . . fortune" might have made Hollingsworth love her, might have made him more godlike, might have spared her her earlier connection with Westervelt which has somehow poisoned her life, or might have made her a man, not "an hereditary bond-slave"? It is hard to say: Zenobia is a complex character, and her complexity is compounded by Hawthorne's ambivalence toward her—and I do not mean deliberate artistic ambivalence, but rather psychological defense-building. Such ambivalence is revealed in Coverdale's final statement on Zenobia, in which he admits the truth of Westervelt's observations: "It was a woful [*sic*] thought, that a woman of Zenobia's diversified capacity should have fancied herself irretrievably defeated on the battle-field of life, and with no refuge, save to fall on her own sword, merely because Love had gone against her. It is nonsense, and a miserable wrong,—the result, like so many others, of masculine egotism,—that the success or failure of woman's existence should be made to depend wholly on the affections, and on one species of affection, while man has such a multitude of other chances that this seems but a mere incident." But then he adds, "For its own sake, if it will do no more, the world should throw open all its avenues to the passport of a woman's bleeding heart." His thoughts start out like Zenobia's "I am a woman" speech, reflecting on the injustice of woman's position, but he does not follow this thought to its logical conclusion—that if the position is false, it should be changed. Instead, his thoughts take him to sympathy for "woman's bleeding heart," and then to a confession of his own love for Priscilla, the pale, submissive helpmeet. This is consistent ambivalence for Coverdale, however; his mind works by a kind of ambivalent logic. His earlier comment, that it is "odd" that "the kind of labor which falls to the lot of women is just that which chiefly distinguishes artificial life," does not lead him to the conclusion that such labor ought to be shared by men, but rather that it is a pity that "housework generally, cannot be left out of our system altogether!" After all, "Eve had no dinner-pot." This is the same kind of reasoning that leads him to feel for "woman's bleeding heart," the same that leads him to reflect that women behave as they do because of "ages of compelled degradation," and that Priscilla, whose "impalpable grace" lies "singularly between disease and beauty"—and who, as I have pointed out earlier, might be the *real* degraded woman—is his ideal. This ambivalence about women comes out most strongly whenever he thinks about Zenobia. He feels "an influence breathing out of her such as we might suppose to come from Eve, when she was just made, and her Creator brought her to Adam, saying, 'Behold! here is a woman!' . . . a certain warm and rich characteristic, which seems, for the most part, to have been refined away out of the feminine system." But he also, imagining her "in Eve's earliest garment," feels that her "free, careless, generous modes of expression" have the effect of creating images which are "hardly felt to be quite decorous when born of a thought that passes between man and woman." Coverdale is *ashamed* of his sexual attraction to Zenobia: "I acknowledged it as a masculine grossness,—a sin of wicked interpretation. . . . Still, it was of no avail to reason with myself, nor to upbraid myself. Pertinaciously the thought, 'Zenobia is a wife,—Zenobia has lived and loved! There is no folded petal, no latent dew-drop, in this perfectly-developed rose!'—irresistibly that thought drove out all other conclusions."

Significantly, all of these reflections about Zenobia are made from Coverdale's "sick-chamber"; in fact, it is probably Zenobia's threatening sexuality which has caused him to retreat into illness. His later dream about Zenobia provides a clue to the anxiety which she arouses. In that dream, it will be remembered, Hollingsworth and Zenobia stand on either side of his bed and exchange a kiss of passion, while Priscilla peeps in at the window and, beholding the kiss, melts gradually away. Clearly Priscilla is only the shadowy snow-maiden, but Hollingsworth and Zenobia are parent figures, and I think there is a connection here between the incest fears aroused by Coverdale's sexual attraction to Zenobia and Hawthorne's ambivalence about full-blooded, powerful, deviant and independent women, like Beatrice Rappaccini, Hester Prynne, Miriam and Zenobia. This is why he has Zenobia, with malicious intent, stick a weed "of evil odor and ugly aspect" in the crown of flowers with which she bedecks Priscilla; flowers are always associated with Zenobia's sexuality, and the weeds are an attempt to degrade it, to make it ugly, like the weeds of her mind and the rank growth of her heart. This is why he associates her with Westervelt, whose identity is symbolized by his walking stick carved in vivid imitation of a serpent: "Whatever stain Zenobia had was caught from him; nor does it seldom happen that a character of admirable qualities loses its better life because the atmosphere that should sustain it is rendered poisonous by such breath as this man mingled with Zenobia's." This is why he makes her a fallen Eve—her fallen state being especially clear when she is removed from the "counterfeit Arcadia" of Blithedale and seen in her "natural" environment, the city. There she wears not a hothouse flower, but a jewelled one, a cold and bright exquisite imitation. There she is involved in some evil and manipulative business with Priscilla and Westervelt, and there she tells Coverdale: "Why should we be content with our homely life of a few months past, to the exclusion of all other modes? It was good, but there are other lives as good, or better."

"Miles Coverdale," Zenobia tells him as Queen Zenobia of the masquerade, "You have come half an hour too late, and you have missed a scene which you would have enjoyed!" And she is right. Hawthorne/Coverdale has created a new woman whose vitality makes her a real person, not a doll; yet he rejects her for Sophia/Priscilla. While he recognizes the restrictiveness of "the sphere of ordinary womanhood" for a person of Zenobia's development, he would rather see her development retarded or halted altogether than her sphere broadened. In death, therefore, he hopes—and his hope "was mingled half with fear"—that she has finally submitted to patriarchal authority. He sees that her "wet garments swathed limbs of terrible inflexibility, . . . [that] her arms had grown rigid in the act of struggling, and were bent before her with clenched hands; her knees, too, were bent, and—thank God for it!—in the attitude of prayer." Coverdale *wants* to see her attitude as one of prayer, but in fact her arms "were bent before her, as if she struggled against Providence in never-ending hostility. Her hands! They were clenched in immitigable defiance." Is Hawthorne suggesting that Zenobia has *chosen* death as a gesture of defiance? This possibility would be a fitting heroic gesture for a tragedy-queen. More-over, Zenobia *knows* all along "that the whole universe, her own sex and yours, and Providence, or Destiny, to boot, make common cause against the woman who swerves one hair's breadth out of the beaten track." She knows that in a patriarchal society there is no place for the new woman, but she also knows that "in the battle-field of life, the downright stroke, that would fall only on a man's steel head-piece, is sure to light on a woman's heart, over which she wears no breastplate, and whose wisdom it is, therefore, to keep out of the conflict." Both, she says, are morals for the story. Silas Foster's observation that Hollingsworth's pole has "wounded the poor thing's breast, . . . close by her heart, too," and Coverdale's hope that her clenched hands represent an atti-tude of prayer, suggest their hope of her submission, and also their fear that even in death Zenobia has defied them all.

The important thing is that Zenobia, the new woman, must die; the fallen Eve is doomed from the beginning. The likelihood of her surviving as an independent woman out-side her prescribed sphere is exactly the same as the likeli-hood of the survival of Blithedale as new Eden in its break with history. "We had imparted a show of novelty to exist-ence, and contemplated it as hopefully as if the soil beneath our feet had not been fathom-deep with the dust of deluded generations," Coverdale reflects. But he holds out little hope for the actual survival of this new way of life: "On the whole, it was a society such as has seldom met together; nor, per-haps, could it reasonably be expected to hold together long. Persons of marked individuality—crooked sticks, as some of us might be called—are not exactly the easiest to bind up into a fagot. . . . Our bond, it seems to me, was not affirmative, but negative. We had individually found one thing or an-other to quarrel with in our past life, and were pretty well agreed as to the expediency of lumbering along with the old system any further." The old system will prevail even in utopia, however, and the most negative aspect of the bond of the communitarians will be the death of Zenobia, the woman who dares to swerve more than a hair's breadth out of the beaten track.

THE UNNATURAL LADY REFORMERS OF BOSTON

Olive Chancellor

James admired Zenobia as Hawthorne's most complete person; yet when he came to create his own lady-reformer, he could hardly have created less of a *person*. Zenobia and Olive Chancellor could not be more different: where Zenobia is almost defined by her sexuality, Olive has "absolutely no figure" and is "unmarried by every implication of her being"; where Zenobia's laugh is mellow, delectable, "not in the least like an ordinary woman's laugh," Olive is "a woman without laughter," her smile is one of exceeding faintness, like "a thin ray of moonlight resting upon the wall of a prison"; where Zenobia is characterized by warmth and associated with hearth-fires, summer sun and hothouse flowers, Olive's eyes have "the glitter of green ice" and she gives "a certain appearance of feeling cold." James had felt the least felicitous part of *The Blithedale Romance* to be the domination of Priscilla by Zenobia; when he came to write his novel about the "new woman," he made the domination of Verena the central issue.[14] Both Hawthorne and James were concerned in these two novels with "that difficult business known as the relations of the sexes." But where Hawthorne equated strength and independence in his women—Hester and Miriam as well as Zenobia—with threatening sexuality and made his lady-reformer the most passionate of his women, James made Olive Chancellor his most perverted woman, stressing the difference between his own time and Hawthorne's, when, because there was not at Brook Farm "the faintest adumbration of a rearrangement" of that difficult business, "the relations of the sexes were neither more nor less than what they usually are in American life, excellent." [15]

Unlike Zenobia, Olive Chancellor hates her sexuality, as her name suggests. Olive connotes greenness—unripeness, the green glitter of her cold eyes, the green of jealousy—and sourness. Although Olive is of an old Boston family, the name Chancellor is more than an ironic reference to qualities of leadership and tradition; it also suggests Olive's guardianship of the chancel, the sacred space of a church. The religious imagery in the book, cited earlier, suggests that as the self-appointed protectress of Verena, it is Olive's greatest wish to keep the girl pure and uncontaminated by men. Olive's focus in the women's movement is not the achievement of sexual equality between women and men, but hatred of men. For her, the great revolution will have come when the scales are reversed and women dominate men. "The unhappiness of women!" she thinks. "The voice of their silent suffering was always in her ears, the ocean of tears that they had shed from the beginning of time seemed to pour through her own eyes. Ages of oppression had rolled over them; uncounted millions had lived only to be tortured, to be crucified. They were her sisters, they were her own, and the day of their delivery had dawned. This was the only sacred cause; this was the great, the just revolution. It must triumph, it must sweep everything before it; it must exact from the other, the brutal, bloodstained, ravening race, the last particle of expiation!"

The exaggerated language—the oceans of tears, the beginning of time, the uncounted millions, and so on—makes the extent of James's mockery of Olive clear. If "she saw the matter through a sort of sunrise-mist of emotion," his own presentation of "the matter" is not without emotion. His hostility here is not sufficiently transmuted by irony because the issue was doubly serious for him. I have mentioned James's notebook entry just prior to beginning *The Bostonians*—his wish to write a very American tale, and his decision that such a tale must describe the "situation of women."

There is, however, another notation—a single word scrawled across the flyleaf of the *Correspondence of Thomas Carlyle and Ralph Waldo Emerson,* which James had reviewed just after the death of his father and of Emerson. The word is "Reformers," and it refers to a passage marked in a letter of Emerson's: "We are all a little wild here with numberless projects of social reform." In this novel, then, James brought together the two subjects which most troubled him and which he saw as the salient conditions of American life— Boston reformers and the "situation of women." [16] James, like Hawthorne, believed that women are supposed to be the preservers of culture ("the keystone of the arch"), but in this capacity they often become manipulative, possessive, destructive. And here is a woman combining these dangerous qualities with a drive to revolutionize society by destroying the "normal" relationship between the sexes. It is appropriate, then, that Olive Chancellor, the potential symbol of a new matriarchal order, be drawn as fanatical, frigid, defensive, destructive and perverted.

Because what she stands for is a serious threat, Olive herself must be made ridiculous. Her "liberation" is a fantasy— the fantasy of an impotent woman. There is nothing that she can *do* on a personal level to transform her fantasies into reality. In response to Mrs. Farrinder's request that she speak publicly, for example, she confesses that she has no self-possession. She can only give her money. Where the logic of sexual oppression has made some women (and men) aware of the extent to which social power is tied to economic power, Olive's "revolution" would never take her to the extreme of upsetting the economic foundations of the social order; she is too much a part of that order. Neither, of course, would she dream of experimenting with alternative life styles, like some of her contemporaries who joined utopian communities for that purpose; she cannot love men in any way. Thus Verena's views about "free unions" (and Verena has been raised in a variety of communal experiments) make Olive "close her eyes in the manner of a person waiting till giddiness passed."

Olive's denial of her own sexuality is brought home in every scene in which she appears. It is there in her shallow smile; it is there in the way she dresses—"in a plain dark dress, without any ornaments"—and in her smooth, color-less, carefully confined hair; it is there in the way she extends her "cold and limp" hand to Ransom, merely placing it in his, "without exerting the smallest pressure," and when she refuses to take his hand at all because "she could not have let him touch her." Olive's cold control masks a deep sense of insecurity which manifests itself as a violent distrust of men. It is this distrust that makes so tense her carriage ride with Basil, so urgent her necessity to get Verena away from her fa-ther, and so decided her refusal to let the journalist Matthias Pardon have anything to do with Verena and herself. "She had not that promise of success which resides in a will-ingness to make use of every aid that offers," James com-ments. "Such is the penalty of being of a fastidious, exclu-sive, uncompromising nature; of seeing things not simply and sharply, but in perverse relations, in intertwisted strands. It seemed to our young lady that nothing could be less attractive than to owe her emancipation to such a one as Matthias Pardon. . . . I suppose it was because he was a man."

Olive recognizes her fear—she has "a fear of every-thing"—but for her fear is an improper emotion and "her greatest fear was of being afraid." Her sister, who has no fear and no sense of propriety, describes Olive as "full of recti-tude." Thus Olive, who dislikes above all to take risks, has nevertheless "erected it into a sort of rule of conduct that whenever she saw a risk she was to take it; and she had frequent humiliations at finding herself safe after all." Poor Olive does suffer frequent humiliations, but this only makes her all the more "strenuous," as Basil calls her. "She gave him an uneasy feeling—the sense that you could never be safe with a person who took things so hard." He realizes that "it was because she took things hard she had sought his acquaintance; it had been because she was strenuous, not because she was genial; she had in her eye—and what an extraordinary eye it was!—not pleasure, but a duty." Olive's compulsive sense of duty, "like a skiff in a stormy sea," seeks its channel through such actions as riding the streetcar when she can afford a carriage, or patronizing penniless shop girls, but is rudderless until in a general way she finds the women's movement and then, in a much more specific way, she finds Verena. She can refight the Civil War now in fighting to free women from slavery as her brothers had fought to free the black slaves, and, on a personal level, she can fight the Southern male chauvinist Basil Ransom for possession of Verena.

The scenes in which Olive "takes possession" of Verena are clearly sexual to twentieth-century readers. Olive speaks always to Verena with passion and with anxiety, as for example, when she attempts to extract a promise from Verena not to marry. We see her throw herself "on Verena's neck with a movement which was half indignation, half rapture. . . . If they were all in all to each other, what more could they want? They would be isolated, but they would be free." A woman who dislikes to be touched, Olive is continuously lifting Verena's hand to her lips, and on one occasion, "She came to her slowly, took her in her arms and held her long—giving her a silent kiss." When she is sure that she has lost Verena to Ransom, she feels "a wild personal passion, a desire to take her friend in her arms again on any terms, even the most cruel to herself." Clearly such scenes were meant by James to portray a perverted relationship, "a matter for whispered communications." But as I have pointed out, I think James was less concerned with whether Olive took actual sexual possession of Verena than with the act of possession itself.[17] He would allow, I think, for strong friendship between women of a sort that is not common in the twentieth century, but sees as perverted the attempt of one human being to dominate and manipulate another and the self-immolation which Olive experiences—even desires—as part of this relationship.

Sadly, ironically, Olive has never even understood Verena. She has seen Verena as a means of winning vicarious triumph and esteem for herself, but she has been blind to the girl's secret wish to be like Mrs. Luna, who is as frivolous as Olive is severe and intense, and who is primarily motivated by a desire to attract men. She has been blind to Verena's own pleasure in the company of men and to the essential fact about Verena—that she has been trained by her father to be a weak and yielding (if attractive) tool, a medium, nothing more. Olive has seen Verena as someone for whom she can sacrifice herself—not, of course, without personal gain—but this martyrdom is a basic part of Olive's nature, not a result of her relationship with Verena. Her final self-immolation, then, is in a way her final triumph. Even though she loses Verena, even though she is about to submit herself to humiliation and disgrace at the close of the novel, James gives the impression that this is what Olive has really wanted all along—to be crucified. As Ransom is about to depart with Verena in that final scene, he looks at Olive and observes that where she had been weak, she is not weak now. "She had straightened herself again, and she was upright in her desolation. The expression of her face was a thing to remain with him forever; it was impossible to imagine a more vivid presentiment of blighted hope and wounded pride. Dry, desperate, rigid, she yet wavered and seemed uncertain; her pale, glittering eyes straining forward, as if they were looking for death. Ransom had a vision, even at the crowded moment, that if she could have met it there and then, bristling with steel or lurid with fire, she would have rushed on it without a tremor, like the heroine that she was." These last words are ironic to say the least, as James underscores by his use of the conditional in his final words on Olive: "If he [Basil] had observed her, it *might have seemed to him* that she hoped to find the fierce expiration she sought. . . . She *might have suggested to him* some feminine firebrand" (emphasis added). But James has not made Olive a heroine; he has made her tragedy pathos, her agony ridiculous.

If Hawthorne was threatened by the powerful and independent new woman, he was also attracted to her; he made her beautiful, compelling, heroic and tragic. But for James she was only dry, strenuous, perverted and ridiculous; she had to be—otherwise her threatening, possessive, manipulative, destructive nature could not be kept within bounds. Olive Chancellor may be a woman without humor, but Henry James was not without humor—a vicious, unhealthy kind of humor that reveals as much about its author as about his character—in creating her.

Miss Birdseye

Miss Birdseye is supposedly modeled on Elizabeth Peabody, Boston reformer and sister of Sophia Peabody Hawthorne. If this is the case, James certainly reduced her, too, to a ridiculous and pathetic caricature, for the real woman was a leader in both social reform and education. One of her most important contributions to American letters is her publication of Thoreau's "Civil Disobedience" as "Resistance to Civil Government" in her journal, *Aesthetic Papers*, in 1849. Her Boston home was the scene of Margaret Fuller's conversational classes, her bookshop was the meeting place of the Transcendentalist Club, she opened the first American kindergarten in 1860, and she was a prolific writer of essays which appeared in *The Dial* and other publications. James's Miss Birdseye has none of the sense of the real achievement of Elizabeth Peabody. Miss Birseye is a beloved old lady; benevolent, well meaning and slightly ridiculous, she is taken seriously only within her own circle. James, however, denied that he had used Elizabeth Peabody in creating Miss Birdseye. His defense in answer to his brother William's protest of his so doing is the typical Jamesian argument about taking only the germ of an idea from actual life and supplying the rest from his imagination:

> I absolutely had no shadow of such an intention. I have not seen Miss P. for twenty years, I never had but the most casual observation of her, I didn't know whether she was alive or dead, and she was not in the smallest degree my starting-point or example. Miss Birdseye was evolved entirely from my moral consciousness, like every other person I have ever drawn, and originated in my desire to make a figure who should embody in a sympathetic, pathetic, picturesque, and at the same time grotesque way, the humanitary and ci-deviant transcendental tendencies which I thought it highly probable I should be accused of treating in a contemptuous manner in so far as they were otherwise represented in the tale. I wished to make this figure a woman, because so it would be more touching, and an old, weary, battered, and simple-minded woman because that deepened the same effect. I elaborated her in my mind's eye—and after I had got going reminded myself that my creation would perhaps be identified with Miss Peabody—*that* I freely admit. . . . The one definite thing about which I had a scruple was some touch about Miss Birdseye's spectacles—I remembered that Miss Peabody's were always in the wrong place; but I didn't see, really, why I should deprive myself of an effect (as regards this point) which is common to a thousand old people. So I thought no more about Miss P. at all, but simply strove to realize my vision.[18]

I think the gentleman doth protest too much; his "after I had got going [I] reminded myself . . ." is no more convincing than Hawthorne's disclaimer about Zenobia and Margaret Fuller. But whether James has reduced Elizabeth Peabody to Miss Birdseye, or whether he has reduced women reformers in general like her and like Susan B. Anthony, Elizabeth Cady Stanton and a number of others to "old, weary, battered, and simple-minded," the point is that he has reduced her, simultaneously reducing the "humanitary and ci-deviant transcendental tendencies" to the pathetic and grotesque. To name his lady-reformer "Miss Birdseye" is to render her diminutive, and that is almost enough. There is more, however.

Miss Birdseye is not only diminutive; she is grotesque. James's description of her head brings to mind some enormous egg balanced on little sticks of legs, a Humpty-Dumpty sort of lady: it is "an enormous head . . .—the vast protuberant, candid ungarnished brow, surmounting a pair of weak, kind, tired-looking eyes, and ineffectually balanced in the rear by a cap which had the air of falling backward, and which Miss Birdseye suddenly felt for while she talked, with unsuccessful irrelevant movements." The movements of the body attached to this enormous head are *irrelevant*—that is, they are uncoordinated, meaningless, frivolous. And the expression on the face of this enormous head is as blurred and vague as the movements of the body: "She had a sad, soft, pale face, which (and it was the effect of her whole head) looked as if it had been soaked, blurred, and made vague by exposure to some slow dissolvent. The long practice of philanthropy had not given accent to her features; it had rubbed out their transitions, their meanings." One senses that this is what James would have liked to do to all the lady-reformers—expose them to some slow dissolvent. As if the egghead were not enough, James made Miss Birdseye harmless by rendering her body sexless: "She always dressed in the same way: she wore a loose black jacket with deep pockets, which were stuffed with papers, memoranda of a voluminous correspondence; and from beneath her jacket depended a short stuff dress. The brevity of this simple garment was the one device by which Miss Birdseye managed to suggest that she was a woman of business, that she wished to be free for action." Her clothes are stuffed not with her feminine body, but with voluminous correspondence, and her short skirts expose not her legs, but that she is a woman of business who wishes to be free for action(!)—until the final point, where James once again cannot contain his viciousness: she is a "confused, entangled, inconsequent, discursive old woman." A very humorous description, this;

clever, too. No wonder James so vehemently disclaimed any identification of Miss Birdseye with an actual person!

Miss Birdseye's sexlessness, like Olive Chancellor's pervertedness, is emblematic of her general meaninglessness, and of the sterility and aridity of American life in which women had become the salient feature. If she is an "essentially formless old woman, who had no more outline than a bundle of hay," then we cannot believe Olive Chancellor's perception that Miss Birdseye is "heroic" and "sublime"— but of course this is just another sign of Olive's perverted vision. Olive is perhaps right, however, when she observes that Miss Birdseye "had the smallest sense of the real," that she is "provincial." But if "the whole moral history of Boston was reflected" in Miss Birdseye's "displaced spectacles," that doesn't say much either for the moral history of Boston or for Miss Birdseye's vision; her glasses reflect that history rather than take it in, and since they are "displaced," her vision is necessarily skewed. Miss Birdseye is, however, relieved by gentle touches of humor of her own. She responds to Basil Ransom's exaggerated Southern politeness—"Wherever you go, madam, it will matter little what you carry. You will always carry your good name"—with "That's the way Olive Chancellor told me you talked." Perhaps James can allow her this because she lacks all the qualities he found so threatening in women: sexuality, possessiveness, assertiveness, manipulation. This seems to be the case when he turns the humor *on* her. She responds to Ransom's "I consider women have no business to be reasonable" with "Do you regard us, then, simply as lovely baubles?" And the effect of this question, "as coming from Miss Birdseye, and referring in some degree to her own venerable identity, was such as to move him [and James] to irresistible laughter."

There is little more to say about Miss Birdseye. She dies at the end of the book as quietly and cheerfully as she has lived, leaving an impression of "simplicity and humility." She has been just a sketch, not a central focus. Basil Ransom probably speaks for James when he reflects during the days following her death that "the absence of pomp and circumstance which had marked her career marked also the consecration of her memory. She had been almost celebrated, she had been active, earnest, ubiquitous beyond anyone else, she had given herself utterly to charities and creeds and causes; and yet the only persons, apparently, to whom her death made a real difference were three young women in a small 'frame-house' on Cape Cod."

Mrs. Farrinder

There is nothing confused and inconsequent about Mrs. Farrinder; she is a "lioness," but her strength is less than fearsome because she is so seldom present. She appears only twice, and both times this "great representative of the enfranchisement of their sex" serves to put down Olive Chancellor. The first time is when Verena Tarrant is introduced to the feminists at Miss Birdseye's. Mrs. Farrinder is described there as the opposite of Miss Birdseye; she is "copious," "handsome" and "angular," but her angularity has been "corrected by the air of success." She has "abundant hair of a glossy blackness," but this potential symbol of sexuality is corrected by "a pair of folded arms, the expression of which seemed to say that rest, in a career such as hers, was as sweet as it was brief, and a terrible regularity of feature." Mrs. Farrinder, it appears, is the Great Mother gone public—she has "a mixture of the American matron and the public character"—and in the description of her "public eye" one feels the threat of the devouring woman: "[it] was large, cold and quiet; it had acquired a sort of exposed reticence from the habit of looking down from a lecture desk, over a sea of heads."

Mrs. Farrinder is a person to reckon with; in any intercourse she sets the pace: "She talked with great slowness and distinctness, and evidently a high sense of responsibility; she pronounced every syllable of every word and insisted on being explicit. If, in conversation with her, you attempted to take anything for granted, or to jump two or three steps at a time, she paused, looking at you with a cold patience, as if she knew that trick, and then went on at her own measured pace." Mrs. Farrinder would reverse the whole social order; "the ends she labored for were to give the ballot to every woman in the country and to take the flowing bowl from every man." But this matriarch would not abandon the hearth to rule from the podium; rather, with her fine manner she is an embodiment of "the domestic virtues and the graces of the drawing room, . . . a shining proof, in short, that the forum, for ladies, is not necessarily hostile to the fireside." The importance of men in this new scheme where ladies rule both the country and the home is indicated by the terseness of the final sentence of this description of Mrs. Farrinder: "She had a husband, and his name was Amariah."

Had James fully developed this combination of the majestic woman and American matron to whom men are mere appendages, one can guess that she would have been like Aunt Maud, like Mrs. Gereth, or perhaps like Mrs. Newsome. She would not, however, have been like Olive Chancellor; to make one feel Mrs. Farrinder's sense of her own power is the main purpose of this description—to show how different a real woman leader is from poor, perverted Olive. Mrs. Farrinder has leadership qualities, self-possession and nobility. She is the only one of the women in the novel who is not at some point described in diminutive terms; Mrs. Farrinder is "copious." She serves—as Basil Ransom cannot serve because he is male, Southern, and as insecure about his masculinity as Olive is about her femininity—to make Olive ridiculous. On that first occasion Mrs. Farrinder brings out great passion in the reserved Olive: "I can't talk to those people, I can't!" Olive tells her. "I want to give myself up to others; I want to know everything that lies beneath and out of sight, don't you know? I want to enter into the lives of women who are lonely, who are piteous. I want to be near to them—to help them. I want to do something—Oh, I should like so to speak!" But Mrs. Farrinder is all business. If she can't speak, then "What *have* you got?" Mrs. Farrinder asks coldly. "Have you got money?" This mercenary handling of the hypersensitive Olive does not humiliate her, but places her under a spell. It is at this point that Olive has her rosy vision of the crucifixion of women and the expiation of the "brutal, bloodstained, ravening race."

The other time we see Mrs. Farrinder is the scene of Olive's great martyrdom, when Ransom comes to prevent Verena from giving her speech and carries her off, leaving Olive to face the angry and impatient crowd alone. Mrs. Farrinder's words—"Well, Miss Chancellor, . . . if this is the way you're going to reinstate our sex!"—are a sudden lash. But they serve to transform Olive from wavering uncertainty to a state of such sudden inspiration that she is ready to offer herself "to be trampled to death and torn to pieces." That is as much as we see of Mrs. Farrinder. It was probably enough for Henry James.

Dr. Prance

Like the name "Birdseye," the name "Prance" has diminutive connotations. Prancing suggests the hurried way in which the doctor moves; it is a series of small, rapid, dancing steps, more like a trot than a gallop. It also suggests, at least to me, the quality of prancing around in a circle, going nowhere. Dr. Prance *is* little; she is always referred to in terms of her smallness—"little Dr. Prance" engaged in her "own little revolution." Her littleness, like Miss Birdseye's, goes along with an absence of sexuality. To Basil Ransom she is "a perfect example of the 'Yankee female'—the figure which, in the unregenerate imagination of the children of the cotton states, was produced by the New England school system, the Puritan code, the ungenial climate, the absence of chivalry. Spare, dry, hard, without a curve, an inflection or a grace, she seemed to ask no odds in the battle of life and to be prepared to give none." Not only does Dr. Prance lack the sexuality which Basil likes to see in a woman, but she is a totally asexual being: "She looked like a boy, and not even like a good boy. It was evident that if she had been a boy, she would have 'cut' school, to try private experiments in mechanics or to make researches in natural history. It was true that if she had been a boy she would have borne some relation to a girl, whereas Doctor Prance appeared to bear none whatever. Except her intelligent eye, she had no features to speak of."

Dr. Prance is a woman without humor, but not like the "lioness," Mrs. Farrinder; she, too, is all business, but not like Olive Chancellor. She is simply a one-track person, completely dedicated to her profession, but as such, totally devoid of any of the "feminine" qualities of softness, grace, charm. "Men and women are all the same to me," she tells Ransom. "I don't see any difference. There is room for improvement in both sexes. Neither of them is up to standard." Dr. Prance is as clipped and to the point as her prose; she is a reduction of a person to its most spare and hard. She looks just about as she speaks: "She was a plain, spare young woman, with short hair and an eyeglass; she looked about her with a kind of nearsighted deprecation, and seemed to hope that she should not be expected to generalize in any way." Yet, although James seems to be saying that a woman who devotes herself to a profession is devoid of all other qualities, there is something likeable about her. Basil, like James, does not know quite how to deal with this reduction of a woman, whether to offer her a cigar or a seat on the fence. He finally goes fishing with her—in silence, one presumes.

Dr. Prance is not of great importance in *The Bostonians;* she is just one of a series of sketches intended to show the possibilities of the feminine sphere removed from that of the male: a dried-up, perverted, hysterical spinster; a confused, entangled, discursive old woman; a noble lioness with a nonentity for a husband; an asexual professional person. The possibilities are not rich; they do not bode well for the increasingly feminized culture of America. Dr. Prance is interesting in her own right, however, as one of the first portraits in American literature of the professional woman. She provides an interesting contrast to her less professional and more womanly counterpart, Howells's Dr. Breen.

THROUGH THE EYE OF THE NEEDLE

Dr. Breen

Howells should have called *Dr. Breen's Practice* "The Romance of Dr. Breen," for Grace Breen has no practice to speak of; the novel describes how she, like any sentimental heroine, mends her broken heart and gets a husband. *Dr. Breen's Practice* was published in 1881, two years before James began to write *The Bostonians,* but James could hardly have used Howells's lady doctor as a model for his own. Dr. Breen is not a new woman; she is but another portrait of "the American girl," whom Howells had delineated as the self-reliant innocent (Kitty) as early as 1873 in *A Chance Acquaintance,* and developed more fully as Lydia Blood in *The Lady of the Aroostook* (1879). Like her predecessors, Grace Breen has a kind of spunk which differentiates her from other women—"dependent and submissive invalids" whom men like Dr. Mulbridge regard with contemptuous amusement.[19] Unlike Howells's earlier heroines, however, Grace Breen is motivated more by a "Puritan" sense of duty than by her instincts, which she suppresses because she has been jilted and is afraid to expose the feeling side of herself again. In writing a story about Grace's rediscovery of her intuitive self, Howells created neither a happy woman nor a believable character. Whatever his intentions, his question—can a woman have both professional satisfaction and marriage?—can only be answered in the negative in this novel. The professional woman, whose husband has "a shrewder knowledge of her own nature than she had herself," is for Howells queer, but "no queerer than the charity to which many ladies devote themselves."

As a "realist" Howells might have modeled his Dr. Breen on such actual female physicians as the Blackwell sisters, who a quarter of a century before had experienced the same sort of self-doubt as Dr. Breen feels in embarking upon a traditionally male profession. Elizabeth Blackwell, like Grace Breen, found that the idea of becoming a doctor was more inspiring than the actual study and practice of medicine. "I am happy," she wrote, "in my steady work as medical practitioner, because in the present age, it has its universal bearings, as a new and noble field for women's work—but also, it has its monotonous routine of poor and insignificant relations, which drives me constantly within, for refreshment, and recreating strength. It is thus I imagine with every work in the present age, no matter how divine in itself, nor how glorious in its enthusiastic initiation—the practical application of grand ideas is necessarily a disappointment, and a degradation of the ideal." [20] What was for Elizabeth Blackwell a passing fear was for her sister Emily a lifelong doubt. "O my God," she wrote in 1856, "is the end of all my aspiration, of my prayers and dreams, to be that this long earnest struggle has been a mistake, that this life of a Physician is so utterly not my life that I can not express myself through it—and worse—worse—that I might have done more in other ways? . . . I could bear anything but the feeling of failure, show me the way, be with me!" [21] Howells could not have been familiar with the correspondence of the Blackwell sisters, but he would have known *about* them and about other women doctors as well, for as early as 1862 such a conservative publication as *Godey's Lady's Book* had advocated "the education of women for the treatment of women" as "the only remedy for concealment and irremediable disease." [22] When Howells created *his* lady doctor, however, he also had to keep in mind "the smiling aspects of American life." Although we get a sense of Dr. Breen's self-doubt, we get a greater sense of her as a lovely woman; although she struggles with self-definition throughout the book, she is really defined in every case by her relationship with men.

Grace Breen's womanliness is present from the first. She does not order her patients to do her bidding, as Dr. Mulbridge does, but pleads with her friend Louise not to sit outside. In dealing with the driver who delivers a prescription, she combines a "lady-like sweetness and a sort of business-like alertness." Howells (like Hawthorne) has his heroine take up her needle and thread on occasion, but ridicules her even in this occupation by having her get so entangled in her threads that Mr. Libby has to cut her loose—a symbol of the way in which he will later rescue her through marriage. Howells further discredits Dr. Breen by showing that her "feminine" concern about her patient's respectability outweighs her concern about her health: "I shall have to be plain and tell you that I can't have them sneering and laughing at any one who is my guest. I can't let you defy public opinion here," she tells Mrs. Maynard. But her patient easily bests Grace by reminding the doctor that she herself is the more scandalous in pursuing an unwomanly profession. We see Dr. Breen blush, we see her cry and we see men continually respond to her as a physically attractive woman. If she is involved in a struggle between her essentially feminine nature and her "Puritan" sense of duty, it isn't much of a struggle; Grace knows all along what she is—she only has to find it out.

Part of Grace's problem is her mother. Mrs. Breen, not her daughter, would have grown up with the Blackwells. Hers is the era of the strong Hawthorne women, but her daughter's is the Victorian era, a time when women were bombarded with homemaking-as-profession advice, the impetus of the women's movement had abated, and novelists were creating Olive Chancellors rather than Zenobias. Mrs. Breen wants Grace to behave as a man would behave, and she praises her with "unwonted recognition." But Grace's self-doubt is articulated when she tells her mother: "No, I am not a man. I have accepted that, with all the rest. I don't rebel against being a woman. If I had been a man, I shouldn't have studied medicine. . . . I wished to be a physician because I was a woman, and because—because—I had failed where—other women's hopes are. . . . I think it's rather hard, mother, that you should be always talking as if I wished to take my calling mannishly; but as for not being a woman about it, or about anything, that's simply impossible. A woman is reminded of her insufficiency to herself every hour of the day."

It is because Dr. Breen is continually reminded of her own insufficiency that she is both so ready to relinquish her patient to a male doctor and so plagued with a sense of guilt about having caused Mrs. Maynard's illness. "I believe that if Mrs. Maynard had had the same confidence in me that she would have had in any man I should not have failed," she later tells Dr. Mulbridge. "But every woman physician has a double disadvantage that I hadn't the strength to overcome,—her own inexperience and the distrust of other women." Grace's biggest problem is her self-distrust. Her failure with Mrs. Maynard has so undermined her confidence in herself that she is ready to give up her profession altogether.

Grace's sense of professional insufficiency is reinforced by her social conditioning—which causes her to tell people, for example, that she does not care whether they call her "Miss Breen" or "Dr. Breen," and to tell Libby that if a woman loves a man, "it wouldn't be anything to give up everything" for him, for "a woman isn't something else first, and a woman afterwards!" Grace is surrounded with this kind of conditioning at Jocelyn's, where one of the ladies discussing Grace says, "Every young couple seen together must be considered in love till they prove the contrary," and another answers, "I like it in her. . . . It shows that she is human, after all . . . like the other girls. It's a relief." Dr. Mulbridge's perceptions are no different; he tells his mother: "the most advanced thinkers among those ladies are not so very different, after all, from you old-fashioned people. When they try to think of the greatest good fortune that can befall an ideal woman, it is to have her married. The only trouble is to find a man good enough; and if they can't find one, they're apt to invent one. They have strong imaginations." Unfortunately, he is right—not only about the ladies, but about Howells himself. When Libby blushes "when required to recognize Grace in her professional quality," one feels that Howells must be blushing, too. Even Miss Gleason, who idealizes Grace and follows her longingly with implicit homosexual attraction, gushingly confesses that "the perfect mastery of the man-physician constitutes the highest usefulness of the woman-physician." [23]

It is Dr. Mulbridge's sense of Grace's professional/personal conflict that makes him think that she will marry him. Although she has "a will and a temper of her own," he tells his mother, she is "cool and careful under instruction, and perfectly tractable and intelligent. . . . And she's made a failure in one way, and then you know a woman is in the humor to try it in another." He says the same thing to Grace: "Under my direction, you have shown yourself faithful, docile, patient, intelligent beyond anything I have seen." Although he offers her a chance to continue her profession in marriage to him, she has not missed the innuendoes of what he really values in her—her docility; nor does she miss the chauvinism in his statement about women: "of all the simpletons, the women who were trying to do something for women, . . . trying to exemplify and illustrate a cause, were the silliest that I came across." But he has misjudged her—he has been raised not by a Mrs. Breen, but by a Mrs. Mulbridge, who "had decided the girl to be particularly forth-putting, from something prompt and self-reliant in her manner . . . and she viewed with tacit disgust her son's toleration of a handsome young woman who had taken up a man's profession." Refusing his offer, Grace tells him, "I think you are a tyrant, and that you want a slave, not a wife. You wish to be obeyed. You despise women. I don't mean their minds,—they're despicable enough, in most cases, as men's are,—but their nature."

Grace is right about Dr. Mulbridge. The reader has earlier been told that "He liked to hear them talk, especially of their ideas of progress, as they called them, at which, with the ready adaptability of their sex, they joined him in laughing when they found that he could not take them seriously. The social, the emotional expression of the new scientific civilization struck him as droll, particularly in respect to the emancipation of women; and he sometimes gave these ladies the impression that he did not value woman's intellect at its true worth. . . . he conveyed the sense of his skepticism as to their fitness for some things to which the boldest of them aspired." Grace's reasons are both intellectual, however, and emotional—like Isabel Archer's. Her bold statement to Dr. Mulbridge occurs on the second occasion when he presses his suit. The first time she is not quite so sure of herself. She tells him then, "I don't believe in myself. I have no right to doubt you. I know that I ought to honor you for what you propose." The difference in the two statements indicates the degree of Grace's self-reliance: she is not afraid of Dr. Mulbridge the second time "Because . . . I'm engaged,—engaged to Mr. Libby!"

Walter Libby is a lightweight, but it is not hard to see why Grace, the ostensibly new woman, not only chooses to marry him, but is willing to renounce her profession to do so. He has been devoted to her from the beginning; he has been gentle; he has not threatened her. What he gives Grace is a renewed sense of self-esteem. Where Dr. Mulbridge praises in a condescending way her professionalism, Libby never pretends to be able to accept her professionally; he never supposes that she would continue to practice medicine married to him: "I knew it was selfish in me, and very conceited, to suppose you would give up your whole life for me," he tells her, but he praises her personally, as a woman. Libby gives her the sense of being needed rather than the sense of being swallowed up in someone else's identity. Under such circumstances, her feminine willingness to submit to him is suggested in her early use of his language: "A woman respects the word a man uses"—in this case "bobbish"—Howells says, "not because she would have chosen it, but because she thinks that he has an exact intention in it, which could not be reconveyed in a more feminine phrase."

In having Dr. Breen accept Walter Libby, and in reestablishing her as a doctor who cares for the children of her husband's employees, so that "the conditions under which she now exercises her skill certainly amount to begging the whole question of woman's fitness for the career she had chosen," Howells has consummated one of those ideal matches for the American girl: "It is thought . . . that he is a man of excellent head, and of a heart so generous that his deference to her in certain matters is part of the devoted flattery which would spoil any other woman, but that she consults his judgment in every action of her life, and trusts his sense with the same completeness that she trusts his love." Thus, *Dr. Breen's Practice* is but one more chapter in the history of the American girl who finds herself when she finds her man. As for the question of how much of herself she has sacrificed in marriage, "perhaps," Howells concludes, "it is not even decorous to ask."

Eveleth Strange

Howells's other "new woman," Eveleth Strange, also finds herself when she finds her man. *The Altrurian Romances* are indeed "romances" in the Hawthornian sense of "moonlight in a familiar room"; but *A Traveller from Altruria, Letters from an Altrurian Traveller* and *Through the Eye of the Needle* are "realistic" as well. They deal with the actual problems of filth in the streets; unemployment; the appalling disparity between rich and poor in manner, living conditions and morals; the ugliness of urbanization as a way of life for rich and poor alike; the discomfort of dressing according to fashion; the ill health of the inhabitants of the nineteenth century due to overwork or hypertension; and the "abyss of inequality" between men and women noted by James. Howells had long been a serious student of these kinds of issues. In *A*

Modern Instance (1881) he dealt with the question of divorce. In *The Rise of Silas Lapham* (1884) Silas's fall from worldly success is his rise in moral stature. In *A Hazard of New Fortunes* (1889) the old values of agrarianism are pitted against the new urban industrialism, and the issues of social and economic displacement, inequality and hypocrisy are explored. *The Altrurian Romances* are concerned with these same issues. One may read them "simply as . . . romance," one reviewer warned his *New York Times* readers, "or . . . as a serious study of sociology." [24]

Howells's Eve does not appear until *Through the Eye of the Needle*. She is appropriately named, for she *is* strange when compared to the "lady" of the nineteenth century, as described by Dolly Makely in *A Traveller from Altruria*:

> In the first place, a lady must be above the sordid anxieties in every way. She need not be very rich, but she must have enough, so that she need not be harrassed about making both ends meet, when she ought to be devoting herself to social duties. . . . She must have a certain kind of house, so that her entourage won't seem cramped and mean, and she must have nice frocks, of course, and plenty of them. She needn't be of the smart set; . . . but she can't afford to be out of fashion. Of course she must have a certain training. She must have cultivated tastes; she must know about art, and literature, and music, and all those kind of things, and though it isn't necessary to go in for anything in particular, it won't hurt to have a fad or two. The nicest kind of fad is charity. . . . A lady is busy from morning to night! She goes to bed perfectly worn out! . . . With making herself agreeable and her house attractive, with going to lunches, and teas, and dinners and concerts, and theatres, and art exhibitions, and charity meetings, and receptions, and writing a thousand and one notes about them, and accepting and declining, and giving lunches and dinners, and making calls and receiving them, and I don't know what all. It's the most hideous slavery!

Eveleth Strange, in contrast, acts according to her own moral law. "I used to be at school with her, and even then she wasn't like any of the other girls," Dolly explains to the Altrurian, Homos. "She was always so original, and did things from such a high motive." Eveleth defines herself as perhaps the only honest American woman, who admits she is unhappy despite Fortune's smiling on her in every way. "I'm quite satisfied," she tells Homos with sad mockery, "that fortune is a man, and an American; when he has given you all the materials for having a good time, he believes that you must be happy." The Altrurian falls in love with her for her very difference; she seems not of the type he has learned to distrust, the woman whose beauty and brilliance masks her inconsequence. They marry, despite some sentimental shilly-shally on Howells's part that seems unworthy of Eve Strange, and the Altrurian takes her "to heaven" with him. Once there, she learns what it is to be a free woman, to share the economic and political power with men, Bellamy-fashion.

Clearly Howells's intentions in his indictment of sexual inequality in nineteenth-century America were serious. But *The Altrurian Romances,* like *Looking Backward,* were written for the middle-class reader, and the Altrurian's condemnation of the status of American women reveals the same kind of unintentional insensitivity to women as do Howells's own "Editor's Easy Chair" columns in *Harper's Monthly Magazine.*[25] Men must pay a severe penalty for excluding women from political affairs, the Altrurian says, "for women are at once the best and the worst Americans: the best because their hearts are the purest, the worst because their heads are the idlest. . . . with all their cultivation, American women have no real intellectual interests, but only intellectual fads; and while they certainly think a great deal, they reflect little, or not at all." Eveleth Strange, then, despite her difference from the "ladies" of the nineteenth century, and despite her finding a new "sphere of duties" to share with men in Altruria, is no more a *person* than Grace Breen or any other Howellsian heroine. As a matter of fact, she is a good deal less "real" than her conventional literary sisters.

EDNA PONTELLIER: THE NEW WOMAN
AS WOMAN

"The nearest approach to the . . . complete creation of a person" in this analysis of women in the American novel of the latter half of the nineteenth century is Isabel Archer. But even she did not satisfy James's contemporaries, like Constance Fenimore Woolson, nor does she satisfy twentieth-century readers as a "real" woman, for James could not portray Isabel from the inside, in terms of her own consciousness. As has been shown, he had to interpret her consciousness in terms of the things and the people that made up her environment. (Later, perhaps because he had come to terms with his own sexuality in his relationship with the artist Hendrik Christian Andersen,[26] he was to create a woman of real vitality— Madame de Vionnet in *The Ambassadors*; but she is distinctly not an American woman.)

In the last year of the nineteenth century, a woman succeeded where the men had failed: Kate Chopin created in *The Awakening* a woman who is a *person*. To say that Edna Pontellier is more like Madame de Vionnet than like any other American heroine in her awareness and frank acceptance of her own sexuality, is to say that she is less like Daisy Miller, Isabel Archer and Maggie Verver than like Emma Bovary and Anna Karenina. Edna is neither deluded nor deludes like Maggie, for example; and she has many "foreign" qualities in common with Emma and Anna—both of whom engage in adulterous love affairs and take their own lives. But Edna is not precisely like these heroines either; she is not seeking "romance" like Emma, nor is she guilt-ridden like Anna. Neither is she like Hawthorne's Zenobia. While she is defined in terms of her suicide, like Zenobia and like Emma Bovary and Anna Karenina, hers is not the doom of a tragedy-queen; it is an awakening.

The difference between male and female perceptions of women can be illustrated by recalling the death of Zenobia and comparing it to the death of Edna Pontellier. The reader does not experience Zenobia's death at all from Zenobia's point of view; we see the midnight search of Silas Foster, Hollingsworth and Coverdale for Zenobia's body; we read Coverdale's description of her drowned corpse; we hear her eulogized by Westervelt and Coverdale. None of the physical aspects of Zenobia's death are sensed—what it feels like, smells like, tastes like *to Zenobia* to drown. Moreover, there is something wrong about her death, something wrong about the conception of the new woman as tragedy-queen, doomed *because* she is a new woman by a male writer who would "turn the whole affair into a ballad." Edna Pontellier, on the other hand, *chooses* to die; her suicide is part of her awakening, the ultimate act of free will. And it is told in terms of Edna: the way in which she preceives the sea, the sun, the sky, her naked body are all there for the reader to see, touch, feel, smell; her thoughts and impressions are there for the reader to share. The suicide scene of *The Awakening* is the fulfillment of Edna's awakening; to understand it, then, is to understand Edna herself.

> Despondency had come upon her there in the wakeful night, and had never lifted. There was no one thing in the world that she desired. There was no human being whom she wanted near her except Robert; and she even realized that the day would come when he, too, and the thought of him would melt out of her existence, leaving her alone. The children appeared before her like antagonists who had overcome her; who had over-powered and sought to drag her into the soul's slavery for the rest of her days. But she knew a way to elude them. She was not thinking of these things when she walked down to the beach.
>
> The water of the Gulf stretched out before her, gleaming with the million lights of the sun. The voice of the sea is seductive, never ceasing, whispering, clamoring, murmuring, inviting the soul to wander in abysses of solitude. All along the white beach, up and down, there was no living thing in sight. A bird with a broken wing was beating the air above, reeling and fluttering.

Edna had found her old bathing suit still hanging, faded, upon its accustomed peg.

She put it on, leaving her clothing in the bath-house. But when she was there beside the sea, absolutely alone, she cast the unpleasant, pricking garments from her, and for the first time in her life she stood naked in the open air, at the mercy of the sun, the breeze that beat upon her, and the waves that invited her.

How strange and awful it seemed to stand naked under the sky! how delicious! She felt like some new-born creature, opening its eyes in a familiar world that it had never known.

The foamy wavelets curled up to her white feet, and coiled like serpents about her ankles. She walked out. The water was chill, but she walked on. The water was deep, but she lifted her white body and reached out with a long, sweeping stroke. The touch of the sea is sensuous, enfolding the body in its soft, close embrace.

She went on and on, . . . thinking of the blue-grass meadow that she had traversed when a little child, believing that it had no beginning and no end.

Her arms and legs were growing tired. . . . Exhaustion was pressing upon and overpowering her. . . . it was too late; the shore was far behind her, and her strength was gone.

She looked into the distance, and the old terror flamed up for an instant, then sank again. . . . There was the hum of bees and the musky odor of pinks filled the air.[27]

All of the patterns of the book are there in this passage; this evocation of Edna's suicide contains all that one needs to know about Edna. It begins with despondency and alienation, but there is also exhilaration and discovery. There is Edna's awareness of herself as the central person in her experience: unlike Zenobia, she does not define herself in terms of a man, but realizes that even Robert would melt out of her existence; unlike her friend Madame Ratignolle, she does not define herself in terms of her husband or in terms of her children—they are antagonists who would drag her down. And there are the images through which we come to understand Edna: the sea, the bird and the bluegrass meadow of her childhood.

The words about the sea frame Edna's experience; in fact, they are repeated almost exactly at the beginning and at the end of the novel: "The voice of the sea is seductive, never ceasing, whispering, clamoring, murmuring, inviting the soul to wander in abysses of solitude." These words convey the traditional love/death identification to be found in the poetry of Emily Dickinson, for example, as well as in the tales of Poe and the novels of Hawthorne, Melville and Henry James, and emphasized in *The Awakening* by the repeated appearance of a pair of lovers at Grand Isle always followed by the ominous presence of the lady in black. More important, there is a very modern awareness of the equation of Transcendental awakening and alienation. Although Edna reads herself to sleep with Emerson, it is the solitariness of her communion with nature that stands out in her "figure of a man standing beside a desolate rock on the seashore," which the piece of music she names "Solitude" suggests to her. Like Edna in the final scene this man is naked; his attitude is one of "hopeless resignation" as he watches a bird "winging its flight *away* from him" (emphasis added). A twentieth-century reader might say that Edna's is a Prufrockian confrontation with nature, remembering that lonely man watching the mermaids ride seaward on the waves, and especially recalling the last line of the poem: "Till human voices wake us, and we drown." * But Edna's is not a stance of ironic detachment; unlike Prufrock, she experiences a real awakening which frees her from her "place" in society. In her illumination she is most like Whitman's awakened self. Recognizing the extent to which Edna's awakening is a Whitmanian song of herself makes clear the radical nature of Chopin's intentions. Edna Pontellier is a *woman* who celebrates herself as a person—a separate person and a sensuous person, defined

---

* Other modern works come to mind also, such as Ibsen's *When We Dead Awaken* and Joyce's *Finnegan's Wake*.

only in terms of her own experience, not in relation to any other person. Whitman's love/death identification with the sea is Edna's: "You sea! I resign myself to you . . ." he chants in *Song of Myself:* "Cushion me soft, rock me in billowy drowse,/ Dash me with armorous wet, . . . / Sea of the brine of life and of unshovell'd yet always-ready graves,/ . . . I am integral with you." But the images of the death scene in *The Awakening* are the images from "Out of the Cradle Endlessly Rocking": the bird, the sea and the child. The poem is about the birth of the artist—the bird's song becomes his song—when the child learns from the sea the word "death." "Never more shall I escape," cries the child to the bird, "Never more the cries of unsatisfied love be absent from me,/ Never again leave me to be the peaceful child I was before . . . / The messenger there arous'd, the fire, the sweet hell within,/ The unknown want, the destiny of me." Then he asks the sea for the "clew," the "word":

> Whereto answering, the sea,
> Delaying not, hurrying not,
> Whisper'd me through the night, and very plainly before
>   daybreak,
> Lisp'd to me the low and delicious word death,
> And again death, death, death, death,
> Hissing melodious, neither like the bird nor like my arous'd
>   child's heart,
> But edging near as privately for me rustling at my feet,
> Creeping thence steadily up to my ears and laving me softly all
>   over,
> Death, death, death, death, death.

To awaken, in the novel and in the poem, is to die; or, to die is to awaken. The child understands the love of the bird in understanding the death of the sea; but the sea gives birth to the artist through the death of the child.

The sea is the dominant image in *The Awakening;* all of the important incidents of the book are connected with the sea, each a kind of journey into the sea until the final immersion. The first stirrings of Edna's awakening and the first passage about the seductive quality of the sea together comprise chapter 6. Here faint glimmerings of an awakened self frighten Edna and make her feel contradictory impulses: one bids her to decline to swim with Robert, the other to follow him to the shore. "A certain light was beginning to dawn dimly within her,—the light which, showing the way, forbids it," Chopin explains. "In short, Mrs. Pontellier was beginning to realize her position in the universe as a human being, and to recognize her relations as an individual to the world within and about her. This may seem like a ponderous weight of wisdom to descend upon the soul of a young woman of twenty-eight—perhaps more wisdom than the Holy Ghost is usually pleased to vouchsafe to any woman." And then the passage about the sea—"The voice of the sea speaks to the soul. The touch of the sea is sensuous, enfolding the body in its soft, close embrace"—indicating that Edna's awakening is clearly sexual, and that it is already equated with being swallowed up, with death.

At this point Edna cannot swim; the sea *is* dangerous to her. Her lack of independence in the water parallels her dependent self: "A certain ungovernable dread hung about her when in the water, unless there was a hand near by that might reach out and reassure her." But the night she learns to swim she is "like the little, tottering, stumbling, clutching child, who of a sudden realizes its powers"—like the child in "Out of the Cradle." As she lifts her body to the surface of the water she feels joy, she feels exultation, and she feels a sense of her own body, a power "to control the working of her body and her soul." Suddenly she wants to "swim far out, where no woman had swum before." It is Edna's body and her soul that have awakened. Where she had accepted her husband's treatment of her as "a valuable piece of personal property" before she learned to swim, now she refuses to obey his whims. She responds to his "I can't permit you to stay out there all night. You must come in the house instantly," for example, by settling herself more securely in the hammock, perceiving "that her will had blazed up, stubborn and resistant." Edna feels "like one who awakens gradually out of a dream, a delicious, grotesque, impossible dream," but which is the dream and which is the reality—the freedom or the confinement—is not clear to her. "Delicious"—a Whitman word—clearly refers to her new-found sense of freedom; it is like her feeling of being in the sea. "Grotesque" refers to the juxtaposition of her emerging self with her preawakened self, living in a marriage which will become increasingly "impossible."

Edna married Léonce Pontellier as a dependent person whose experience in love has taught her to feel insecure; he is for her a father figure. Her own father represented not love, but "Puritan" repressiveness: Edna's most vivid childhood memory is of "running away from prayers, from the Presbyterian service, read in a spirit of gloom by my father that chills me yet to think of"; and her later impression of him is of a man "with padded shoulders, his Bible reading, his 'toddies' and ponderous oaths" whom she is glad to be rid of. In response to this cold father, Edna developed such "reserve of . . . character" that she has only been able to love in fantasy, and all her loves have disappeared. There was the "dignified and sad-eyed cavalry officer" who melted imperceptibly out of her existence. There was "a young gentleman who visited a lady on a neighboring plantation," and "the realization that she herself was nothing, nothing, nothing" to him was a "bitter affliction to her"; he, too, went "the way of dreams." Then "the face and figure of a great tragedian began to haunt her imagination and stir her senses"; the hopelessness of this infatuation "colored it with the lofty tones of a great passion," expressed on Edna's part only by kissing the cold glass which frames his photograph. All of these early loves were, like her father, unattainable. So her marriage to Léonce Pontellier was "purely an accident." His absolute devotion flattered her, and with him she felt safe: *he* would not abandon her, but more importantly, she was taking no risk herself because "no trace of passion or excessive and fictitious warmth colored her affection, thereby threatening its dissolution." Add to this "the violent opposition of her father . . . and we need seek no further for the motives which led her to accept Monsieur Pontellier for her husband."

Even in her passive dream world, however, there is something unresolved about Edna in this marriage. "She is not one of us; she is not like us," Adèle Ratignolle, one of the women at Grand Isle, observes about her. Edna *is* unlike Madame Ratignolle, that "sensuous Madonna" with her "spun-gold hair that comb nor confining pin could restrain; the blue eyes that were like nothing but sapphires; two lips that pouted, that were so red one could only think of cherries or some other delicious crimson fruit in looking at them." Adèle is a fairy-tale heroine, but there is "no suggestion of the . . . stereotyped fashion-plate" about Edna. She is "different from the crowd" with her "long, clean and symmetrical" body, her quick and bright yellowish brown eyes, which she has "a way of turning . . . swiftly upon an object and holding them there as if lost in some inward maze of contemplation or thought." Edna's habit of introspection and her difference in appearance from other women suggest what is really different about her: she is not a "mother-woman." Mother-women prevail at Grand Isle; they are women who idolize their children, worship their husbands and esteem it "a holy privilege to efface themselves as individuals and grow wings as ministering angels." With these extended, protecting wings—very different from the kind of wings Edna will need to achieve her freedom—they flutter about their precious broods in the face of any harm, real or imaginary. The mother-woman, then, is one who thinks always about others, like Adèle Ratignolle, keeping up her music only for the sake of her family and cutting out patterns for her children's winter underwear in the middle of summer. Edna, on the other hand, thinks only of herself; she paints because she feels like painting and cannot "see the use of anticipating and making winter night garments the subject of her summer meditations." She explains to Madame Ratignolle on another occasion that she would never sacrifice herself for her children or for anyone: "I would give up the unessential; I would give up my money, I would give up my life for my children; but I wouldn't give up myself. I can't make it more clear; it's only something which I am beginning to comprehend, which is revealing itself to me." Edna's husband is unhappy that she is not more of a mother-woman; he reproaches her "with her inattention, her habitual neglect of the children," but he has been "a rather courteous husband so long as he met a certain tacit submissiveness in his wife." Once she has begun to awaken from her dream, however, her "new and unexpected line of conduct" completely bewilders and shocks him, and her "absolute disregard for her duties as a wife" angers him. "She's got some sort of notion in her head concerning the eternal rights of women; and—you understand—we meet in the morning at the breakfast table," he finally complains to the doctor.

What has happened to Edna between the time when Léonce regards her "inattention" with vague irritation and that when her "absolute disregard" angers him to the point where he cannot eat his food is Grand Isle and the sea. At Grand Isle Edna is awakened to a sense of herself as a person, rather than as a piece of valuable personal property. When she learns to swim, she becomes aware of the sensations of her body—the feel of the water against her limbs, the feel of the hot sun on her skin, the feel of the wind beating in her face; and with the awakened sense of her body comes sexual arousal. In her sexual desire for Robert, which she interprets as love, she is not unlike Whitman's child on the beach. In fact, her awakening is a kind of rebirth of her childhood, and her love for Robert is similar to the fantasy-love she experienced before her marriage. Edna establishes the connection between her awakening and her renewed sense of childhood freedom in that final suicide scene. Standing naked in the open air she feels "like some new-born creature opening its eyes in a familiar world that it had never known." The sea makes her think of the "blue-grass meadow

that she traversed when a little child," and the reader remembers another time, in the initial stages of her awakening, when the sea has reminded her of the blue-grass
meadow. "I can trace . . . a meadow that seemed as big as
the ocean to the very little girl walking through the grass,
which was higher than her waist. She threw out her arms as
if swimming when she walked, beating the tall grass as one
strikes out in the water," she tells Madame Ratignolle. "I
could only see the stretch of green before me, and I felt as if I
must walk on forever . . . sometimes I feel this summer as if
I were walking through the green meadow again; idly, aim-
lessly, unthinking and unguided." As a child she walked
through the meadow to escape her gloomy Presbyterian father; as a woman she walks into the sea first to escape her
husband and then to escape all the antagonists who would
drag her down—even Robert. Edna's awareness that it is not
Robert, but her own awakening that has happened to her is
clear when she tells him toward the end of the book, "You
have been a very, very foolish boy, wasting your time
dreaming of impossible things when you speak of Mr. Pontellier setting me free! I am no longer one of Mr. Pontellier's
possessions to dispose of or not. I give myself where I
choose. If he were to say, 'Here, Robert, take her and be
happy; she is yours,' I should laugh at you both."

At Grand Isle, however, Edna has not so much self-
awareness, partially because by the time she and Robert are
reunited in New Orleans she has already experienced another lover, Alcée Arobin, and begun to realize that what she
craves most of all is personal freedom. The experience of
Edna and Robert at Grand Isle is a beautiful pastoral interlude where each awakens with a sense of wonder to the
other. The full realization of their feelings for one another
comes when they take their journey across the sea to *Chênière
Caminada*. As they sail across the bay Edna feels "as if she
were being borne away from some anchorage which had held
her fast, whose chains had been loosening—had snapped the
night before when the mystic spirit was abroad, leaving her

252

free to drift whithersoever she chose to set her sails." They go, she and Robert, ostensibly to attend church, but Edna reacts to the service with the same sense of oppression that she had experienced as a child forced to listen to her father's Presbyterian prayers. She becomes drowsy, her head begins to ache and the lights on the altar sway before her eyes. Her one thought is "to quit the stifling atmosphere of the church and reach the open air." Her feeling of giddiness indicates that she is approaching a crisis—a sexual crisis and an identity crisis. Her long sleep is like the swoon of "Sleeping Beauty" in the fairy tale, and when she awakens, Robert, her waiting Prince Charming, tells her: "You have slept precisely one hundred years. I was left here to guard your slumbers." The scene is reminiscent of the awakening of another princess, Maggie Verver, to a sense of her sexuality; but where Maggie awakens to the knowledge that she must give up her father in order to put a stop to her husband's adulterous affair and win him for herself, Edna awakens *to* adulterous love. Where Maggie gives up her childhood identity and learns to play the role of wife, Edna gives up all role-playing and awakens to a rediscovered sense of childhood freedom. It is the male versus the female interpretation of the myth.

So significant is this awakening for Edna, that she carries out her own religious ritual when she arises: she washes herself in a kind of baptismal rite, and then she bites a piece of bread from a brown loaf, "tearing it with her strong, white teeth," and drinks some wine. While she washes, she looks in the mirror, confronting herself in a way that heroines seldom do, and perceives her literally new face. But the mirror in which she peers is "distorted," and while it shows her a face that is "wide awake," the vision is distorted because this is only an idyllic interlude in her life. While Edna is awake in sensual terms—she has slept deeply, awakens ravenously hungry, is vividly aware of the color of the gray houses against the orange trees, the taste of the cool water, the cleanliness and softness of the snow-white bed, the ache in her strong limbs, the feel of her fingers in her loosened hair, the sizzle of the broiled fowl and the crumbs of the crusty loaf—she will not be spiritually awake until the final scene of the novel. But clearly the interlude has been significant, so significant for Robert that he will have to go away from Edna because his relationship with her has gone beyond the boundaries of the game he usually plays with attractive female summer guests, and so significant for Edna that when she returns to New Orleans with her husband they will both become aware that "she was becoming herself and daily casting aside that fictitious self which we assume like a garment with which to appear before the world." By the time Robert leaves her, however, she has only come to the point of recognizing "the symptoms of infatuation which she had felt incipiently as a child, as a girl in her earliest teens, and later as a young woman. The recognition did not lessen the reality, the poignancy of the revelation by any suggestion or promise of instability. The past was nothing to her; offered no lesson which she was willing to heed. The future was a mystery which she never attempted to penetrate. The present alone was significant; was hers, to torture her as it was doing then with the biting conviction that she had lost that which she had held, that she had been denied that which her impassioned, newly awakened being demanded." This reflection occurs midway through the novel; by the time Edna returns to the sea at the end of the novel, past, present and future will have come together for her in her final act.

If Edna learns the word "death" from the sea in that final scene where she stands naked at the mercy of the waves that invite her she has, like Whitman's child, learned the word "love" from the bird. If this bird with the broken wing is an image of Edna's self, it is a reminder that the word "self" is never really separated for her from the word "love." And suddenly the bird that has been singing to Edna throughout the novel wings its way across the reader's mind. The first words in the book are about a caged green and yellow parrot who keeps repeating "Allez vous-en!"—Go away—and speaks mostly "a language which nobody understood, unless

it was the mocking bird"—like Whitman's mocking-bird—
"whistling his fluty notes out upon the breeze with madden-
ing persistence."

"Go away" is what all of the men in Edna's life have done;
it is what Edna sees herself doing in the story she tells her father, her husband and the doctor; and it is what she will finally do. That series of dinner-table stories provides a neat
microscopic glimpse of Edna as she has been, as others see
her, and as she sees her newly awakened self. The Colonel,
Edna's father, relates "a somber episode of those dark and
bitter days, in which he had acted a conspicuous part and
always formed a central figure." The Doctor tells "the old,
ever new and curious story of the waning of a woman's love,
seeking strange, new channels, only to return to its legiti-
mate source after days of fierce unrest." Edna's story is of "a
woman who paddled away with her love one night in a
pirogue and never came back. They were lost amid the Bara-
tarian Islands, and no one ever heard of them or found trace
of them from that day to this." Chopin likens Edna's story to
a dream, "But every glowing word seemed real to those who
listened. They could feel the hot breath of the Southern
night; they could hear the long sweep of the pirogue through
the glistening moonlit water, the beating of the birds' wings,
rising startled from among the reeds in the salt-water pools;
they could see the faces of the lovers, pale, close together,
rapt in oblivious forgetfulness, drifting into the unknown."
Love, death, bird and journey across the water into the unknown again come together in Edna's story. But the bird that
beats the air in the final scene, which this story foreshadows,
reels and flutters because it has a *broken* wing, reminding
one of the advice given Edna by Mademoiselle Reisz, the
pianist who has recognized Edna's awakening spirit in her
unusual response to music: "The bird that would soar above
the level plain of tradition and prejudice must have strong
wings." Edna's wings have been strong enough to break out
of her cage as wife to Mr. Pontellier by resuming her painting, abandoning the housekeeping and social duties which

she has never liked, sending her children off to her mother-in-law's farm, and most significantly by leaving her husband's expensive house for her own "pigeon-house." But the name Edna gives her house, as well as the image of the bird in the final scene, suggest the actual strength of Edna's wings. Although she feels that this descent in the social scale implies "a corresponding sense of having risen in the spiritual," the reader is aware that the pigeon is a domesticated bird, and that a pigeonhole is a compartment for filing something away in its proper place. A pigeon, in fact, is a member of the dove family, and when one recalls the doves of this study—Priscilla, Hilda, Sophia Peabody and Milly Theale—the parallel image of the dovecote comes to mind. It is significant that in ascending to her dovecote Hilda removed herself from the world of men, while in moving to her pigeon-house with the help of Alcée Arobin and in receiving Robert there, Edna frees herself from one man only to transfer her feelings of dependency to other men. Thus, the pigeon-house is no more a symbol of real independence than her "coup d'état," her farewell dinner for herself and her new friends given in her husband's house and paid for with his money, is a real revolution.

Edna's self-perception is reminiscent of Theron Ware's as well as of Whitman's: "Every step which she took toward relieving herself from obligations added to her strength and expansion as an individual. She began to look with her own eyes; to see and to apprehend the deeper undercurrents of life. No longer was she content to 'feed upon opinion' when her own soul invited her." While it is true, as she tells the doctor, that "I don't want anything but my own way," Edna has been unable to realize what her own way is. Painting has not satisfied her; the races which she attends (like Anna Karenina) with her new social set of not-quite-respectable friends have not satisfied her; sexual warmth, while it gives her a certain badly needed validation as a woman in contrast to her cold father, her indifferent husband and her fantasy-loves, has not satisfied her. While Arobin, with "effrontery in his eyes repelled the old, vanishing self in her, yet drew all her awakening sensuousness," he also awakens her guilt, and after he leaves her she cries, feeling "multitudinous emotions" assailing her, among them "an overwhelming feeling of irresponsibility."

The "something" that Edna wants to happen—"something, anything; she did not know what"—is not Arobin, but neither, finally, is it Robert. It is not really his note, "Good-by—because I love you," that drives her to the sea for the final time. She is on her way to Robert, in fact, believing that their love is about to be consummated, when she tells the doctor of the "periods of despondency and suffering" which take possession of her. Not wanting "anything but my own way," she tells him, "is wanting a good deal, of course, when you have to trample upon the lives, the hearts, the prejudices of others—but no matter—still I shouldn't want to trample upon the little lives." That Robert is not waiting for her when she returns from attending the birth of the Ratignolles' child only intensifies her despondency; it has not been the cause. The "torture scene" there and Adèle's words to Edna—"Think of the children; think of them"—have been far more upsetting; the determination to "think of them" has "driven into her soul like a death wound."

And so it is the birth of the child which is a death wound, an interlude between shared love and vanished love—a reversal of the earlier interlude of awakened love framed by Edna's prior caged existence and her subsequent return to New Orleans determined to break free—that drives her back to the sea, the scene of her original awakening, and now of her death. Edna's is not a noble death. The tone of that scene is set by the first word: "despondency." It is reinforced by such words as "antagonists," "slavery," "broken" and finally "exhaustion." It is a return to the womb of the sea, a return to the freedom of the blue-grass meadow, a choice to be a free child rather than a tortured mother-woman. Edna chooses to die because it is the one, the ultimate act of free will open to her through which she can elude those who would drag her down. In becoming one with the sea she is free. She has achieved a kind of rebirth. Edna Pontellier is not a tragic heroine; she is not a fairy-tale princess. She is a woman, a real woman living in a world which has no place for her.

> White
> Godiva, I unpeel—
> Dead hands, dead stringencies.
>
> And now I
> Foam to wheat, a glitter of seas.
> The child's cry
>
> Melts in the wall.
> And I
> Am the arrow,
>
> The dew that flies
> Suicidal, at one with the drive
> Into the red
>
> Eye, the cauldron of morning.
> —Sylvia Plath, from "Ariel"

Notes

PREFACE

1 R. W. B. Lewis, *The American Adam: Innocence, Tragedy and Tradition in the Nineteenth Century* (Chicago: University of Chicago Press, 1955), p. 1. During the final stages of the preparation of this manuscript, Ernest Earnest's *The American Eve in Fact and Fiction* was published (Bloomington: Indiana University Press, 1975). It is, I believe, the first study of the American Eve, but its focus is primarily historical, while the focus of this book is literary.

CHAPTER I
The Myth of America as New World Garden of Eden

1 Leo Marx, *The Machine in the Garden: Technology and the Pastoral Ideal in America* (New York: Oxford University Press, 1964), p. 228.

2 John Humphrey Noyes, *History of American Socialisms* (New York: Hillary House Publishers, 1961 reprint of 1870 edition), p. 24.

3 See Charles L. Sanford, *The Quest for Paradise: Europe and the American Moral Imagination* (Urbana: University of Illinois Press, 1961).

4 Henry James, *The Art of the Novel: Critical Prefaces* (New York: Scribners, 1934), pp. 31–32.

5 Lewis, *American Adam*, p. 5.

6 David Potter, "American Woman and the American Character," *Stetson University Bulletin* LXII (Jan. 1962). Potter made some mistaken assumptions and perpetrated some myths of his own, especially about the dependence of the frontier woman and opportunities for independence for women in the city, but his thesis is still sound and, for 1962, far-reaching. For more recent

and more accurate analyses of women in American history see Betty E. Chmaj, "Even Good Guys Make Mistakes: Answers to Potter's 'American Woman and the American Character,' " in *Image, Myth and Beyond: American Women and American Studies*, vol. II (Pittsburgh: Know, Inc., 1972). See also Gerda Lerner, *The Woman in American History* (Menlo Park, Cal.: Addison-Wesley, 1972); Helen Papashivly, *All the Happy Endings* (New York: Harper & Brothers, 1956).

7 Mircea Eliade, *The Sacred and the Profane: The Nature of Religion*, translated by Willard Trask (New York: Harper & Row, 1959). See also the works of Joseph Campbell, especially *The Hero with a Thousand Faces* (Cleveland: World, 1956).

8 Henry James, *The American*, 1877 version (New York: Holt, Rinehart and Winston, 1949). Subsequent references are to this edition.

9 Theodore Roszak, "The Hard and the Soft: The Force of Feminism in Modern Times," in Theodore Roszak and Betty Roszak, eds., *Masculine/Feminine: Readings in Sexual Mythology and the Liberation of Women* (New York: Harper & Row, 1969), pp. 91–92.

10 Ibid., pp. 99–100.

11 Cited in Roszak, ibid., p. 89.

12 Henry James, *The Bostonians*, 1886 (New York: Modern Library, 1956). Subsequent references are to this edition.

13 Barbara M. Cross, ed., *The Educated Woman in America: Selected Writings of Catharine Beecher, Margaret Fuller, and M. Carey Thomas* (New York: Teachers College Press of Columbia University, 1965), pp. 14–19.

14 Cited in Miriam Schneir, ed., *Feminism: The Essential Historical Writings* (New York: Random House Vintage Books, 1972), p. 78.

15 Allan Nevins, *The Emergence of Modern America: 1865–1878* (New York: Macmillan, 1927), p. 178.

16 Vernon L. Parrington, *Main Currents in American Thought*, vol. III: *The Beginnings of Critical Realism in America* (New York: Harcourt, Brace, 1930; Harbinger paperback edition used), pp. 74–75.

17 See Richard Hofstadter, *The Age of Reform: From Bryan to F. D. R.* (New York: Knopf, 1955).

18 Stephan Thernstrom, "Urbanization, Migration and Social Mobility in Late Nineteenth-Century America," in Barton J. Bernstein, ed., *Towards a New Past: Dissenting Essays in American History* (New York: Pantheon, 1968), pp. 158–59. Thernstrom states that in 1860 less than one-fourth of the American population lived in a city or town. By 1910 one-half of the American people lived in cities. 101 American communities grew by 100% or more in the 1880s. His point that the exodus to the city caused a "great social transformation" is not really so new. "Old-fashioned" historians have also commented on the confrontation of the old and the new orders during this period: the values of agrarianism versus those of industrialism; the spirit of frontier independence and the "noisy enthusiasms of the new coonskin democracy" against the more sophisticated traditionalism of the city; the clash of Pagan-

ism, representatives of the God of love come from the free spaces of the West, and Puritanism, representatives of the God of wrath abiding in the respectable East (Parrington, vol. III, p. 11; pp. 74–75).

19 Cited in Constance Mayfield Rourke, *Trumpets of Jubilee* (New York: Harcourt, Brace, 1927), p. 142.

20 See Lerner, *Woman in American History*, p. 23; Papashvily, *All the Happy Endings*, pp. 19–20.

21 Catharine Beecher and Harriet Beecher Stowe, *The American Woman's Home* (New York: Ford, 1869), p. 19.

22 Catharine Beecher, "How to Redeem Woman's Profession from Dishonor," *Harper's New Monthly Magazine* XXXI (Nov. 1865), 710.

23 For additional information see Barbara Welter, "The True Cult of American Womanhood: 1820–1860," *American Quarterly* XVIII (Summer 1966), 151–74. In her survey of ladies' magazines, gift books, women's diaries, autobiographies, memoirs, personal papers and novels of the period Welter finds that women were expected to have four qualities: piety, purity, submissiveness and domesticity.

24 Willard Parker, M.D., "A Psychological View of the Woman Question," *Hearth and Home* I (Nov. 20, 1869), 760.

25 H. S. Pomeroy, M.D., *The Ethics of Marriage* (New York: Funk & Wagnalls, 1888), p. 128.

26 Horace Greeley, "My Notion of Women's Rights," *Hearth and Home* I (Sept. 18, 1869), 616–17.

27 Kate Field, "A Conversation on the Stage," *Atlantic Monthly* XXI (March 1868), 274.

28 Alexis de Tocqueville, *Democracy in America,* translated by George Lawrence, edited by J. P. Mayer (Garden City, N.Y.: Doubleday, 1969), p. 601.

29 James Bryce, *The American Commonwealth,* vol. III (London: Macmillan, 1888), pp. 506, 523.

30 Jane Trahey, ed., *Harper's Bazaar: 100 Years of the American Female* (New York: Random House, 1967), pp. 2–3.

31 Frank Luther Mott, *A History of American Magazines,* vol. III: *1865–1885* (Cambridge: Harvard University Press, 1938), p. 7.

32 Ibid. The largest circulation of any periodical of the time was that of the *New York Weekly* at 350,000.

33 Nevins, *Emergence of Modern America*, p. 342.

34 Ibid., p. 280.

35 Cross, *Educated Woman*, p. 3.

36 Nevins, *Emergence of Modern America*, p. 280.

37 *The Round Table* I (Feb. 27, 1864), 164–65.

38 F. O. Matthiessen and Kenneth B. Murdock, eds., *The Notebooks of Henry James* (New York: Oxford University Press, 1947; paperback edition used), p. 47.

39 Henry Nash Smith, *Virgin Land: The American West as Symbol and Myth*

(Cambridge: Harvard University Press, 1950; Vintage paperback edition used), pp. 126 ff.

40 Ibid., pp. 130–31.

41 Cross, *Educated Woman*, pp. 37–38.

42 Letter to Mrs. John Van Vorst reprinted in the introduction to her book, *The Woman Who Toils* (New York: Doubleday, Page, 1903), pp. vii–ix. The fear of race suicide could hardly have been allayed by the increasing divorce rate—9,937 divorces in the nation in 1867 and 16,089 in 1878, an increase of more than 60% (Nevins, *Emergence of Modern America*, p. 215), an indication of the increasing independence of women and of social and economic changes as well.

43 Whitney R. Cross, *The Burned-Over District: The Social and Intellectual History of Enthusiastic Religion in Western New York, 1800–1850* (Ithaca, N.Y.: Cornell University Press, 1950; Harper Torchbook edition used), p. 237.

44 R. Palme Dutt, "Women in the Class Struggle," in Samuel D. Schmalhausen and V. F. Calverton, eds., *Woman's Coming of Age: A Symposium* (New York: Liveright, 1931), p. 550. He cites Engels in *The Origin of the Family:* "The emancipation of women and their equality with men are impossible and remain so, as long as women are excluded from social production and restricted to domestic labor. The emancipation of women becomes feasible only then when women are enabled to take part extensively in social production" (p. 556).

45 Donald Drew Egbert and Stow Persons, eds., *Socialism in American Life*, vol. II (Princeton: Princeton University Press, 1952), p. 319.

46 V. F. Calverton, *Where Angels Dared to Tread* (Indianapolis: Bobbs Merrill, 1941), p. 200.

47 Amelia Russell, "Home Life of the Brook Farm Association," *Atlantic Monthly* XLII (Oct. 1878), 466.

48 Margaret Fuller, "The Great Lawsuit: Man versus Men; Woman versus Women," *The Dial* IV (July 1843), 11; later reprinted as *Woman in the Nineteenth Century*.

49 Ralph Waldo Emerson, "Lectures on the Times," *The Dial* III (July 1842), 11.

50 Noyes, *History of American Socialisms*, p. 636.

51 Erich Fromm's introduction to Edward Bellamy, *Looking Backward* (New York: New American Library, 1960), pp. v–vi. Subsequent references are to this edition.

52 Herbert Marcuse, for example, in *Eros and Civilization* (Boston: Beacon Press, 1955), calls the condition where women, and therefore acceptable sexual activity, belong only in the home, repressed out of social consciousness by men and women alike, "genital supremacy," because sex is limited to the procreative function. He points out that psychoanalytic theory (which also arises out of Western industrial civilization) contradicts this fallacy, insisting that sexuality exists in all of life's activities. See David Bleich, "Eros and Bellamy," *American Quarterly* XVI (Fall 1964), 455.

53 Charles Bellamy, *An Experiment in Marriage* (Albany, N.Y.: Weed, Parsons, 1899), p. 24.

54 Sylvia Bowman, "Bellamy's Missing Chapter," *New England Quarterly* XXXI (March 1958), 47.

55 Ibid.

56 Ibid., 51.

57 Ibid., 55–56.

CHAPTER II
The Temptress

1 John Milton, *Paradise Lost*, Book IX, ll. 232–34, 816–24, in Merritt Y. Hughes, ed., *John Milton: Complete Poems and Major Prose* (New York: Odyssey, 1957), pp. 384, 397. A variation on the "standard" myth of creation is that God created man and woman at the same time—Adam and Lilith. "Like him she had been created out of the dust of the ground. But she remained with him only a short time, because she insisted upon enjoying full equality with her husband. She derived her rights from their identical origin. With the help of the Ineffable Name of God, which she pronounced, Lilith flew away from Adam, and vanished in the air. Adam complained before God that the wife He had given him had deserted him, and God sent forth three angels to capture her. They found her in the Red Sea, and they sought to make her go back with the threat that, unless she went, she would lose a hundred of her demon children daily by death. But Lilith preferred this punishment to living with Adam." Louis Ginzberg, *The Legends of the Jews*, vol. I, p. 65, cited in Wolfgang Lederer, M.D., *The Fear of Women* (New York: Harcourt-Brace-Jovanovich, 1968), p. 61.

2 See Philip Rahv's essay by that title in *Literature and the Sixth Sense* (New York: Houghton Mifflin, 1970), pp. 55–75. See also D. H. Lawrence, *Studies in Classic American Literature* (New York: Viking, 1923), and Leslie Fiedler, *Love and Death in the American Novel*, rev. ed. (New York: Stein and Day, 1966). For more recent feminist criticism of the "dark lady" see Elizabeth Hardwick, *Seduction and Betrayal* (New York: Random House, 1974); Carolyn Heilbrun, *Toward a Recognition of Androgyny* (New York: Knopf, 1973); and Wendy Martin, "Seduced and Abandoned in the New World: The Image of Woman in American Fiction" in Vivian Gornick and Barbara K. Moran, eds., *Woman in Sexist Society* (New York: Basic Books, 1971), pp. 329–46.

3 This poster appears as an illustration in Carl G. Jung, *Man and his Symbols* (Garden City, N.Y.: Doubleday, 1964), p. 180.

4 Kai T. Erikson, *Wayward Puritans: A Study in the Sociology of Deviance* (New York: Wiley, 1966), pp. 6, 11. Interestingly, all of Erikson's case studies in deviance are women—Anne Hutchinson, the Quakers, the Salem witches—and all of them are treated by Hawthorne (with considerably less

sympathy). They are all ostracized, all punished. In Hawthorne's America, however, no one community had a monopoly on the Edenic myth. There were alternative communities which experimented with differing behavior patterns and roles, especially, as has been shown, for women. Each new community, of course, had its own set of definitive boundaries.

5 Cf. Clarence P. Oberndorf's introduction to *The Psychiatric Novels of Oliver Wendell Holmes* (New York: Columbia University Press, 1943), which argues that Holmes's "medicated novels" were fictionalized psychiatric case studies, antedating Freud by over a quarter of a century.

6 Oliver Wendell Holmes, *Elsie Venner* (Boston: Houghton Mifflin, 1891), pp. ix–x. Subsequent references are to this edition.

7 Nathaniel Hawthorne, "Rappaccini's Daughter," in *The Complete Short Stories of Nathaniel Hawthorne* (Garden City, N.Y.: Hanover House, 1959), pp. 256–75. Subsequent references are to this edition.

8 Lederer, in *The Fear of Women,* suggests that both *la femme fatale* and *l'homme fatale,* the lady killer, are typical of nineteenth-century Romanticism. Don Juan, he says, "is fascinated by the danger of woman; but his game is not to become a victim, but to taunt destruction like a mountaineer or a parachutist or a race driver or anyone else who seeks danger in order to experience its thrill, to tease death and prove superior to it" (p. 230). Mario Praz also makes this point in *The Romantic Agony* (London: Oxford University Press, 1933): ". . . just as the Byronic hero's origin was often said to be mysterious and extremely noble, so, too was the origin of the Fatal Woman. And like the Byronic superman, the superwoman also assumes an attitude of defiance to society" (p. 261).

9 See Frederick Crews, *The Sins of the Fathers: Hawthorne's Psychological Themes* (New York: Oxford University Press, 1966), for a complete analysis of the incest question in Hawthorne.

10 F. O. Matthiessen, *American Renaissance: Art and Expression in the Age of Emerson and Whitman* (New York: Oxford University Press, 1941), p. 502. Matthiessen also noted Melville's later notations on Hawthorne's preoccupation with the Fall in *The Marble Faun* and his underscoring in Schopenhauer's *Studies in Pessimism:* "Accordingly the sole thing that reconciles me to the Old Testament is the story of the Fall. In my eyes, it is the only metaphysical truth in that book, even though it appears in the form of an allegory" (ibid.).

11 Herman Melville, *Pierre, or, The Ambiguities,* 1852 (New York: Grove Press, 1957). Subsequent references are to this edition.

12 Melville wrote to Hawthorne after reading "Ethan Brand": "I stand for the heart. To the dogs with the head!" Cited in Matthiessen, *American Renaissance,* p. 468.

13 If Freud knew *Pierre,* which I doubt, he would have found it a perfect illustration of his theory about psychic impotence in males who separate their feelings of tenderness and passion. A man who idealizes his mother,

Freud argued, similarly idealizes a woman he loves, and cannot experience passion for her without simultaneously feeling incestuous guilt. Thus, he often needs to prove his manliness with a woman who is degraded, in contrast to his "pedestalled mother," as Pierre calls her. See "The Most Prevalent Form of Degradation in Erotic Life," in Ernest Jones, ed., *The Collected Papers of Sigmund Freud*, vol. IV (New York: Basic Books, 1959), pp. 203–16. Paul Morel, in D. H. Lawrence's *Sons and Lovers*, has a problem similar to Pierre's, and Simon O. Lesser uses this essay to explain Paul's different attractions to Miriam and Clara in *Fiction and the Unconscious* (Boston: Beacon Press, 1957), pp. 175–78. This is, of course, an explanation for the creation of the dark and light ladies quite different from that of the phenomenon of projection, discussed elsewhere in this book.

14 "The typical Victorian heroine," reports Susan Gorsky in a study of novels from 1840 to 1920, has hair that is "blond or light brown, occasionally darker, but never red." "The Gentle Doubters," in Susan Koppelman Cornillon, ed., *Images of Women in Fiction: Feminist Perspectives* (Bowling Green, Ohio: Bowling Green University Popular Press, 1972), p. 31.

15 Harold Frederic, *The Damnation of Theron Ware*, 1896 (New York: Holt, Rinehart and Winston, 1958). Subsequent references are to this edition.

16 John Henry Raleigh, in his introduction to *The Damnation of Theron Ware*, sees Celia as a representative of "Catholicism *cum* Art," likening her to late nineteenth-century English culture with its "memories of the Pre-Raphaelites and the *Yellow Book* and Aubrey Beardsley, redolent of secular incense, private altars, diabolical poetry devoted to God, pictures of the Virgin overhanging nude statuary," etc., p. xiii.

17 Nathaniel Hawthorne, *The Marble Faun*, 1860 (New York: New American Library, 1961). Subsequent references are to this edition.

18 "The complete dark lady is the Jewess," Charles Blinderman writes. "The Jewish Dark Lady is a most tempting and dangerous creature for the Christian lover. . . . She is an exotic . . . with the cutomary grandiloquence of orientalism, with the poetic exaggeration . . . [which] is the breath of destruction." "The Servility of Dependence: The Dark Lady in Trollope," in Cornillon, *Images of Women in Fiction*, p. 63.

19 This idea of "uncleanness" is, strangely, close to that of the orthodox Jewish doctrine of the uncleanness of women (because they menstruate) and the separation, therefore, of men and women in the orthodox synagogue. When one recalls Miriam's describing the jewel within her not as a pearl, but as a bloody red carbuncle (later symbolized by the red jewel on her breast when Kenyon sees her in a carriage with a Roman official), Hawthorne's own squeamishness about sex, always sensed, is vividly revealed. Jew equals female sexuality, then, and sex is corrupt, unclean and threatening.

20 Hawthorne, however, insists on defining art as masculine and feminine. Miriam is an anomaly, but "original" feminine art in his country con-

sists of "pretty fancies of snow and moonlight; the counterpart in picture of so many feminine achievements in literature!" Hawthorne is clearly threatened by really original women like Miriam, for he tries to tone her down (or at least insist that women can never be as serious as men about art—"Our own sex is incapable of any such byplay aside from the main business of life . . .") by picturing her sewing. "There is something extremely pleasant, and even touching—at least, of very sweet, soft, and winning effect—in this peculiarity of needlework," Hawthorne writes. "Methinks it is a token of healthy and gentle characteristics when women of high thoughts and accomplishments love to sew; especially as they are never more at home with their own hearts than while so occupied."

21 Cited in Allen Flint, "The Saving Grace of Marriage in Hawthorne's Fiction," *Emerson Society Quarterly* XIX (1973), 112.

22 Nathaniel Hawthorne, *The Scarlet Letter,* 1850 (New York: Rinehart, 1960). Subsequent references are to this edition.

23 Cited in Malcolm Cowley, *The Portable Hawthorne* (New York: Viking, 1948), pp. 611–18.

24 See Carolyn Heilbrun, *Toward Androgyny;* and Nina Baym, "The Blithedale Romance: A Radical Reading," *Journal of English and Germanic Philology* LXVII (Oct. 1968), 545–69; "Hawthorne's Women: The Tyranny of Social Myths," *Centennial Review* XV (Summer 1971), 250–72; "Passion and Authority in *The Scarlet Letter,*" *New England Quarterly* XLIII (June 1970), 209–30; "The Romantic *Malgré Lui:* Hawthorne in the Custom House," *Emerson Society Quarterly* XIX (1973), 14–25.

25 Nathaniel Hawthorne, "Mrs. Hutchinson," in *Biographical Sketches of Nathaniel Hawthorne,* vol. XII (Boston: Houghton Mifflin, 1883), pp. 217–19.

26 Ibid., p. 224.

27 John Winthrop, "A Modell of Christian Charity," *Winthrop Papers,* vol. II (Massachusetts Historical Society, 1931), pp. 283–94.

28 John Winthrop, *Journal,* vol. II, James K. Hosmer, ed. (New York: Scribners, 1908), p. 239.

29 These are the words of John Winthrop explaining why a woman of his acquaintance had become mentally ill (*Journal,* vol. II, p. 225). For a discussion of woman's place in the Puritan community see Edmund S. Morgan, *The Puritan Family: Religion and Domestic Relations in Seventeenth-Century New England* (New York: Harper & Row, 1944). For a discussion of this problem with specific reference to Anne Hutchinson see Kai Erikson, *Wayward Puritans,* pp. 71–107.

CHAPTER III
The American Princess

1 Frederick I. Carpenter, "Puritans Preferred Blondes," *New England Quarterly* IX (1936), 253–54.

2 America's first best seller, Susanna Rowson's *Charlotte Temple,* for example, sold 25,000 copies within a few years of its publication in 1794. During the first quarter of the nineteenth century it outdistanced in popular favor every competitor in the field, and by 1905 it had gone through 104 editions. Fred Lewis Pattee, *The First Century of American Fiction, 1770–1870* (New York: Appleton-Century, 1935), p. 88. Susan Warner's *Wide Wide World,* issued in 1850 under the pseudonym Elizabeth Wetherell, was another best seller: in three months it sold 1500 copies and by 1852 was in its 14th edition. Pattee, *The Feminine Fifties* (New York: Appleton-Century, 1940), p. 56.

3 Ralph Waldo Emerson, "The Transcendentalist," in Stephen E. Whicher, ed., *Selections from Ralph Waldo Emerson* (Boston: Houghton Mifflin, 1957), p. 195.

4 Nathaniel Hawthorne, *The Blithedale Romance,* 1852 (New York: Norton, 1958). Subsequent references are to this edition.

5 See Allan and Barbara Lefcowitz, "Some Rents in the Veil: New Light on Priscilla and Zenobia in *The Blithedale Romance," Nineteenth Century Fiction* XXI (Dec. 1966), 263–75.

6 William W. Sanger, *History of Prostitution: Its Extents, Causes and Effects Throughout the World* (New York, 1858), p. 524, points out that women employed in the needle trades were second only to servants in entering prostitution. Cited in A. and B. Lefcowitz, ibid., p. 269.

7 In the nineteenth century, according to Mary Black and Jean Lipman, copying was not regarded with disdain, but rather was *the* mode of instruction for American artists, especially young ladies, who after 1800 began to go beyond their study of the essentials to add "the gracious art of painting in watercolor and oil. For schoolgirls, aids to inspiration were readily available. They came from paintings copied by their instructors; from stencils, . . . colored prints and Bible illustrations." One of the interesting original paintings cited by the authors, however, is a depiction of Venus winged through the sky by a brace of doves. "Art Instruction for Young Ladies," in *American Folk Art* (New York: Bramhall House, 1966), pp. 205–15.

8 Henry James, *The Art of the Novel: Critical Prefaces* (New York: Scribners, 1934), p. 268.

9 Cited in Leslie Fiedler, *Love and Death in the American Novel,* rev. ed. (New York: Stein and Day, 1966), p. 311. Fiedler also notes that as late as 1936 one literary historian still found Daisy a confused caricature, arguing that any lady really endowed with "active innocence" and "personal daintiness" would not have acted like Daisy because "she would not have cared to be conspicuous" (ibid.).

10 James, *The Art of the Novel,* p. 270.

11 Henry James, *Daisy Miller* in Philip Rahv, ed., *The Great Short Novels of Henry James* (New York: Dial, 1944). Subsequent references are to this edition.

12 Ralph Waldo Emerson, "Self-Reliance," in Whicher, ed., *Selections*, p. 151.

13 Sasha Davis, in Alix Kates Shulman's *Memoirs of an Ex-Prom Queen* (New York: Knopf, 1969), makes essentially the same discovery in Rome from a feminist point of view—that wearing one's wedding ring puts a woman in a different category. It is significant that Sasha reads Henry James while she sips coffee in cafés.

14 For background on Minny Temple see F. O. Matthiessen, *The James Family* (New York: Knopf, 1947), pp. 259–64, where the entire letter of Henry James to his brother William on Minny's death is quoted, and Henry James, *Notes of a Son and Brother* (New York: Scribners, 1914), the last chapter of which is devoted to Minny Temple. For a discussion of James and Hawthorne see Marius Bewley, *The Complex Fate: Hawthorne, Henry James and Some Other American Writers* (London: Chatto and Windus, 1952), and for a discussion of the influence of Ibsen on James in the matter of light and dark heroines see Michael Egan, *Henry James: The Ibsen Years* (London: Vision Press, 1972).

15 Henry James, Preface to *The Wings of the Dove*, 2 vols., 1902 (New York: Modern Library, 1930), p. xxx. Subsequent references are to this edition.

16 For example, as Susan and Milly embark for Europe, the sound is of "a Wagner overture. It was the Wagner overture that practically prevailed, up through Italy." In the opera, King Mark is promised Isolde, who loves Tristan, in marriage; the lovers die while King Mark lives on. In light of the way Lord Mark would use Milly to gain Kate, it is significant that Densher and Kate seal their compact to use Milly for their ends in St. Mark's Square; it is there that she pledges to come to his rooms as "payment."

17 William James was among those who was dismayed by his brother's method of indirection, writing: "I have read *The Wings of the Dove* (for which all thanks!) but what shall I say of a book constructed on a method which so belies everything that *I* acknowledge as law? You've reversed every traditional canon of story-telling (especially the fundamental one of telling the story, which you carefully avoid) and have created a new *genre littéraire* which I can't help thinking perverse, but in which you nevertheless succeed, for I read with interest to the end (many pages, and innumerable sentences twice over to see what the dickens they could possibly mean) and all with unflagging curiosity to know what the upshot might become. It's very *distingué* in its way, there are touches I don't know whether it's fatal and inevitable with you, or deliberate and possible to put off and on. At any rate it is your own, and no one can drive you out or supplant you. . . ." Cited in Matthiessen, *The James Family*, p. 338.

18 According to Carl Jung, the moral qualities of the wise old man in the fairy tale lead to his identification with God: 'The old man . . . represents knowledge, reflections, insight, wisdom, cleverness, and intuition on the one hand, and on the other moral qualities such as good will and readiness

to help." *The Archetypes and the Collective Unconscious,* translated by R. F. C. Hull (Princeton: Princeton University Press, 1951), p. 222.

19 Cited in Leon Edel, *Henry James,* vol. I: *The Untried Years* (Philadelphia: Lippincott, 1953), p. 326. Edel demonstrates that this theme of men and women preying upon one another, one living only by another's death, is present in James's fiction from his earliest tales on.

20 Joseph Campbell, *The Hero with a Thousand Faces* (Cleveland: World, 1949), p. 52.

21 Jean Cocteau, the French director, made a superb film from this story in 1946. Jung also treats the legend in some depth in *Man and His Symbols* (Garden City, N.Y.: Doubleday, 1964), pp. 137–40. "In this story," he writes, "we . . . see that Beauty is any young girl or woman who has entered into an emotional bond with her father, no less binding because of its spiritual nature. Her goodness is symbolized by her request for a white rose, but in a significant twist of meaning her unconscious intention puts her father and then herself in the power of a principle that expresses not goodness alone, but cruelty and kindness combined. It is as if she wished to be rescued from a love holding her to an exclusively virtuous and unreal attitude. By learning to love Beast she awakens to the power of human love concealed in its animal (and therefore imperfect) but genuinely erotic form. Presumably this represents an awakening of her true function of relatedness, enabling her to accept the erotic component of her original wish, which had to be repressed because of a fear of incest. To leave her father she had, as it were, to accept the incest-fear, to allow herself to live in its presence in fantasy until she could get to know the animal man and discover her own true response to it as a woman" (p. 138).

22 Henry James, *The Golden Bowl,* 2 vols., 1904 (New York: Scribners, 1909). Subsequent references are to this edition.

23 One is reminded of Mark Twain's Satan in *The Mysterious Stranger,* who unlike the citizens of Esledorf (Ass-ville), does not possess the moral sense. Hawthorne's already cited preface to *The Marble Faun* also comes to mind with its discussion of the difficulty of writing a romance about a country with no shadows. "Romance," interestingly, is the word the Prince uses about himself.

24 For a review of the criticism on both sides of the Maggie question, see Oscar Cargill's chapter on "The Golden Bowl" in *The Novels of Henry James* (New York: Macmillan, 1961), pp. 383–440.

25 Cited in Edel, *Henry James,* vol. III: *The Middle Years* (1962), pp. 88–89.

26 Henry James, 1909 Preface to *The Portrait of a Lady,* 1881 (New York: Modern Library reprinting of the New York edition, 1951), pp. xxxiv–xxxvii. Subsequent references are to this edition.

27 Henry James, Preface to *The Princess Casamassima* in *The Art of the Novel,* pp. 64–65.

28 The goddess, of course, is Diana, as Isabel's surname suggests. Cecil

Hunt in *Word Origins: The Romance of Language* (New York: Philosophical Library, 1949) defines her as the woman "intent upon remaining single. . . . She was the patron of virgins until they were married." In art she is usually depicted as a "woman of slender grace and beauty." He adds, interestingly, "The phrase 'Great is Diana of the Ephesians' (*Acts,* xix, 28) is often used to imply that self-interest can breed deceit" (pp. 54–55).

29 Place is a metaphor for the self in James. As Edel points out in the biography, James was preoccupied throughout most of his life with the right place. He seems to have found it, finally, in Lamb House at Rye, of which Edel writes: "There was a . . . garden. . . . There were peaches—a memory of Albany." He cites James's statement that his house was "really good enough to be a kind of little becoming, high door'd, brass knockered *façade* to one's life." *Henry James,* vol. IV: *The Treacherous Years* (1969), pp. 196–97.

30 Edel, *Henry James,* vol. II: *The Conquest of London* (1962), p. 429. Modern biographers, with the psychological sophistication of a post-Freudian age, are not the only ones to see an author's personality in the characters he or she creates. Edel cites James Herbert Morse, for example, who wrote in *Century Magazine* a year after the publication of the novel that there was in nearly every personage of *The Portrait* "an observable infusion of the author's personality." He went on to say that a shrewd critic could reconstruct James from his novels, and that in *The Portrait,* "The person thus fashioned would be one of fine intellectual powers, incapable of meannesses; of fastidious tastes, and of limited sympathies; a man, in short, of passions refined away by the intellect" (pp. 428–29). This sounds like a combination of Isabel and Osmond—which is precisely Edel's point.

CHAPTER IV
The Great Mother

1 Erich Neumann, *The Great Mother: An Analysis of the Archetype,* translated by Ralph Manheim (Princeton: Princeton University Press, 1955), pp. 65–66.

2 F. O. Matthiessen and Kenneth B. Murdock, eds., *The Notebooks of Henry James* (New York: Oxford University Press, 1947), p. 42. "To have been the 'keystone' of the James family arch," Leon Edel comments, "required strength and firmness and an ability to control and weather high emotional tempests." As she wrote to her son Wilkinson, "Holding a firm rein is especially my forte." Mary James was not only strong and firm; she was to her favorite son Henry the "so widely open yet so softly enclosing lap . . . of all our securities. . . . She *was* each of us." Cited in *Henry James,* vol. I: *The Untried Years* (Philadelphia: Lippincott, 1953), pp. 41, 48.

3 Edel, *Henry James,* vol. III: *The Middle Years* (1962), p. 38.

4 Ibid., p. 144.

5 James, *Notebooks*, p. 129.

6 See, for example, Robert Heilman, "The Turn of the Screw as Poem," *The University of Kansas City Review* XIV (Summer 1948), 277–89; in Gerald Willen, ed., *A Casebook on Henry James's "The Turn of the Screw"* (New York: Crowell, 1969), pp. 174–88.

7 Cited in John Lydenberg, "The Governess Turns the Screws," *Nineteenth Century Fiction* XII (June 1957), 36–58; in Willen, *Casebook*, p. 275. Lydenberg insists, and I agree, that whatever James may have intended to do—or not do—he has made the governess a character with eminently discussable characteristics.

8 Henry James, *The Turn of the Screw* in *The Two Magics: The Turn of the Screw, Covering End* (New York: Macmillan, 1898). Subsequent references are to this edition.

9 Although Lydenberg, cited in note 7 above, also sees the governess as the focus of *The Turn of the Screw,* he does not link her to or see her as a prototype for other Jamesian mother figures as I do.

10 Henry James, *A Small Boy and Others* (New York: Scribners, 1913), pp. 16, 18.

11 C. Knight Aldrich, M.D., "Another Twist to *The Turn of the Screw,*" *Modern Fiction Studies* XIII (Summer 1967), 167–78; in Willen, *Casebook*, pp. 367–78.

12 Since writing this analysis of Mrs. Bread, I have come across John A. Clair's article, *"The American:* A Reinterpretation," *PMLA* LXXIV (Dec. 1959), 613–18. Clair goes so far as to make Mrs. Bread the *real* villain of the piece and absolves Madame de Bellegarde from guilt—a position which I feel is highly speculative rather than one based on textual evidence.

13 Henry James, *What Maisie Knew,* 1897 (Garden City, N.Y.: Doubleday, 1954). Subsequent references are to this edition.

14 Adapted from *Playboy* Magazine (March 1964), p. 94, by Norman N. Holland in *The Dynamics of Literary Response* (New York: Oxford University Press, 1968), p. 4.

15 Henry James, "The Pupil," in Clifton Fadiman, ed., *The Short Stories of Henry James* (New York: Modern Library, 1945). Subsequent references are to this edition.

16 Neumann, *The Great Mother*, pp. 148–49.

17 Henry James, "De Grey," in Leon Edel, ed., *The Ghostly Tales of Henry James* (New York: Grosset and Dunlap, 1963), p. 67.

18 Henry James, "Osborne's Revenge," in Leon Edel, ed., *The Complete Tales of Henry James,* vol. II (Philadelphia: Lippincott, 1962), p. 45.

19 Cited in Edel, *The Untried Years,* p. 127.

20 James, *Notebooks,* p. 348 (Jan. 4, 1910).

21 Leon Edel, Introduction to Henry James, *The Other House* (London and New York: Macmillan, 1948), p. vii. Subsequent references are to this edition.

22 James, *Notebooks*, pp. 140–41.

23 This is James's account of Hedda Gabler after seeing her interpreted by Elizabeth Robins in 1891. As Edel writes in his introduction to *The Other House*, "Rose Armiger leads us to Miss Robins and Miss Robins leads us straight to Henrik Ibsen" (p. xv).

24 Neumann, *The Great Mother*, p. 27.

CHAPTER V
The New Woman

1 From Betty Miles, "Atalanta and the Race," in *Ms.* Magazine (March 1973), 75–78. In the original Greek myth, Melanion won the race by enlisting the help of Aphrodite, who gave him three golden apples. During the race, he dropped the apples, and Atalanta, stopping to pick them up, lost to him. They were married, but they didn't live happily ever after; they lay in a place sacred to Zeus, who punished them by turning them into lions. Richmond Y. Hathorn, *Crowell's Handbook of Classical Drama* (New York: Crowell, 1967), pp. 208–209.

2 Patriarchal culture is roughly five thousand years old, but for a period at least five times as long as that, women were worshipped as goddesses in matriarchal cultures as, for example, Sumerian, Babylonian, Mesopotamian and African ruins reveal. See Joseph Campbell, *The Hero with a Thousand Faces* (Cleveland: World, 1949), and other works, and Erich Neumann, *The Great Mother: An Analysis of the Archetype*, translated by Ralph Manheim (Princeton: Princeton University Press, 1955). In *The First Sex* (Baltimore: Penguin Books, 1972), Elizabeth Gould Davis cites as the earliest recorded account of creation: "When above the heavens had not been formed, when the earth beneath had no name, Tiamat brought forth them both. . . . Tiamat, the Mother of the Gods, Creator of All." "In *all* myths throughout the world," she writes, "the first creator . . . is a goddess" (p. 33).

3 Neumann, Preface to *The Great Mother*, p. xlii.

4 Larzer Ziff, *The American 1890s: Life and Times of a Lost Generation* (New York: Viking, 1966), p. 283. The analogy between slavery of blacks and women is by now an obvious one. As pointed out in Chapter I, women attracted to the secular utopian communities were those actively engaged in the abolition movement. For further examples see Nancy F. Cott, ed., *Root of Bitterness: Documents of the Social History of American Women* (New York: Dutton, 1972).

5 Ziff, *American 1890s*, p. 304.

6 Henry James, *Hawthorne* (New York: Harper & Brothers, 1879), p. 130.

7 Julian Hawthorne, *Nathaniel Hawthorne and His Wife*, vol. I (Boston: Houghton Mifflin, 1884), p. 257.

8 James, *Hawthorne*, pp. 130–31. Elsewhere in this critical biography,

James writes of Hawthorne: "We may be sure that in women his taste was conservative" (p. 78). The same, I think, may be said for James. His statement that Margaret Fuller "represented feminine culture in the suburbs" is a clue to his own view of the lady reformers in *The Bostonians*, as is his observation: "It was a strange history and a strange destiny, that of this brilliant, restless, and unhappy woman—this ardent New Englander, this impassioned Yankee, who occupied so large a place in the thoughts, the lives, the affections, of an intelligent and appreciative society, and yet left behind her nothing but the memory of a memory. Her function, her reputation, were singular, and not altogether reassuring; she was a talker, she was *the* talker, she was the genius of talk. She had a magnificent, though by no means an unmitigated, egotism; and in some of her utterances it is difficult to say whether pride or humility prevails . . ." (p. 76).

9 Newton Arvin, ed., *The Heart of Hawthorne's Journals* (Boston: Houghton Mifflin, 1929), pp. 270–72. Margaret Fuller's opinion of Hawthorne was quite different from his of her. Her diary entry, "I feel more like a sister to Hawthorne, or rather more that he might be a brother to me, than ever with any man before," cited in Randall Stewart, ed., *The American Notebooks of Nathaniel Hawthorne* (New Haven: Yale University Press, 1932), p. 315, suggests that his simultaneous attraction/repulsion of the dark lady might be based on subconscious incest fears. In this connection see Frederick Crews, *The Sins of the Fathers: Hawthorne's Psychological Themes* (New York: Oxford University Press, 1966).

10 Hawthorne, *American Notebooks*, pp. 293–94.

11 Margaret Fuller, "The Great Lawsuit: Man versus Men; Woman versus Women," *The Dial* IV (July 1843), 11; later reprinted as *Woman in the Nineteenth Century*.

12 Ibid., 47.

13 Cf. the words of Milton's Adam, cited in Chapter II: ". . . nothing lovelier can be found/ In Woman than to study household good,/ And good works in her Husband to promote. . . ."

14 James, *Hawthorne*, p. 132. I think James placed more importance on this aspect of *The Blithedale Romance* than Hawthorne intended it to have; Hawthorne probably meant Zenobia's domination over Priscilla as one more example of the impossibility of returning to the timeless world of perfection, even in a utopian community. Marius Bewley, in *The Complex Fate: Hawthorne, James and Some Other American Writers* (London: Chatto and Windus, 1952), compares the two novels and mentions this issue of dominance; however, *he*, in concentrating on the domination of Verena by Olive, misses James's point—that Verena is caught in a struggle between Olive *and* Basil Ransom.

15 James, *Hawthorne*, p. 79. In the context of this passage, James seems perfectly serious, although it is hard to believe, in light of his own novels, which stress possessiveness and perversion in sexual relations, that he

thought their quality in American life excellent. Probably he means that mo-
nogamy prevailed at Brook Farm, because as we know, he had no love for
reform movements in general.

16 Leon Edel, *Henry James*, vol. III: *The Middle Years* (Philadelphia: Lippincott, 1962), p. 137. Unlike—and perhaps because of—his father, whose
utopian socialist views are discussed in F. O. Matthiessen's *The James Family*
(New York: Knopf, 1961), Henry Jr. was interested in psychological (individual) evil. Like Hawthorne, he would never consider social institutions as the
root of evil. This is part of the Europe-America theme pursued in most of his
novels and is a clue to his presentation of Madame de Vionnet, despite—or
perhaps because of—her connection with a corrupt society, as more worthy,
more sympathetic than the righteous representatives of Woollett, Massachusetts, for example, in *The Ambassadors*.

17 Leon Edel makes the interesting point that "had Olive obtained physical possession of Verena, her need of her as an instrument of power would
have diminished considerably." *Henry James: The Middle Years*, p. 140.

18 Cited in F. O. Matthiessen and Kenneth B. Murdock, eds., *The Notebooks of Henry James* (New York: Oxford University Press, 1947), pp. 67–68.

19 William Dean Howells, *Dr. Breen's Practice* (Boston: Houghton Mifflin,
1881). Subsequent references are to this edition.

20 Elizabeth Blackwell to Barbara Bodichon, September 25, no year given,
Columbia University Library, cited in Andrew Sinclair, *The Emancipation of
the American Woman* (New York: Harper & Row, 1965), pp. 147–48.

21 Emily Blackwell, *Diary*, June 20, 1858, Radcliffe Women's Archives,
cited in Sinclair, *Emancipation*, pp. 148–49.

22 *Godey's Lady's Book* (Dec. 1862), cited in Sinclair, *Emancipation*, p. 146.

23 Miss Gleason is an interesting case, tangential to the portrayal of the
professional woman here, but one which must have influenced James along
with *The Blithedale Romance* when he came to write *The Bostonians*, where he
would make central the relationship of two women and the manipulation in
that relationship of one by the other. Although Grace is not only unattracted
to Miss Gleason, but repulsed by her, Miss Gleason pursues Grace with "repressed tumult," longing and luminous looks and "devouring fondness." At
one point she tells Grace that her influence upon herself has been a "delicious . . . sense of self-surrender."

24 Cited in Clara and Rudolf Kirk in their introduction to *The Altrurian
Romances* (Bloomington: Indiana University Press, 1968), p. xxxiii. These
Romances were originally published in *Cosmopolitan* Magazine in 1892–93,
1893–94 and 1907. Subsequent references are to the Kirks' edition.

25 See, for example, William Dean Howells, "Editor's Easy Chair," *Harper's Monthly Magazine*, CXI (Oct. 1905), 794–97; CXVIII (May 1909), 965–68;
CXXIV (Feb. 1912), 470–74; CXXVII (June 1913), 148–51; CXL (March 1920),
565–68.

26 Edel, in *Henry James*, vol. IV: *The Treacherous Years* (1969), p. 313, cites

this letter of 1902 from James to Andersen: "The sense that I can't help you, see you, talk to you, touch you, hold you close and long, or do anything to make you rest on me, and feel my participation—this torments me, dearest boy, makes me ache for you, and for myself; makes me gnash my teeth and groan at the bitterness of things. . . . I wish I could go to Rome and put my hands on you (oh, how lovingly I should lay them!) but that, alas, is odiously impossible. . . . I am in town for a few weeks but I return to Rye April 1st, and sooner or later to *have* you there and do for you, to put my arms around you and *make* you lean on me as on a brother and a lover, and keep you on and on, slowly comforted or at least relieved of the first bitterness of pain. . . . There I am, at any rate, and there is my house and garden and my table and my studio . . . and your room, and your welcome, and your place everywhere—and I press them upon you, oh so earnestly, dearest boy. . . . I will *nurse* you through your dark passage. . . . I embrace you with almost a passion of pity." Edel further suggests in *Henry James,* vol. V: *The Master* (1972), that James's relationship with Jocelyn Persse made him able to write his one consummated love story, *The Golden Bowl*.

27 Kate Chopin, *The Awakening,* 1899 (New York: Capricorn Books, 1964). Subsequent references are to this edition.

Bibliography

Core List of Novels and Tales and Related Works of Literature

Bellamy, Charles. *An Experiment in Marriage*. Albany, N.Y.: Weed, Parsons and Co., 1899.

Bellamy, Edward. *Equality*, 1897. Upper Saddle River, N.J.: The Gregg Press, 1968.

———. *Looking Backward: 2000–1887*, 1888. New York: New American Library, 1960.

Chopin, Kate. *The Awakening*, 1899. New York: Capricorn Books, 1964.

Emerson, Ralph Waldo. "The Transcendentalist," "Self-Reliance," in *Selections from Ralph Waldo Emerson*, edited by Stephen E. Whicher. Boston: Houghton Mifflin Company, 1957.

Frederic, Harold. *The Damnation of Theron Ware*, 1896. New York: Holt, Rinehart and Winston, 1958.

Hawthorne, Nathaniel. *The American Notebooks*, edited by Randall Stewart. New Haven: Yale University Press, 1932.

———. *The Blithedale Romance*, 1852. New York: W. W. Norton & Company, 1958.

———. "Grandfather's Chair," 1840. *The Centenary Edition of the Works of Nathaniel Hawthorne*, vol. VI. Columbus: Ohio State University Press, 1972, pp. 9–67.

———. *The Heart of Hawthorne's Journals*, edited by Newton Arvin. Boston: Houghton Mifflin Company, 1929.

———. *The Marble Faun*, 1860. New York: New American Library, 1961.

———. "Mrs. Hutchinson," in *Bibliographical Sketches, Works of Nathaniel Hawthorne*, vol. XII. Boston: Houghton Mifflin Company, 1883, pp. 217–26.

———. "Rappaccini's Daughter" in *The Complete Tales of Nathaniel Hawthorne*. Garden City, N.Y.: Hanover House, 1959.

Bibliography

———. *The Scarlet Letter*, 1850. New York: Rinehart & Co., 1960.

Holmes, Oliver Wendell. *Elsie Venner*, 1861. Boston: Houghton Mifflin Company, 1891.

Howells, William Dean. *The Altrurian Romances: A Traveller from Altruria*, 1894; *Letters of an Altrurian Traveller*, 1893–94; *Through the Eye of the Needle*, 1907; edited by Clara and Rudolph Kirk. Bloomington: The University of Indiana Press, 1968.

———. *Dr. Breen's Practice*. Boston: Houghton Mifflin Company, 1881.

James, Henry. *The Ambassadors*, 1903. New York: Holt, Rinehart and Winston, 1967.

———. *The American*, 1877. New York: Holt, Rinehart and Winston, 1949.

———. *The Art of the Novel: Critical Prefaces*, edited by R. P. Blackmur. New York: Charles Scribner's Sons, 1934.

———. *The Bostonians*, 1886. New York: Modern Library, 1956.

———. *The Complete Tales of Henry James*, 12 vols., edited by Leon Edel. Philadelphia: J. B. Lippincott Company, 1962.

———. *The Ghostly Tales of Henry James*, edited by Leon Edel. New York: Grosset and Dunlap, 1963.

———. *The Golden Bowl*, 1904, 2 vols. New York: Charles Scribner's Sons, 1909.

———. *Hawthorne*. New York: Harper & Brothers, 1879.

———. *The Notebooks of Henry James*, edited by F. O. Matthiessen and Kenneth B. Murdock. New York: Oxford University Press, 1947.

———. *Notes of a Son and Brother*. New York: Charles Scribner's Sons, 1914.

———. *The Other House*, 1896. London and New York: Macmillan, 1948.

———. *The Portrait of a Lady*, 1881. New York: Modern Library, 1951.

———. "The Pupil," 1891, in *The Short Stories of Henry James*, edited by Clifton Fadiman. New York: Modern Library, 1945.

———. *A Small Boy and Others*. New York: Charles Scribner's Sons, 1913.

———. *The Turn of the Screw* in *The Two Magics: The Turn of the Screw, Covering End*. New York: Macmillan, 1898.

———. *What Maisie Knew*, 1897. Garden City, N.Y.: Doubleday and Company, 1954.

———. *The Wings of the Dove*, 1902. New York: Modern Library, 1930.

Melville, Herman. *Pierre, or, The Ambiguities*, 1852. New York: Grove Press, 1957.

Milton, John. *Paradise Lost*, in *John Milton: Complete Poems and Major Prose*, edited by Merritt Y. Hughes. New York: Odyssey Press, 1957.

Literary Criticism: Books

Adams, Frederick B. *Radical Literature in America*. Stamford, Conn.: Overbrook Press, 1939.

Bibliography

Anderson, Quentin. *The American Henry James*. New Brunswick, N.J.: Rutgers University Press, 1957.

Bewley, Marius. *The Complex Fate: Hawthorne, Henry James and Some Other American Writers*. London: Chatto and Windus, 1952.

Bodkin, Maud. *Archetypal Patterns in Poetry: Psychological Studies of Imagination*. London: Oxford University Press, 1934.

Cantwell, Robert. *Nathaniel Hawthorne: The American Years*. New York: Rinehart & Company, 1948.

Cargill, Oscar. *The Novels of Henry James*. New York: Macmillan, 1961.

Carpenter, Frederic I. *American Literature and the American Dream*. Freeport, N.Y.: Books for Libraries Press, 1955.

Chapman, Elizabeth Rachel. *Marriage Questions in Modern Fiction*. New York: John Lane the Bodley Head, 1897.

Cornillon, Susan Koppelman, ed. *Images of Women in Fiction: Feminist Perspectives*. Bowling Green, Ohio: Bowling Green University Popular Press, 1972.

Crews, Frederick C. *The Sins of the Fathers: Hawthorne's Psychological Themes*. New York: Oxford University Press, 1966.

Deegan, Dorothy Yost. *The Stereotype of the Single Woman in American Novels: A Social Study with Implications for the Education of Women*. New York: Octagon Books, 1969.

Edel, Leon. *Henry James*, 5 vols. Philadelphia: J. B. Lippincott Company, 1953–1972.

Egan, Michael. *Henry James: The Ibsen Years*. London: Vision Press, 1972.

Ellman, Mary. *Thinking About Women*. New York: Harcourt Brace Jovanovich, 1968.

Feidelson, Charles, Jr. *Symbolism and American Literature*. Chicago: University of Chicago Press, 1953.

Fiedler, Leslie A. *Love and Death in the American Novel*. New York: Stein and Day, revised 1966 edition.

Fuller, Edmund. *Man in Modern Fiction: Some Minority Opinions on Contemporary American Fiction*. New York: Random House, 1949.

Hardwick, Elizabeth. *Seduction and Betrayal*. New York: Random House, 1974.

Hathorn, Richmond Y. *Crowell's Handbook of Classical Drama*. New York: Thomas Y. Crowell Company, 1967.

Hawthorne, Julian. *Nathaniel Hawthorne and His Wife*, 2 vols. Boston: Houghton Mifflin Company, 1884.

Heilbrun, Carolyn G. *Toward a Recognition of Androgyny*. New York: Alfred A. Knopf, 1973.

Henderson, Harry B. III. *Versions of the Past: The Historical Imagination in American Fiction*. New York: Oxford University Press, 1974.

Hicks, Granville. *The Great Tradition: An Interpretation of American Literature since the Civil War*. New York: Macmillan, revised 1935 edition.

Bibliography

Hoffman, Daniel G. *Form and Fable in American Fiction*. New York: Oxford University Press, 1961.

Holland, Norman. *The Dynamics of Literary Response*. New York: Oxford University Press, 1968.

Howe, Irving. *Politics and the Novel*. New York: Horizon Press, 1957.

Kaul, A. N. *The American Vision: Actual and Ideal Society in Nineteenth Century Fiction*. New Haven: Yale University Press, 1963.

Krook, Dorothea. *The Ordeal of Consciousness in Henry James*. London: Cambridge University Press, 1963.

Lawrence, D. H. *Studies in Classic American Literature*. Garden City, N.Y.: Doubleday & Company, 1923.

Lesser, Simon O. *Fiction and the Unconscious*. New York: Random House, 1957.

Lewis, R. W. B. *The American Adam: Innocence, Tragedy, and Tradition in the Nineteenth Century*. Chicago: University of Chicago Press, 1955.

Leyburn, Ellen Douglass. *Strange Alloy: The Relation of Comedy to Tragedy in the Fiction of Henry James*. Chapel Hill, N.C.: University of North Carolina Press, 1968.

Male, Roy R. *Hawthorne's Tragic Vision*. New York: W. W. Norton & Company, 1957.

Marx, Leo. *The Machine in the Garden: Technology and the Pastoral Ideal in America*. New York: Oxford University Press, 1967.

Matthiessen, F. O. *American Renaissance: Art and Expression in the Age of Emerson and Whitman*. New York: Oxford University Press, 1941.

———. *Henry James: The Major Phase*. London: Oxford University Press, 1944.

———. *The James Family: Selections from the Writings of Henry James, Senior, William, Henry, & Alice James*. New York: Alfred A. Knopf, 1961.

Murray, Michele, ed. *A House of Good Proportion: Images of Women in Literature*. New York: Simon & Schuster, 1973.

Negley, Glenn and J. Max Patrick. *The Quest for Utopia: An Anthology of Imaginary Societies*. New York: Henry Schuman, 1952.

Noble, David. *The Eternal Adam and the New World Garden: The Central Myth in the American Novel since 1830*. New York: George Braziller, 1968.

Oberndorf, Clarence P., M.D. *The Psychiatric Novels of Oliver Wendell Holmes*. New York: Columbia University Press, 1943.

Parrington, Vernon L. *Main Curents in American Thought*, vol. III: *The Beginnings of Critical Realism in America*. New York: Harcourt, Brace & World, 1930.

Parrington, Vernon Louis, Jr. *American Dreams: A Study of American Utopias*. Providence: Brown University, 1947.

Pattee, Fred Lewis. *The Feminine Fifties*. New York: Appleton-Century Company, 1940.

Bibliography

Pattee, Fred Lewis. *The First Century of American Fiction, 1770–1870*. New York: Appleton-Century Company, 1935.

Poirier, Richard. *The Comic Sense of Henry James: A Study of the Early Novels*. New York: Oxford University Press, 1960.

Praz, Mario. *The Romantic Agony*, translated by Angus Davidson. London: Oxford University Press, 1933; 1970 revised edition used.

Rahv, Philip. *Literature and the Sixth Sense*. Boston: Houghton Mifflin Company, 1969.

Rogers, Katherine M. *The Troublesome Helpmate: A History of Misogyny in Literature*. Seattle: University of Washington Press, 1966.

Samuels, Charles Thomas. *The Ambiguity of Henry James*. Urbana, Ill.: University of Illinois Press, 1971.

Shurter, Robert F. *The Utopian Novel in America, 1865–1900*. New York: The AMS Press, 1973.

Tanner, Tony, ed. *Henry James, Modern Judgments*. London: Macmillan, 1968.

Waggoner, Hyatt H. *Hawthorne: A Critical Study*. Cambridge, Mass.: The Belknap Press of Harvard University Press, 1963.

Wasserstrom, William. *Heiress of All the Ages: Sex and Sentiment in the Genteel Tradition*. Minneapolis: University of Minnesota Press, 1959.

Willen, Gerald, ed. *A Casebook on Henry James's "The Turn of the Screw,"* second edition. New York: Thomas Y. Crowell Company, 1969.

Literary Criticism: Articles

Adkins, Nelson F. "An Early American Story of Utopia," *Colophon* I (July 1935), 123–32.

Bailey, J. O. "An Early American Utopian Fiction," *American Literature* XVI (Nov. 1942), 285–93.

Baym, Nina. "*The Blithedale Romance:* A Radical Reading," *Journal of English and Germanic Philology* LXVII (Oct. 1968), 545–69.

———. "Hawthorne's Women: The Tyranny of Social Myths," *Centennial Review* XV (Summer 1971), 250–72.

———. "Passion and Authority in *The Scarlet Letter*," *New England Quarterly* XLIII (June 1970), 209–30.

———. "The Romantic *Malgré Lui:* Hawthorne in the Custom House," *Emerson Society Quarterly* XIX (1973), 14–25.

Bleich, David. "Eros and Bellamy," *American Quarterly* XVI (Fall 1964), 445–59.

Bowman, Sylvia E. "Bellamy's Missing Chapter," *New England Quarterly* XXXI (Mar. 1958), 47–65.

Carpenter, Frederic I. "Puritans Preferred Blondes: The Heroines of Melville and Hawthorne," *New England Quarterly* IX (1936), 253–72.

Chernaik, Judith. "Henry James as Moralist: The Case of the Late Novels," *Centennial Review* XVI (Spring 1972), 105–21.

Bibliography

Clair, John A. "*The American:* A Re-interpretation," *PMLA* LXXIV (Dec. 1959), 613–18.

Colacurio, Michael J. "Footsteps of Ann Hutchinson: The Context of *The Scarlet Letter,*" *English Literary History* XXXIX (Sept. 1972), 459–94.

Crane, Verner W. "A Lost Utopia of the First American Frontier," *Sewanee Review* XXVII (Jan. 1919), 48–61.

Erlich, Gloria Chasson. "Deadly Innocence: Hawthorne's Dark Women," *New England Quarterly* XLI (June 1968), 163–79.

Flint, Allen. "The Saving Grace of Marriage in Hawthorne's Fiction," *Emerson Society Quarterly* XIX (1973), 112–16.

Forbes, Allyn B. "The Literary Quest for Utopia," *Social Forces* VI (Dec. 1927), 179–89.

Gottfried, Alex and Sue Davidson. "Utopia's Children: An Interpretation of Three Political Novels," *Western Political Quarterly* XV (Mar. 1962), 17–32.

Heilbrun, Carolyn. "The Masculine Wilderness of the American Novel," *Saturday Review* LV (Jan. 29, 1972), 41–44.

Hofstadter, Beatrice K. "Popular Culture and the Romantic Heroine," *American Scholar* XXX (Winter 1960–61), 98–116.

Knox, George. "Romance and Fable in James's *The American,*" *Anglia* LXXXIII (1965), 308–322.

Lefcowitz, Allan and Barbara. "Some Rents in the Veil: New Light on Priscilla and Zenobia in *The Blithedale Romance,*" *Nineteenth Century Fiction* XXI (Dec. 1966), 263–75.

McMaster, Juliet. "The Portrait of Isabel Archer," *American Literature* XLV (Mar. 1973), 50–66.

Martin, Wendy. "Seduced and Abandoned in the New World: The Image of Women in American Fiction," in Vivian Gornick and Barbara K. Moran, eds., *Woman in Sexist Society*. New York: Basic Books, 1971, pp. 329–46.

Perloff, Marjorie. "Cinderella Becomes the Wicked Stepmother: *The Portrait of a Lady* as Ironic Fairy Tale," *Nineteenth Century Fiction* XXIII (Mar. 1969), 413–33.

Schroeder, John W. "The Mothers of Henry James," *American Literature* XXII (Jan. 1951), 424–31.

Schultz, Elizabeth. "*The Bostonians:* The Contagion of a Romantic Illusion," *Genre* IV (Mar. 1971), 45–59.

Shurter, Robert L. "The Utopian Novel in America, 1888–1900," *The South Atlantic Quarterly* XXXIV (Apr. 1935), 137–44.

Silverstein, Henry. "The Utopia of Henry James," *New England Quarterly* XXXV (Dec. 1962), 458–64.

Trilling, Diana. "The Image of Women in Contemporary Literature," in Robert J. Lifton, ed., *The Woman in America*. Boston: Beacon Press, 1964, pp. 52–71.

Wolff, Cynthia Griffin. "A Mirror for Men: Stereotypes of Women in Literature," *Woman: An Issue, Massachusetts Review* XIII (Winter–Spring 1972), 205–18.

Bibliography

Works Having to Do with the Status and Role of Women: Books

Battis, Emory. *Saints and Sectaries*. Chapel Hill, N.C.: University of North Carolina Press, 1962.

Calverton, V. F. *The Bankruptcy of Marriage*. New York: Macaulay Company, 1928.

Calverton, V. F. and S. D. Schmalhausen, eds. *Sex in Civilization*. New York: Macaulay Company, 1929.

Chesler, Phyllis. *Women and Madness*. New York: Doubleday and Company, 1972.

Coser, Rose Laub, ed. *The Family: Its Structure and Functions*. New York: St. Martin's Press, 1966.

Cott, Nancy F., ed. *Root of Bitterness: Documents of the Social History of American Women*. New York: E. P. Dutton & Co., 1972.

Cross, Barbara M. *The Educated Woman in America: Selected Writings of Catharine Beecher, Margaret Fuller, and M. Carey Thomas*. New York: Teachers College Press of Columbia University, 1965.

Davis, Elizabeth Gould. *The First Sex*. Baltimore: Penguin Books, 1972.

Dingwall, Eric John. *The American Woman*. London: Gerald Duckworth & Co., 1956.

Earnest, Ernest. *The American Eve in Fact and Fiction, 1775–1914*. Urbana: University of Illinois Press, 1974.

Firestone, Shulamith. *The Dialectic of Sex*. New York: William Morrow and Company, 1970.

Forsyth, P. T. *Marriage: Its Ethic and Religion*. New York: Hodder and Stoughton, 1912.

Fuller, Margaret. *Woman in the Nineteenth Century*, 1845. New York: W. W. Norton & Company, 1971.

Gornick, Vivian and Barbara K. Moran, eds. *Woman in Sexist Society*. New York: Basic Books, 1971.

Harding, M. Esther. *The Way of All Women*. London: Longmans, Green and Co., 1933.

Lederer, Wolfgang, M.D. *The Fear of Women*. Harcourt Brace Jovanovich, 1968.

Lerner, Gerda. *The Woman in American History*. Menlo Park, Cal.: Addison-Wesley, 1972.

Lifton, Robert J., ed. *The Woman in America*. Boston: Beacon Press, 1964.

Papashvily, Helen. *All the Happy Endings*. New York: Harper & Brothers, 1956.

Pomeroy, H. S., M.D. *The Ethics of Marriage*. New York: Funk & Wagnalls Company, 1888.

Riegel, Robert E. *American Women: A Story of Social Change*. Rutherford, N.J.: Fairleigh Dickinson University Press, 1970.

Ross, Ishbel. *Charmers and Cranks: Twelve Famous American Women Who Defied the Conventions*. New York: Harper & Row, 1965.

Bibliography

Roszak, Betty and Theodore, eds. *Masculine/Feminine: Readings in Sexual Mythology and the Liberation of Women*. New York: Harper & Row, 1969.

Schmalhausen, Samuel D. and V. F. Calverton, eds. *Woman's Coming of Age: A Symposium*. New York: Horace Liveright, 1931.

Sinclair, Andrew. *The Emancipation of the American Woman*. New York: Harper & Row, 1965.

Smith, Page. *Daughters of the Promised Land: Women in American History*. Boston: Little, Brown and Company, 1970.

Trahey, Jane, ed. *Harper's Bazaar: 100 Years of the American Female*. New York: Random House, 1967.

Van Vorst, Mrs. John and Marie Van Vorst. *The Woman Who Toils*. New York: Doubleday, Page & Company, 1903.

Woolson, Abba Gould. *Woman in American Society*. Boston: Roberts Brothers, 1873.

Works Having to Do with the Status and Role of Women: Articles

An American Mother. "What the American Girl Has Lost," *Ladies Home Journal* XCII (May 1900), 17.

Beecher, Catharine. "How to Redeem Woman's Profession from Dishonor," *Harper's New Monthly Magazine* XXI (Nov. 1865), 710–16.

Beecher, Henry Ward. "Do the Scriptures Forbid Women to Preach?" Feb. 11, 1872, in *The Original Plymouth Pulpit*, vol. VII. Boston: The Pilgrim Press.

———. "The Family as an American Institution," Nov. 26, 1868, in *The Original Plymouth Pulpit*, vol. I. Boston: The Pilgrim Press.

———. "The Strange Woman," in *Lectures to Young Men on Various Important Subjects*. Salem: John P. Jewett & Co., 1846.

———. "The True Law of the Household," Jan. 21, 1872, in *The Original Plymouth Pulpit*, vol. VII. Boston: The Pilgrim Press.

Bell, Lillian. "The Management of Husbands," *Harper's Bazar* XXXVI (Mar. 1902), 203–207.

Buell, Jennie. "Household Heroines," *Good Housekeeping* V (Oct. 1, 1887), 285.

Chambers, William and Robert. "A Specimen of Feminine Journalism," *Chambers Journal* XLVIII (July 15, 1871), 433–36.

de Varigny, M. C. "The American Woman," *Popular Science Monthly* XLIII (July 1893), 383–88.

Greeley, Horace, "My Notions of Women's Rights," *Hearth and Home* I (Sept. 18, 1869), 616–17.

Harrison, Mrs. Burton. "Home Life as a Profession," *Harper's Bazar* XXXIII (May 19, 1900), 148–50.

Hart, Lavinia. "The Ideal Wife & Helpmeet," *Cosmopolitan* XXX (Apr. 1901), 638–42.

Bibliography

Howells, William Dean. "Editor's Easy Chair," *Harper's Monthly Magazine* CXI (Oct. 1905), 794–97; CXVIII (May 1909), 965–68; CXXIV (Feb. 1912), 470–74; CXXVII (June 1913), 148–51; CXL (Mar. 1920), 565–68.

Linton, Mrs. E. Lynn. "The Wild Women as Social Insurgents," *The Nineteenth Century* XXX (Oct. 1891), 596–605.

Parker, Willard, M.D. "A Psychological View of the Woman Question," *Hearth and Home* I (Nov. 20, 1869), 760.

Potter, David M. "American Women and the American Character," *Stetson University Bulletin* LXII (Jan. 1962).

Schreiner, Olive. "The Woman's Movement of Our Day," *Harper's Bazar* XXXVI (Jan.–Mar. 1902), 3–8, 103–107, 222–27.

Sheldon, Frederick. "Various Aspects of the Woman Question," *Atlantic Monthly* XVIII (Oct. 1866), 425–34.

Stowe, Harriet Beecher. "My Wife and I," *Christian Union* III (May 31, 1871), 339; (May 17, 1871), 309.

Sutherland, Millicent. "Woman and her Sphere," *North American Review* CLXXXIV (Mar. 1902), 632–39.

H. W. T. "Commandments for Women," *Harper's Bazar* XXXVIII (July 1904), 706–707.

Welter, Barbara. "The True Cult of Womanhood: 1820–1860," *American Quarterly* XVIII (Summer 1966), 151–74.

Wright, Sylvia. "*Whose World? . . . and Welcome to It.*" *Harper's* Magazine CCX (May 1955), 35–38.

Historical and Social Thought: Books

Andrews, Edward Deming. *The People Called Shakers,* New York: Oxford University Press, 1953.

Bestor, Arthur E., Jr. *Backwoods Utopias: The Sectarian and Owenite Phases of Communitarian Socialism in America: 1663–1829.* Philadelphia: University of Pennsylvania Press, 1950.

Black, Mary and Jean Lipman. "Art Instruction for Young Ladies," in *American Folk Art.* New York: Bramhall House, 1966, pp. 205–15.

Bryce, James. *The American Commonwealth.* New York: The Macmillan Company, 1893.

Calverton, V. F. *Where Angels Dared to Tread.* Indianapolis: The Bobbs-Merrill Company, 1941.

Carden, Maren Lockwood. *Oneida: Utopian Community to Modern Corporation.* Baltimore: Johns Hopkins Press, 1969.

Codman, John Thomas. *Brook Farm: Historic and Personal Memoirs.* Boston: Arena Publishing Company, 1894.

Cross, Whitney R. *The Burned-Over District: The Social and Intellectual History of Enthusiastic Religion in Western New York, 1800–1850.* Ithaca, N.Y.: Cornell University Press, 1950.

Bibliography

Dollard, John. *Caste and Class in a Southern Town.* New York: Harper & Brothers, 1937.

Egbert, Donald Drew, Stow Persons and T. D. Seymour Bassett, eds. *Socialism in American Life,* 2 vols. Princeton, N.J.: Princeton University Press, 1952.

Erikson, Kai T. *Wayward Puritans: A Study in the Sociology of Deviance.* New York: John Wiley & Sons, 1966.

Fried, Albert. *Socialism in America: From the Shakers to the Third International.* Garden City, N.Y.: Doubleday & Company, 1970.

Haller, William. *The Rise of Puritanism.* New York: Columbia University Press, 1938.

Hill, Marvin S. and James B. Allen, eds. *Mormonism and American Culture.* New York: Harper & Row, 1972.

Hinds, William Alfred. *American Communities.* Chicago: Charles H. Kerr & Company, 1902.

Holloway, Mark. *Heavens on Earth: Utopian Communities in America, 1680–1880.* New York: Library Publishers, 1951.

Kanter, Rosabeth Moss. *Commitment and Community: Communes and Utopias in Sociological Perspective.* Cambridge: Harvard University Press, 1972.

Lasch, Christopher. *The New Radicalism in America: The Intellectual as a Social Type.* New York: Vintage Books, 1965.

Lockwood, George Browning. *The New Harmony Communities.* Marion, Ind.: Chronicle Company, 1902.

——. *The New Harmony Movement.* New York: D. Appleton and Company, 1905.

Lockwood, Maren. "The Experimental Utopia in America" in *Utopias and Utopian Thought,* edited by Frank E. Manuel. Boston: Houghton Mifflin Company, 1966, pp. 183–200.

Morgan, Edmund S. *The Puritan Family: Religion and Domestic Relations in Seventeenth-Century New England.* New York: Harper & Row, 1944.

Mott, Frank Luther. *A History of American Magazines,* vol. III: *1865–1885.* Cambridge, Mass.: Harvard University Press, 1938.

Nevins, Allan. *The Emergence of Modern America, 1865–1878.* New York: Macmillan, 1927.

Nordhoff, Charles. *The Communistic Societies of the United States.* New York: Schocken Books, 1966 reprint of the 1875 edition.

Noyes, John Humphrey. *History of American Socialisms.* New York: Hillary House Publishers, 1961 reprint of the 1870 edition.

Robertson, Constance Noyes. *Oneida Community, An Autobiography, 1851–1876.* Syracuse, N.Y.: Syracuse University Press, 1970.

Rourke, Constance. *The Roots of American Culture.* New York: Harcourt, Brace and World, 1942.

——. *Trumpets of Jubilee.* New York: Harcourt, Brace and Company, 1927.

Sams, Henry W., ed. *Autobiography of Brook Farm.* Englewood Cliffs, N.J.: Prentice-Hall, 1958.

Bibliography

Sanford, Charles L. *The Quest for Paradise: Europe and the American Moral Imagination.* Urbana: University of Illinois Press, 1961.

Seitz, Don C. *The Dreadful Decade, Detailing Some Phases in the History of the United States from Reconstruction to Resumption, 1869–1879.* Indianapolis: Bobbs-Merrill Company, 1926.

Sibley, Mulford Q. "Oneida's Challenge to American Culture," in *Studies in American Culture: Dominant Ideas and Images,* edited by Joseph J. Kwiat and Mary C. Turpie. Minneapolis: University of Minnesota Press, 1960.

Smith, Goldwyn, D. C. L. *Essays on Questions of the Day, Political and Social.* New York: Macmillan, 1894.

Smith, Henry Nash. *Virgin Land, The American West as Symbol and Myth.* Cambridge, Mass.: Harvard University Press, 1950; Vintage paperback edition used.

Swift, Lindsay. *Brook Farm.* Secaucus, N.J.: Citadel Press, 1973 reprint of the 1900 edition.

Thernstrom, Stephan. "Urbanization, Migration, and Social Mobility in Late Nineteenth-Century America," in *Towards a New Past: Dissenting Essays in American History,* edited by Barton J. Bernstein. New York: Pantheon Books, 1968, pp. 158–75.

Tocqueville, Alexis de. *Democracy in America,* 1835, translated by George Lawrence, edited by J. P. Mayer. Garden City, N.Y.: Doubleday & Co., 1969.

Tyler, Alice Felt. *Freedom's Ferment: Phases of American Social History from the Colonial Period to the Outbreak of the Civil War.* Minneapolis: University of Minnesota Press, 1944.

Webber, Everett. *Escape to Utopia.* New York: Hastings House, 1959.

Wilson, William E. *The Angel and the Serpent: The Story of New Harmony.* Bloomington, Ind.: Indiana University Press, 1964.

Ziff, Larzer. *The American 1890s: Life and Times of a Lost Generation.* New York: Viking, 1966.

Historical and Social Thought: Articles

Bushee, Frederick A. "Communistic Societies in the United States" *Political Science Quarterly* XX (Sept. 1905), 625–64.

The Dial, vols. I–IV, 1840–1844. New York: Russell & Russell, 1961.

Flower, B. O. "The Latest Social Vision," *Arena* XVIII (Oct. 1897), 517–34.

"Fourierism and the Socialists," in *The Dial* III (July 1842), 86–96.

Gates, Susa Young. "Family Life Among the Mormons—by a Daughter of Brigham Young," *North American Review* CL (Mar. 1890), 339–50.

Larsen, Louis W. "Childhood in a Mormon House," *American Mercury* XXIX (Aug. 1933), 480–87.

Russell, Amelia. "Home Life of the Brook Farm Association," *Atlantic Monthly* XLII (Oct., Nov. 1878), 458–66, 563–66.

Bibliography

Sedgwick, Ora Gannett. "A Girl of Sixteen at Brook Farm," *Atlantic Monthly* LXXXV (Mar. 1900), 394–404.

Psychological, Philosophical and Anthropological Studies of Mythology

Campbell, Joseph. *The Flight of the Wild Gander: Explorations in the Mythological Dimension.* Chicago: Henry Regnery Company, 1951.
———. *The Hero with a Thousand Faces.* Cleveland: The World Publishing Company, 1956.
———. *Myths to Live By.* New York: Viking, 1971.
Eliade, Mircea. *The Sacred and the Profane: The Nature of Religion,* translated by Willard R. Trask. New York: Harper & Row, 1959.
Erikson, Erik H. *Childhood and Society.* New York: W. W. Norton & Company, second revised edition, 1963.
Freud, Sigmund. "The Most Prevalent Form of Degradation in Erotic Life," in *The Collected Papers of Sigmund Freud,* edited by Ernest Jones. New York: Basic Books, 1959, pp. 203–16.
Jung, Carl G. *The Archetypes and the Collective Unconscious,* translated by R. F. C. Hull. Princeton, N.J.: Princeton University Press, 1951.
———. *Man and his Symbols.* Garden City, N.Y.: Doubleday & Company, 1964.
Murray, Henry A. *Myth and Mythmaking.* New York: George Braziller, 1960.
Neumann, Erich. *The Great Mother: An Analysis of the Archetype,* translated by Ralph Manheim. Princeton, N.J.: Princeton University Press, 1963.

Bibliographies

Bentley, Wilder. *The Communication of Utopian Thought.* San Francisco: San Francisco State College Bookstore, 1959.
Chambers, Clarke A. *Woman in America.* Minneapolis: University of Minnesota History Department, 1970.
Jacobs, Sue-Ellen. *Women in Persepective: A Guide for Cross-Cultural Studies.* Urbana: University of Illinois Press, 1974.
Sense and Sensibility Collective. *Women and Literature: An Annotated Bibliography of Women Writers,* second revised edition. Cambridge, Mass.: Sense and Sensibility, 1973.
Sibley, Mulford Q. and Kenneth C. Zimmerman. *Utopias and Utopian Thought.* Minneapolis: University of Minnesota Political Science Department, 1970.

Index

Adam, 5, 6, 23, 27, 37, 43, 45, 54, 55, 62, 63, 68, 68n, 70-71, 78, 80, 86, 87, 112, 208, 214, 216. *See American Adam, The* (Lewis)
Adams, Henry, 15
Alcott, Bronson, 18
Aldrich, C. Knight, 162
Altrurian Romances, The (Howells), 25, 26, 207, 208, 240-42
Ambassadors, The (James), 243
American, The (James), 5, 6, 25, 58, 112, 126, 165-68, 182, 183, 185, 189-95, 203
American Adam, The (Lewis), 5
American Commonwealth, The (Bryce), 12-13
American Woman's Home, The (Beecher, Stowe), 11
Andersen, Hendrik Christian, 243
androgyny, 17, 74, 84, 128
Anna Karenina (Tolstoy), 243, 256
Anthony, Susan B., 13, 16, 227
"Ariel" (Plath), 258
Atalanta (myth), 204, 208
"Atalanta and the Race" (Miles), 204-206
"Author of Beltraffio, The" (James), 183, 188

Awakening, The (Chopin), 25, 207, 208, 243-58

"Beauty and the Beast" (fairy tale), 112-13, 141
Beecher, Catharine, 11
Beecher, Henry Ward, 11
Bellamy, Charles, 21
Bellamy, Edward, 4, 16, 19, 20, 21, 22, 208, 242
Billy Budd (Melville), 6
"Birthmark, The" (Hawthorne), 42, 161
Blackwell, Antoinette Brown, 16
Blackwell, Elizabeth, 207, 235, 236
Blackwell, Emily, 235, 236
Blithedale Romance, The (Hawthorne), 20, 24, 25, 28, 66, 76, 86, 89-93, 96, 105, 108, 109, 128, 182, 206-207, 208-20, 221, 236, 243-44, 245, 256
Bloomer, Amelia, 16
Bok, Edward, 13
Bostonians, The (James), 8, 25, 128, 143, 147-52, 153, 172, 192, 194, 199, 207, 208, 220-34, 236
Brook Farm, 18-19, 20, 24, 28, 73, 76, 208, 210, 211, 220

Browning, Robert, 130
Brownson, Orestes, 18
Bryce, James, 12, 13, 15, 24
Bushnell, Horace, 11

Campbell, Joseph, 112
Carlyle, Thomas, 222
Carpenter, Frederick I., 85
Cenci, Beatrice, 64, 67, 71
Chance Acquaintance, A (Howells), 234
Channing, William Ellery, 18
Channing, William Henry, 18
Chopin, Kate, 25, 26, 207, 208, 243, 258 246
"Christabel" (Coleridge), 29, 38
Clemens, Samuel. *See* Twain, Mark (pseud.)
Cleopatra, 71
Clytemnestra, 194
Coleridge, Samuel Taylor, 27, 29, 33
community, 28, 30, 31, 40, 54, 72, 74, 75, 76, 77, 81, 83, 84, 100, 127, 206. *See* utopian communities
Cooper, James Fenimore, 14, 25, 26, 27
Croly, Mrs. J. C., 13
Cross, Whitney, 16

Daisy Miller (James), 24-25, 86, 97-101, 105, 113, 120, 126, 128, 243
Damnation of Theron Ware, The (Frederic), 24, 28, 42, 54-62, 63, 72, 181, 208, 256
Dana, Charles, 18
Dante, 41
"De Grey" (James), 183
Delilah, 55
Democracy in America (Tocqueville), 12-13
Democratic Vistas (Whitman), 9
deviance, 28, 39, 40, 48, 68n, 75, 76, 78, 79, 81-82, 100, 127, 208, 217
Dial, The, 226

Dickens, Charles, 127
Dickinson, Emily, 9, 26, 246
dime-novel heroine, 14-15
Dr. Breen's Practice (Howells), 25, 26, 207, 208, 234-40, 242
Downing, Andrew Jackson, 11
Draper, E. D., 13
Dutt, R. Palme, 16
Dwight, John Sullivan, 18

Edel, Leon, 126, 142, 148, 184
Eden, America as New World Garden of, 3, 4, 5, 6, 16, 20, 23, 24, 26, 31, 38, 40, 41, 42, 76, 77, 79, 99, 151, 211, 218, 219. *See* garden imagery
Edgar, Pelham, 153
"Egotism, or The Bosom Serpent" (Hawthorne), 40
Electra, 194
Eliade, Mircea, 6
Eliot, George (pseud.), 130
Eliot, T. S., 175
Elsie Venner (Holmes), 24, 28, 29-40, 41, 43, 45, 48, 50, 54, 62, 72, 79
Emerson, Ralph Waldo, 6, 9, 18, 19, 22, 53, 86, 98, 142, 222, 246
Equality (E. Bellamy), 21, 22
Erikson, Kai T., 28, 77
"Ethan Brand" (Hawthorne), 161, 210
Eve, 6, 16, 23, 24, 26, 27, 28, 29, 30, 33, 38, 40, 43, 44, 47, 54, 58, 62, 63, 68n, 70-71, 78, 81, 85, 86, 104, 105, 112, 113, 119, 128, 144, 198, 213, 216, 217, 218, 219, 241
Experiment in Marriage, An (C. Bellamy), 21-22

fairy tale, 46, 105, 109, 112, 120, 125, 126, 134, 141, 161, 170, 171, 206, 250, 258
Fall of Man (Original Sin), 5, 6, 18, 23, 24, 29, 30, 41, 45, 47, 50, 55, 62, 63, 68, 71, 79, 118, 128, 139, 142, 210

Finnegan's Wake (Joyce), 246n
Fitzgerald, F. Scott, 101n
Fourier, Charles, 18
Frederic, Harold, 23, 24, 28, 55
Freud, Sigmund, 150, 153, 154
Fruitlands, 24
Fuller, Margaret, 9, 19, 130, 210, 211, 212, 213, 226, 227

garden imagery, 30, 31, 40, 41, 42, 43, 46, 47, 55, 56, 69, 98, 112, 113, 121, 122, 129, 131-32, 133, 134, 136, 139, 140, 141, 144-45, 154, 155, 183, 187, 193, 196-97, 202. *See* Eden
Garrison, William Lloyd, 6
"Georgina's Reasons" (James), 102
Gilded Age, The (Twain), 9
Godey's Lady's Book, 13, 235
Godkin, E. L., 9
Golden Bowl, The (James), 6, 24, 86, 87, 101, 112-26, 141, 196n, 243, 253, 256
Gounod, Charles, 130
Great Mother, The (Neumann), 143, 182, 189, 191
Greeley, Horace, 12
Grimke, Angelina and Sarah, 16
Grimm, Jakob and Wilhelm, 143
Guido, 64, 65
Guy Domville (James), 185

Hale, Sarah Josepha, 13
Hall, G. Stanley, 15
Harper's Bazar, 13
Hawthorne (James), 208-209, 211-12, 220-21
Hawthorne, Nathaniel, 4, 5, 22, 23, 24, 25, 28, 29, 33, 40, 43, 44, 45, 47, 50, 54, 63, 71, 72, 77, 80, 83, 95n, 101, 110n, 128, 153, 161, 208, 210, 215, 222, 236, 240, 246; on America, 4, 68; as artist, 72-74, 92, 93, 127; at Brook Farm, 18, 20, 24, 28, 73; on Margaret Fuller, 212-13; to Long-

fellow, 72; on women, 74-75, 78, 210, 211, 218, 220, 226
Hawthorne, Sophia Peabody, 22, 72, 73, 74, 92, 210, 213, 218, 226, 256
Hazard of New Fortunes, A (Howells), 241
Hearth and Home, 11, 12
Hecker, Isaac, 19
Hedda Gabler (Ibsen), 185
Heilbrun, Carolyn, 17
Henry James (Edel), 126
Herodias, 67
Higginson, Thomas Wentworth, 14
Holland, Norman, 170
Holmes, Oliver Wendell, 23, 24, 28, 29, 40, 47, 50
Holofernes, 64, 67
Howe, Julia Ward, 13
Howells, William Dean, 5, 22, 23, 25, 26, 97, 234, 235, 236, 238, 239, 240, 242
Huckleberry Finn (Twain), 6, 86
Hutchinson, Anne, 75, 76, 77, 95. *See* "Mrs. Hutchinson" (Hawthorne)

Ibsen, Henrik, 27, 185, 246n

Jael, 55, 67, 71
James, Henry, 5, 6, 8, 22, 23, 24, 25, 97, 101, 110n, 118, 120, 128, 129, 142, 161, 168, 170, 182, 183, 184, 225, 226, 231, 232, 246; on America, 10, 14, 147, 221, 222, 229; and H. C. Andersen, 243; as artist, 127, 127n, 184, 227; and the Civil War, 151; on Hawthorne, 208-209, 211-12, 220; and Mary James, 147-48; and William James, 111-12, 226-27; and Minny Temple, 101, 111-12; on women, 10, 14, 127, 128, 147, 148, 149, 162, 168, 194, 220-21, 222, 226, 228-29, 233, 240, 243; and Constance Fenimore Woolson, 126
James, Henry Sr., 222

James, Mary, 147-48
James, William, 111, 226
John the Baptist, 67
Joyce, James, 160, 246n
Judith, 55, 64, 67, 71
Juno, 195, 197

Keats, John, 27, 29, 33, 190

"La Belle Dame sans Merci" (Keats), 190
Ladies' Home Journal, The, 13
Lady of the Aroostook, The (Howells), 234
"Lamia" (Keats), 29, 38
Lee, (Mother) Ann, 17, 19, 23
Lerner, Gerda, 10
Lewis, R. W. B., 5
Longfellow, Henry Wadsworth, 72
"Longstaff's Marriage" (James), 183
Looking Backward (E. Bellamy), 4, 19-21, 22, 25, 208, 242
"Love Song of J. Alfred Prufrock, The" (Eliot), 246
Lydenberg, John, 156

Madame Bovary (Flaubert), 243
Marble Faun, The (Hawthorne), 4, 24, 28, 29, 55, 62-71, 72, 79, 86, 90, 93-97, 105, 133, 182, 208, 217, 220, 256
Marcuse, Herbert, 20
Marvell, Andrew, 87
Marx, Karl, 20
Marx, Leo, 3
Mary (Virgin), 56, 57, 63, 81, 93, 94, 174, 250
Master Builder, The (Ibsen), 185
"Maypole of Merry Mount, The" (Hawthorne), 95
Medusa, 187
Melville, Herman, 23, 24, 28, 33, 47, 49, 50, 54, 95n, 101, 246
Menelaus, 194

Milton, John, 27, 28, 62, 104, 213
Modern Instance, A (Howells), 241
Modern Times, 208
Mormons, 17, 24, 208
"Mrs. Hutchinson" (Hawthorne), 74-75, 76-77
Mysterious Stranger, The (Twain), 52
myth, 23, 25, 29, 46, 112, 119, 143; of America as New World Garden, 3, 4, 5, 6, 23, 26, 119; of the eternal return, 4, 6; female version of, 206, 253; mythologizing women, 7; new myth of Atalanta, 204-206, 208; patriarchal myth, 6, 182, 206, 253
My Wife and I (Stowe), 11

Neumann, Erich, 25, 143, 189, 190, 206
"New Adam and Eve, The" (Hawthorne), 4, 40
New Harmony, 18, 208
"Next Time, The" (James), 127n
Niobe, 195
Noyes, John Humphrey, 4, 6, 17, 19, 20, 42n

Oneida Perfectionists, 6, 17-18, 19, 24, 25, 42n, 207
Orestes, 194
Original Sin. *See* Fall of Man
"Osborne's Revenge" (James), 183
Other House, The (James), 25, 101, 182, 183, 184-89
"Out of the Cradle Endlessly Rocking" (Whitman), 247, 248, 251, 254, 255
Owen, Robert, 18
Owen, Robert Dale, 18

Pandora (James), 204
Papashvily, Helen, 10
Paradise Lost (Milton), 27, 28, 47, 62, 70-71, 104, 109, 139, 141, 203, 213

Index

Parker, Theodore, 18

Parker, Willard, 11

Peabody, Elizabeth, 18, 226, 227

Phillips, Wendell, 10, 11

Pierre, or, The Ambiguities (Melville), 24, 28, 47-54, 62, 63, 66, 72, 79, 86, 87-89, 95n

Plath, Sylvia, 258

Poe, Edgar Allan, 25, 26, 27, 33, 42, 161, 246

Pomeroy, H. S., 12

Portrait of a Lady, The (James), 25, 38, 56, 85, 86, 102, 126-42, 177-82, 195-203, 239, 243

Potter, David, 6, 10

Praxiteles, 68

Pudd'nhead Wilson (Twain), 26

"Pupil, The" (James), 25, 175-77

puritanical traditions, 12, 18, 30, 34, 40, 75, 76, 77, 81, 95, 127, 130, 232, 234, 236, 249

Quakers, 76, 95

"Rappaccini's Daughter" (Hawthorne), 24, 28, 29, 40-47, 48, 50, 55, 62, 63, 72, 79, 161, 217

"Rapunzel" (fairy tale), 105, 143

"Rapunzel" (Sexton), 144-47

Rich, Adrienne, 3

Richard II (Shakespeare), 47

Ripley, George, 19

Rise of Silas Lapham, The (Howells), 111, 241

Robins, Elizabeth, 185

romance, 5, 26, 29, 132, 211, 240

Romersholm (Ibsen), 185

Roosevelt, Theodore, 15

Rossi, Alice, 17

Roszak, Theodore, 7, 8

Roth, Henry, 160

Sacred Fount, The (James), 183

Salome, 67, 71

Sand, George (pseud.), 9

Satan, 52, 56, 65

Scarlet Letter, The (Hawthorne), 24, 26, 28, 29, 42, 72-84, 86, 90, 95, 127, 128, 208, 210-11, 217, 220

Scott, Sir Walter, 127, 132

"Self-Reliance" (Emerson), 98

Seneca Falls convention, 9, 207

serpent imagery, 29, 33, 34, 35, 37-38, 39, 40, 41, 43, 45n, 46, 47, 55, 56, 59, 65-66, 69, 79, 80, 108, 138, 146, 181, 187, 198, 218, 245

Sexton, Anne, 144-47

Shakers, 16-18, 23, 25, 207

Shakespeare, William, 47, 127

Sisera, 67

"Sleeping Beauty" (fairy tale), 105, 253

Small Boy and Others, A (James), 162

"Snapshots of a Daughter-in-Law" (Rich), 3

"Song of Myself" (Whitman), 247

Stanton, Elizabeth Cady, 13, 16, 227

Stowe, Harriet Beecher, 11

Tempest, The (Shakespeare), 3

Temple, Mary (Minny), 101, 109, 111-12

Thernstrom, Stephan, 9

Thomas, M. Carey, 14

Thoreau, Henry David, 6, 226

Through the Eye of the Needle (Howells). *See Altrurian Romances, The*

Tocqueville, Alexis de, 12, 13, 15, 24

"Tragedy of Error, A" (James), 183

Transcendentalism, 53, 86, 87, 95n, 128, 129, 131, 142, 211, 226, 227, 246

"Transcendentalist, The" (Emerson), 86, 142

"Tree of Knowledge, The" (Hawthorne), 4

Tristan and Isolde (Wagner), 102

Trollope, Anthony, 27

Index

Turn of the Screw, The (James), 25, 153-65, 166, 172, 173, 188

Twain, Mark (pseud.), 9, 25, 26, 52

"Uriel" (Emerson), 53

utopia, 4, 16, 20, 22, 23, 24, 76, 127n, 151, 219

utopian communities, 4, 8, 16-19, 24, 28, 53n, 76, 206, 211, 218, 219-20, 222

utopian novels, 4, 8, 19-22, 24, 76, 89-93, 206, 208-20, 240-42

"Wakefield" (Hawthorne), 74

Waste Land, The (Eliot), 5

Weininger, Otto, 8

What Maisie Knew (James), 25, 120, 168-74, 177

When We Dead Awaken (Ibsen), 246n

Whitman, Walt, 9, 84, 246, 247, 249, 251, 254, 255, 256

Whittaker, Frederick, 14

Wilkinson, Jemima, 19

Willett, Edward, 14

Wilson, John, 77

Wings of the Dove, The (James), 25, 86, 93, 101-12, 113, 136, 137, 256

Winthrop, John, 77

witches, 76, 95, 105, 119, 120, 143, 144-47, 152, 164-65, 170, 171, 172, 182, 183

Wollstonecraft, Mary, 9

Woman in the Nineteenth Century (Fuller), 9, 207, 213

Woman's Journal (Revolution), 13

Woodhull, Victoria, 208

Woolson, Constance Fenimore, 126, 128, 243

Wright, Frances, 24

"Young Goodman Brown" (Hawthorne), 45, 80, 95, 161

Ziff, Larzer, 207

The myth of America as a New World Garden of Eden was the major shaping force of the American imagination in the nineteenth century. The American Adam, the simple and self-reliant man who lives in harmony with nature, is a stock figure in the analyses of literary critics and intellectual historians. But what about Eve, the woman in the Garden? Long ignored by critics, the figure of Eve is Judith Fryer's subject, and she offers an incisive analysis of what women meant to such writers as Hawthorne, Melville, Holmes, Frederick, James, Howells, and Chopin.

Within the gardens of newborn, pristine, and sterile innocence, or of Old World decadent experience, the heroine was of primary importance to American novelists. Usually, according to Fryer, these novelists, products of their patriarchal culture, cast heroines as types, projections of their own limited vision:

The Temptress—a deviant from societal norms. Sexually alluring, she is dangerously suggestive of Adam's fall from purity. For this reason, from Holmes's Elsie Venner to Hawthorne's Hester Prynne, she is an outcast in her own community.

The American Princess—Eve before the fall. Innocent and self-reliant, she is the psychosexual opposite of the Temptress,